D0096216

FIRST EDITION

WHO SHAPED THE AMERICAN CRIMINAL JUSTICE SYSTEM?

Innovators, Pioneers, and Trailblazers

By James Windell

cognella® | ACADEMIC PUBLISHING

Bassim Hamadeh, CEO and Publisher

Mary Jane Peluso, Senior Specialist Acquisitions Editor

Leah Sheets, Associate Editor

Jess Estrella, Cover Designer

Alexa Lucido, Licensing Coordinator

Joyce Lue, Interior Designer

Kassie Graves, Director of Acquisitions and Sales

Jamie Giganti, Senior Managing Editor

Copyright © 2018 by Cognella, Inc. All rights reserved. No part of this publication may be reprinted, reproduced, transmitted, or utilized in any form or by any electronic, mechanical, or other means, now known or hereafter invented, including photocopying, microfilming, and recording, or in any information retrieval system without the written permission of Cognella, Inc. For inquiries regarding permissions, translations, foreign rights, audio rights, and any other forms of reproduction, please contact the Cognella Licensing Department at rights@cognella.com.

Trademark Notice: Product or corporate names may be trademarks or registered trademarks, and are used only for identification and explanation without intent to infringe.

Cover credits: Underwood & Underwood / Public Domain.
      George W. Harris and Martha Ewing / Public Domain.
      Source: https://commons.wikimedia.org/wiki/File:Clarence_Darrow.jpg.
      Public Domain.
      Marion S. Trikosko / U.S. News & World Report / Public Domain.
      Copyright © by Depositphotos/georgios.
      Copyright © by Depositphotos/georgios.

Printed in the United States of America

ISBN: 978-1-5165-1300-0 (pbk) / 978-1-5165-1301-7 (br)

CONTENTS

PART IV. COURT PIONEERS

PART V. CORRECTIONS INNOVATORS

PREFACE

How much would you learn about such notable criminal justice figures as Cesare Beccaria, August Vollmer, J. Edgar Hoover, and James Q. Wilson from reading the best criminal justice textbooks that we have? The answer is simple: little or nothing.

This is not to say that most introductory criminal justice and criminology textbooks do a poor job of teaching what students need to learn about criminal justice and criminology. Far from it. By and large, they do a great job of introducing students to the key elements of the criminal justice field. But students will come away from introductory courses with almost no appreciation of the great pioneers and innovators who helped shape our criminal justice system.

Over the years, in teaching various criminal justice courses, I was frequently frustrated by the dearth of information about the individuals who helped develop the American criminal justice system. I wanted to know more about some of these innovators; not only about their accomplishments, but also about their personal lives. Who were these people? How did they come to initiate new theories, procedures, and practices that made them criminal justice heroes? Furthermore, I wanted my students to have a better sense of the people whose ideas and work built the foundations of our criminal justice system.

The leading textbooks typically allot few pages to biographies of the important people in criminal justice history. Of course, when the people most instrumental in shaping and designing our criminal justice system are noted, most often that mention is no more than a paragraph. As a result of my personal desire to teach my students more about the personalities who contributed to our justice system, I began putting together biographies in my lectures. From that grew my interest in writing a book of biographies of some of the most influential figures in the American criminal justice system. The result is this book.

Who Shaped the American Criminal Justice System? is designed to be a supplementary textbook for courses as varied as Introduction to Criminal Justice, History of Criminal Justice, Criminological Theory, and Corrections. It starts with biographies of two pioneers in criminal justice law—Cesare Beccaria and James Madison. But in addition to Beccaria and Madison, you will discover biographies of the great policing trailblazers August Vollmer and J. Edgar Hoover, along with court and legal pioneers and the great corrections innovators.

Since many, if not most, introduction to criminal justice and introduction to criminology textbooks follow a similar formatting of the contents, this book is also designed to fit in with the major introductory textbooks. For instance, there are fourteen biographies, which conforms to the typical term or semester of fourteen weeks. The book is divided into five parts, with two or more biographies in each part. The two historical figures of Beccaria and Madison are discussed in Part I. These chapters can be assigned to students as readings when the primary textbooks deal with the history of criminal justice. Part II, titled Criminological Pioneers, is positioned to supplement discussion of criminological theories. Part III contains the biographies of three policing innovators, and these will best accompany a class section on policing and law enforcement. Often following law enforcement is one of the other major components of a survey of criminal justice: the courts. Part IV devotes chapters to three court pioneers: Lucy Flower, Clarence Darrow, and Earl Warren. The final section likewise is aimed at corresponding to corrections, one of the last components typically discussed in introductory courses. Part V, thus, includes biographies of John Augustus, Samuel Gridley Howe, Zebulon Brockway, and Thomas Mott Osborne.

Each biography includes a review of the individual's formative years and influences. The development of their major theories is discussed and usually set within a social or cultural time period. The significance of their writings and work are explored, and each biography ends with an assessment of the pioneer's legacy in criminal justice. At the end of each biography are Discussion Questions, Important Names and Terms, Recommended Readings for more information about the individual profiled, and References. These features allow instructors to use individual chapters as readings for class discussion or written assignments. Instructors will also find that lecture PowerPoint slides are available as well as a test bank. Active learning features that will aid students include the material at the end of each biography, along with flash cards and sample test questions on a textbook website.

I would like to acknowledge the people who have contributed to this book in one way or another. First, I would like to thank my wife, Jane, and our friend David Cutting, who patiently listened to my initial ideas for this book. Next, I would like to thank the Cognella team, including Mary Jane Peluso, Jamie Giganti, and Leah Sheets, for their assistance in bringing this book to fruition. Their ideas and suggestions have been invaluable. I am also grateful for the comments and suggestions offered by Professor Marvin Zalman, whose understanding and knowledge of the history of criminal justice played a significant part in some of my decisions to include or exclude certain biographies in this book. Thank you also to the following reviewers who provided feedback on the book: Dr. James C. Brown, Utica College, and Deb Brydon, Mount Mercy University.

In attempting to understand how ideas, policies, and practices have become standard in the field of criminal justice, it's always important to attempt to understand the people who brought innovations and new ideas to the field. This book focuses on fourteen key people who truly had a major impact on the development of our criminal justice system. I hope that these biographies spark the interest of criminal justice students and, in turn, inspire them to become innovators and trailblazers of the future.

INTRODUCTION

The idea for this book grew out of the author's curiosity. When reading criminal justice textbooks and teaching various criminal justice courses, I was intensely curious about the pioneers and innovators of criminal justice. Names—Cesare Beccaria, August Vollmer, John August, Thomas Mott Osborne, to name just four—would show up in textbooks, but typically with little more than a few sentences that generally only told about the person's most significant achievement. So, I would ask myself, "But who was this person, and what led him (or her) to be a leading figure in this field? What were they really like?"

That curiosity developed into the concept of this book. As the concept developed, I found that I had several primary goals:

1. To provide both students and professors with more in-depth information about some of the criminal justice pioneers who are frequently mentioned in textbooks;
2. To deliver readable and engrossing short biographies that included personal and family details that would enable students to gain a broader understanding of the people who shaped our criminal justice system;
3. To place the ideas and theories of the pioneers of criminal justice in the context of their lives and times; and
4. To organize a book in such a way that it would be a useful and practical supplement to go along with the most popular criminal justice introductory textbooks.

Before describing the organization of this book, I would like to comment on the selection of the people whose biographies are contained in this book. As might be expected, it was not easy to decide which figures to include and which to leave out. There are some biographies among the chapters of this book that I am sure most people would agree belong here. For instance, I think few would quibble with the decision to include James Madison, Thomas Mott Osborne, John Augustus, and August Vollmer. Less obvious choices are Cesare Beccaria, Zebulon Brockway, James Q. Wilson, Lucy Flower, and Jack Maple.

Beccaria, many would agree, should be included in any book about the history of criminal justice. But since he was not an American, does he deserve a place in this book that purports to give the stories of individuals who helped shape the American criminal justice system? I contend that he does, and the reasons will become clear when you read that chapter.

Lucy Flower is perhaps the least well-known figure in this book, yet her influence in the development of the juvenile court should not, in my opinion, be overlooked. Also, it could be argued that she was the first woman to have a significant impact on the American criminal justice system.

And, while many criminal justice instructors might insist that James Q. Wilson and George Kelling's 1982 "Broken Windows" article is a must for any criminal justice reading list, the same instructors and professors might take issue with including Wilson in this book. However, I believe his influence was so pervasive in the years from the early 1960s right up to today that it seemed essential to include him so students could see him as a person as well as an outstanding researcher and writer.

The reasoning that led to the inclusion of James Q. Wilson and Lucy Flower is related to what was extremely important to me as both a criminal justice lecturer and as an ongoing criminal justice student. The people who actually had an impact on the evolution of the American criminal justice system should be included in a book like this. I tried to include people in various areas of criminal justice. And not only was it important in the planning of these chapters to present them as individuals who contributed to criminal justice, but to show them as people who were influenced by their experiences, as well as by family and friends. In short, I wanted to portray them as people who were more than innovators or creative thinkers.

I don't blame the authors of textbooks for not including more information about the great thinkers or innovative geniuses. Having written textbooks, I fully understand that although the author might like to go more in depth to explain who certain people were and how they contributed to the field, there are often practical limitations imposed on authors.

Of course, anyone who is truly interested in learning more about an important figure in criminal justice history could search out biographies, autobiographies, and articles about them. However, as will become evident by reviewing the references at the end of each chapter, you will find that biographies, particularly of individuals who were born prior to the beginning of the twentieth century, sometimes require extraordinary persistence in tracking down the resources needed to gain a well-rounded portrait of these pioneers. Certainly, it would be difficult for students, many of whom are often less skilled at research and frequently less resourceful at ferreting out lesser-known references, to devote the time and energy to learning about people in this book.

It is also important to understand more about the organization in this book. As indicated, one of my goals was to make this book a valuable supplemental text for teachers and professors of criminal justice. To accomplish this, I paid careful attention to the leading criminal justice and criminology textbooks and how they were organized. What I discovered was that most textbooks (including my own, *The American Criminal Justice System*) are organized in terms of the main components of the criminal justice system. That is, most are organized around what we usually refer to as cops, courts, and corrections. While many textbooks start with an overview of the history of criminal justice, ways to measure the amount of crime in our society, and the causes of crime, these introductory and background chapters are usually followed by a few chapters on law enforcement, several on courts, and a handful on corrections. Therefore, this book is organized so that instructors can assign readings from this book as they teach more or less in the order dictated by a majority of the most popular textbooks.

For example, when teaching about the history of criminal justice, the chapters devoted to Cesare Beccaria and James Madison can be assigned and discussed to enhance student's understanding of the history of how the American criminal justice evolved. When discussing criminological theories, the biographies in Part II on James Q. Wilson and Travis Hirschi can be assigned. When covering the chapters on policing and law enforcement, the three chapters comprising Part III (August Vollmer, J. Edgar Hoover, and Jack Maple) may be assigned to provide students with a more intimate understanding of three important people from three different eras in the field of law enforcement. The succeeding parts of the book (Court Pioneers and Corrections Innovators) can be used to supplement the student's grasp of key figures in courts and corrections.

One final note about the number of biographies in this book: I find that most textbooks have from thirteen to twenty chapters, and most semesters or terms run about fourteen weeks. Thus, there was a purpose in limiting the number of biographies to fourteen, since this would allow approximately one assigned chapter per week.

I sincerely hope that this book and its fourteen biographies will complement and increase the student's understanding of how our criminal justice developed, and the people behind the theories, the development, and the ever-evolving field of criminal justice. I believe this is what every teacher wants for their students.

1

CESARE BECCARIA
The Father of Criminology

Cesare Beccaria was an Enlightenment philosopher who wanted to apply the rationalist perspective to the judicial, penal, and criminal justice systems of his time. He was born in Italy in the eighteenth century and rarely ventured far from his home in Milan. His seminal work, *Dei delitte e delle pene* (*On Crimes and Punishments*), was first published anonymously. However, the influence of this small, somewhat disjointed book reached every country in Europe and colonial America. His criminal courts reforms were praised by rulers, philosophers, and American founding fathers, such as Thomas Jefferson and John Adams, and his ideas seeped into the United States Constitution and the Declaration of Independence. His concepts of criminal justice still resound today, and on the strength of *On Crimes and Punishments*, a strong case can be made that, indeed, Cesare Beccaria is the Father of Criminology.

Born in Milan, Italy, on March 15, 1738, Cesare Beccaria's father was an aristocrat born of the Austrian Habsburg Empire, although he earned only a modest income. Cesare Beccaria received his primary education at a Jesuit school in Parma, Italy, and he would later describe his early education as "fanatical" and oppressive of "the development of human feelings" (Monachesi, 1973). Despite his frustration at school, Beccaria was an excellent math student, which is evident in some parts of *On Crimes and Punishments.* Following his education at the hands of the Jesuits, he attended the University of Parma, receiving a degree in law in 1758.

Showing a rebellious spirit, he proposed to sixteen-year-old Teresa Blanco against his father's wishes, and they eloped in 1761. However, with the birth of a baby girl in 1762, and following the persuasive arguments of his friends, he asked his father for forgiveness. The couple was forgiven, and they returned to the Beccaria family fold and later would have two additional children. Family and family life, as it turned out, were important to Beccaria, who was described as shy and prone to mood swings, which alternated from fits of anger to bursts of enthusiasm, followed by periods of depression and lethargy (Paolucci, 1963).

A Portrait of Cesare Beccaria

https://commons.wikimedia.org/wiki/File:Beccaria_-_Opere,_Milano,_1821_(page_6_crop).jpg.
Copyright in the Public Domain.

He made two friends early in life, and these two friends, the brothers Pietro Verri and Alessandro Verri, would exert powerful influences on him and his work. Pietro was ten years older than Cesare Beccaria, and Beccaria always looked up to him, especially because Pietro had a literary career followed by a stint in the Austrian army, attaining the rank of captain. Returning to Milan in 1760, Pietro and Alessandro began advocating for political, social, and literary reforms. As part of their reform efforts, they formed a society—later called the "academy of fists"—which waged war against what they saw as disorder in the economy of Milan, the tyranny of bureaucrats, the narrow-mindedness of religious institutions, and intellectual pedantry.

Beccaria became a member of this forward-looking and revolutionary group, attending meetings of the "academy of fists," which were usually held in the Verri home and featured lively discussions. Reportedly, Beccaria listened carefully to the discussions and debates, and began, under the guidance of Pietro, to avidly read the Enlightenment authors of France and England, including Montesquieu, Helvetius, Diderot, Buffon, and Hume (Paolucci, 1963). During the often animated discussions in the

Verri home, Beccaria remained quiet—listening, rather than taking part in conversations—and only wrote when assigned a topic by his friends.

Not only did Beccaria rely on his friends to assign him topics for writing, but often his friends helped him elaborate on certain subjects and sometimes even pieced together his fragmented ideas and thoughts. That was true for his first publication, titled *On Remedies for the Monetary Disorder of Milan in the Year 1762*. That monograph, according to Monachesi (1973), while original and thought provoking and showing he had the ability to write clearly and perhaps forcibly, was not a significant work. However, his next—and literally last—work was his *Dei delitte e delle pene*, *On Crimes and Punishments*, published anonymously in 1764.

As with his first written work, *On Crimes and Punishments* was completed only because of the help and prodding of Pietro Verri. Later, Beccaria would acknowledge that Pietro "gave me the strength to write" (Paolucci, 1963, p. xiii). Given his emotional state, which may have been overly stimulated by the discussions during the day at the academy of fists meetings that often left him drained and without energy, Beccaria tried to write in the evenings. However, writing was such a laborious task that he couldn't put much time into it, and much of his efforts resulted in scattered notes or ideas scribbled on scraps of paper. That's where Pietro, perhaps his closest friend, would provide invaluable assistance. Sometime after publication of *On Crimes and Punishments*, Pietro Verri described his role: "I suggested the topic to him and most of the ideas came out of daily conversation between Beccaria, Alessandro, Lambertenghi, and myself" (Paolucci, 1963, p. xiii). Beyond this help, though, Pietro would eventually collect the assorted random ideas on pieces of paper, write them out, arrange them in a logical order, and ultimately make a book of them.

Alessandro played an important role in Beccaria's *On Crimes and Punishments*, too, since Beccaria had no firsthand knowledge of the criminal justice system of his time. Alessandro, however, had the job of "protector of prisoners" in Milan and had direct experience with then current penal practices. Also, Pietro had an interest in torture and was able to supply Beccaria with details about how torture was used in the European justice system.

On Crimes and Punishments was published anonymously because Beccaria was fearful that he was being too bold in his recommended reforms; he didn't want to get into trouble with the authorities in Milan. However, Beccaria would be surprised that not only was his book well received in other parts of Europe, but the political authorities in Milan welcomed the book. Thus, when it was reprinted, Beccaria's name appeared as author.

In *On Crimes and Punishments*, Beccaria touched a nerve wherever it was published: it seemed to be the right book at the right time. So, despite his fears that it would be too controversial, his treatise on the reforms needed in the criminal justice system found wide acceptance. Receptive audiences all over Europe and even in the American colonies recognized that it was time for long and harsh punishments, torture, and even the death penalty to be abandoned.

As a result of the critical acclaim for his book, Beccaria was invited to go to Paris. Given his retiring personality, he was reluctant to travel to Paris, but with Alessandro Verri at his side (Pietro was unavailable to go with him), he went. As might be expected, he found being in the spotlight arduous and quite uncomfortable. Not only was he extremely anxious in social situations, but he came across as nervous and somber. He soon left France and returned home, leaving Alessandro to attend salons and talk about needed justice reforms. Paolucci, the man who translated a 1963 English edition of his book, wrote in an introduction to that translation that Beccaria realized that on a personal level he was not able to live up to the reputation of his book.

Once he returned home to Milan, he never ventured away again. But the success of his work led the government to appoint him to various offices and positions. From 1768 until his death in 1794, he did not publish any writings that garnered public attention.

ON CRIMES AND PUNISHMENTS

What were the contents of the book that found so many champions and caused such a stir in many parts of the world? It is important to examine more closely the ideas and proposals Beccaria put forward in his book.

On *Crimes and Punishments* is a short book of forty-two chapters, each of which ranges from a paragraph to a few pages. In his introduction, Beccaria pays tribute to some of his inspirations, such as "the immortal Montesquieu" and others, and then goes on to write that he plans to "examine and distinguish the various kinds of crimes and modes of punishment" (Beccaria, 1963, p. 9). Then, in his introduction, he raises questions he plans to address in this work; questions related to appropriate punishments, torture, and the death penalty.

In Chapter II, "The Origins of Punishments, and the Right to Punish," Beccaria lays out a philosophical justification for laws and for punishment of crimes. His philosophical underpinning is the social contract theory of the state. He writes that "Laws are the conditions whereby free and independent men unite to form society" (Beccaria, 1963, p. 11). He explains that the basis of punishment is the necessity to restrain men from encroaching upon the freedom of one another. An orderly social existence, he argues, is dependent on laws and on punishment of violations of laws.

In subsequent chapters, Beccaria continues to build upon arguments to construct a foundation for the legitimacy of punishment. He declares that only laws can decree punishments and only legislators can decide which punishments are consequences for particular crimes. Furthermore, judges in criminal cases do not have the authority to interpret laws. They must follow the dictates of the law, which means that they cannot decide the length or type of punishment for a particular offender. Punishments, he states, should not be arbitrary, but fixed by law. This, he says, provides a sense of security for citizens because then each person can "calculate accurately the inconveniences of a misdeed" (Beccaria, 1963, p. 17). Finally, he concludes that making the laws and the punishments for violations of laws available in writing to more citizens will decrease crime because ignorance and uncertainty of punishments lead to more—not less—crime.

By Chapter VI, Beccaria has moved on from punishment to imprisonment. First, he rails at judges who imprison people at their own pleasure and for frivolous matters. And, he writes, men should be convicted only on the basis of evidence, and this evidence must be determined by law—not by judges. Next, he asserts that men ought to be judged innocent or guilty by their peers. But in so judging the guilt of an accused man, the credibility of witnesses and the proofs of a crime need to be considered. He states that the credibility of a witness must be deduced through his or her association and closeness to the accused. But Chapter IX is a sort of aside in which Beccaria declares that accusations of wrongdoing should never be secret. Beccaria refers to Montesquieu and writes that "Montesquieu has said that public accusations are more suited to a republic, in which the principal passion of citizens ought to be for the public good, than to a monarchy, where that feeling is extremely weak owing to the very nature of the government ..." (Beccaria, 1963, p. 27). He ends Chapter IX by suggesting that governments ought to punish people who bring false accusations against others with the very punishment that the accused would have received if found guilty.

Beginning in Chapter X, Beccaria takes on the issue of torture, suggesting in this chapter that torture is likely to bring about a false confession. In succeeding chapters, he questions the helpfulness of witnesses, especially the accused, swearing an oath to tell the truth, and provides arguments against the various justifications for the use of torture in criminal procedures. Then, Beccaria discusses the importance of swift punishment but at the same time stating that there should be sufficient time allowed both for the prosecution and the defense to prepare their cases prior to trial. In Chapter IX, he argues for immunity for accomplices in order to learn about other crimes that have been committed or are in the planning stages.

In another chapter (XV), Beccaria goes back to punishment to take up another issue: the intensity of punishment. In effect, in this chapter, he wants to answer the question: How severe does punishment need to be in order to accomplish its purpose? And soon enough, he answers the question with this statement: "For a punishment to attain its end, the evil which it inflicts has only to exceed the advantage derivable from the crime" (Beccaria, 1963, p. 43). Anything beyond this, he goes on to write, is superfluous and unlikely to achieve its purpose. He continues, though, to state that when punishment becomes severe and resembles torture, it actually makes people immune to its effects and may lead them to commit the wrongs the punishment is supposed to be preventing.

Having written that excessive punishment is unproductive, Beccaria begins to reflect on the ultimate punishment and torture: the death penalty. He addresses various arguments that had been advanced for the death penalty, but his main argument against capital punishment emerges as this: It is absurd that the laws of the state punish the taking of a life, yet when executing a criminal, the state itself is committing murder. He would prefer that criminals who take the life of others be banished, rather than killed by the government. Although he is generally opposed to capital punishment, he is in favor of punishments. For punishments to be effective, he contends, they must be promptly applied after the commission of a criminal act. The reason for this, Beccaria writes, is because the crime and the punishment must be linked in the minds of citizens. Long delays between the act and the consequence weaken that association. In addition, the punishment should be certain. If men who do wrong believe they might escape punishment, then that punishment is useless. Furthermore, he states that punishment should be suitable to the criminal event.

Continuing to discuss the suitability of punishment, Beccaria argues that if two unequal crimes result in the same punishment, then men may reason that they might as well commit the more serious crime. To argue this, he reiterates a primary philosophical belief: that men are motivated by obtaining pleasure and avoiding pain. People strive to maximize their pleasure and to minimize their pain. If the fear of pain is minimal, then there is little or no deterrence to violate the law.

Starting in Chapter XXIV, Beccaria spends several chapters discussing measuring and classifying crimes. While he takes the position that every crime injures society, he also believes that crimes against people should always result in corporal punishment. This seemingly is an inconsistency in Beccaria's philosophy, as he appears to say that the state shouldn't take the lives of criminals except in some instances. On the other hand, he believes that crimes that dishonor people should result in infamy for the offender, and thefts should result in a fine. Smuggling should result in the loss of the goods smuggled and whatever else the offender possesses at the time. Suicide and expatriation also enter into Beccaria's discussion of classifications of crime. He sees suicide as harming society less than expatriation. The person who takes his wealth to live in another country certainly deprives his own country; however, he states that to discourage expatriation, a state should strive to improve the well-being of all citizens.

After spending some time discussing the crimes of adultery, pederasty (male homosexuality), infanticide, witchcraft, and heresy, Beccaria turns his attention at the end of his book to the prevention of crime. He offers several proposals for preventing crimes after asserting that it is better to prevent criminal acts than to punish them. His first proposal is to make sure that laws are clear and simple. Second, see to it that men fear the laws and nothing else in society. Third, ensure that enlightenment accompanies liberty; "... For no enlightened person can fail to approve of the clear and useful public compacts of mutual security ..." (Beccaria, 1963, p. 95). Fourth, make sure that judges observe the laws rather than corrupt the laws. Fifth, reward virtue. Sixth, perfect education. While he doesn't explain this final proposed idea, it is apparent that he believes that educated youth and adults are more easily directed away from evil and toward the virtuous in life.

Cesare Beccaria

Copyright © 1823 (CC by 4.0) at https://commons
.wikimedia.org/wiki/File:Portrait_of_Marchese_Cesare_
Beccaria_Bonesana,_1738-1794_Wellcome_L0015131.
jpg#/media/File:Portrait_of_Marchese_Cesare_Beccaria_
Bonesana,_1738-1794_Wellcome_L0015131.jpg

Finally, in his conclusion, a one-paragraph ending chapter, Beccaria provides this summing up of his philosophy concerning crimes and punishment: "In order for punishment not to be, in every instance, an act of violence of one or of many against a private citizen, it must be essentially public, prompt, necessary, the least possible in the given circumstances, proportionate to the crimes, dictated by the laws" (Beccaria, 1963, p. 99).

~ THE INTERPRETATION OF
ON CRIMES AND PUNISHMENTS

Beccaria is credited with being a classicist. In criminological theory, the classical position is that people have free will and are rational. Criminals commit crimes, classical criminologists say, because they make rational decisions based on the potential risks and rewards. In other words, offenders—like nonoffenders—exercise their free will. However, a careful reading of *On Crimes and Punishments* suggests that Beccaria was not proposing a theory of carte-blanche volition. Instead, his is a determined will rather than a free will. Thus, his proposals for punishment were predicated on a rational and calculating human being (Beirne, 1993). This calculating man will weigh the pros and cons of committing a criminal act and, if the punishment is swift enough and severe enough, he will desist from offending. If the benefits, however, outweigh the potential risks, he will violate the law.

It can be said that Beccaria's theories were based on three tenets: 1.) Free will leads to people making choices; 2.) Laws exist to preserve the social contract, but people's self-interest often conflicts with what's best for society; people sometimes commit criminal acts out of self-interest; and 3.) Manipulability—people act in predictable ways out of rational self-interest. But if punishment poses a considerable risk for them, they will be dissuaded from violating the law; at that point—when people are reacting to their calculations of risks and rewards—they are no longer operating based on free will.

~ THE RESPONSE TO *ON CRIMES AND PUNISHMENTS*

The response to *On Crimes and Punishments* was uniformly positive. And, as Newman and Marongiu (1990) point out, the ideas expressed in Beccaria's book quickly found advocates in Europe and became important in debates about criminal law, penology, and criminology. But Newman and Marongiu contend that this was mostly due to the strong support of Beccaria's recommendations by Voltaire (Newman & Marongiu, 1990).

While Monachesi (1973) also notes the role of Voltaire in promoting the book, he indicates that in order to properly understand why *On Crimes and Punishments* created such excitement and enthusiasm in Europe, it is important to understand the state of criminal law in Europe at that time. Monachesi describes the criminal justice system in eighteenth-century Europe as repressive, uncertain, and barbaric (Monachesi, 1973). There was a great deal of arbitrariness in how the process of accusing and trying a defendant was carried out, and this process often included many abusive practices (Monachesi, 1973). Prosecutors and judges were given wide latitude in dealing with people accused of crimes. The concept of due process, as we know it today, literally did not exist, and torture was frequently used to elicit confessions. And a great many types of crimes were punished by the death penalty.

Newman and Marongiu (1990) and others have stated that Beccaria's ideas were important because they laid out some basic principles of judicial policy. The criticism, however, was that several of the reforms that Beccaria proposed were already included in the reforms and the writings of others from his day, including Voltaire and Montesquieu.

Further criticism was made of his lack of consistency and even his contradictions. For instance, in one place he indicates that he is in favor of mild punishments, but in other places, he says that the penalties for some crimes (such as those acts of aggression against others) should always be corporal punishment. Similarly, he says that torture should be banned, but at other times, he says that a person who refuses to answer questions during interrogation should receive punishment of the severest kind.

Despite these criticisms, there is no doubt that *On Crimes and Punishments* had an influence on other reformers. Perhaps, though, the reformers—much like the sovereigns who were so enthusiastic about his work, such as Empress Catherine II of Russia, the Grand Duke Leopold of Tuscany, and Frederick II of Prussia—were already inclined toward judicial reform (Newman & Marongiu, 1990).

However, there can be little doubt that the ideas of the Enlightenment philosophers, of whom Beccaria was one, brought about change in many aspects of social and political life, including penal punishment (Newman & Marongiu, 1990).

⌐ THE WIDESPREAD INFLUENCE OF
ON CRIMES AND PUNISHMENTS

The influence of Beccaria's major work after being published in many languages all over the world was felt from Russia, where Catherine the Great praised the work, to the American colonies, where Thomas Jefferson and John Adams quoted from him. It led to the creation and reform of penal systems in many countries. The success of the treatise is explained by the author Maestro (1942) who stated, "Moreover, the great merit of Beccaria's book—and this explains its great success and the practical impact that it would soon have in many countries lies in the fact that for the first time the principles of a penal reform were expressed in a systematic and concise way, and the rights of humanity were defended in the clearest terms, with the most logical arguments" (Maestro, 1942, p. 34).

The popularity of the book may well have centered around the fact that Beccaria discussed issues that were being widely expressed at that time. In addition, more than one country or, in the case of America, group of colonies, were moving toward overthrowing monarchies and instituting a republican form of government. In fact, it was just after *On Crimes and Punishments* was published that the American Revolution occurred. Many of the American founding fathers were well read, and several were greatly influenced by Beccaria, Jeremy Bentham, and other contemporary philosophers. As a result, the Constitution and Bill of Rights, which include many of the rights that United States citizens accept as fundamental, come from the works of these classical criminologists.

As Maestro (1942) suggests, the principles of penal reform were articulated in Beccaria's work, and that influenced many advocates of prison reform. That was particularly true in Europe, where both William Eden, who wrote *Principles of Penal Law* in 1771 and John Howard, who was an English prison reformer, could be counted among the followers of Beccaria (Bessler, 2009). By 1777, John Howard had written *The State of the Prisons in England and Wales*, describing in this book the terrible conditions of British prisons. He was appalled by the filthy conditions in prisons and the fact that prisoners were charged fees, which fed into both the greed of jailers and their neglect of inmates. Based on his observations, Howard made various recommendations for improving prisons (Bessler, 2009).

Also in England, the philosopher Jeremy Bentham read *On Crimes and Punishments* and was so impressed by the book that he wrote glowing praise of Beccaria's work but also commented that the Italian had made a major contribution to his own development while referring to Beccaria as "my master" (Bessler, 2009, p. 205). Another Englishman who had high praise for Beccaria was William Blackstone, the jurist who wrote *Commentaries on the Laws of England.* Blackstone referred to Beccaria as an ingenious writer who understood human nature; he wrote that Beccaria was right in stating that crimes are more likely prevented by the certainty, rather than by the harshness, of punishment (Bessler, 2009).

Blackstone disagreed with Beccaria in terms of the types and ranges of punishments. It was Blackstone's opinion that, in diverging from Beccaria in regard to deciding which punishments ought to be imposed, it is difficult to decide on punishments, and decisions about appropriate punishments should be left up to legislators. In his *Commentaries*, Blackstone laid out some foundational principles, some of which seemed to be inspired by Beccaria's book. Echoing Beccaria, Blackstone wrote that punishment should be rationally imposed and that it should not be arbitrary or overly harsh. And, like Beccaria, Blackstone took the position that punishment should take into account the many complexities of aggravating and extenuating circumstances, and that the effectiveness of a particular punishment should be considered when trying to prevent future crimes (Bessler, 2009).

～ THE INFLUENCE ON EARLY AMERICANS

William Blackstone and Cesare Beccaria were both authors read by many of America's founding fathers. Since they shared similar views on the law and criminal justice, it is certain that both men played a role in the shaping of the Constitution and the Bill of Rights. Some historians have gone so far as to cite *On Crimes and Punishments* as the most influential book in America around the time of the Revolution (Bessler, 2009). Historical writings by America's founders strongly suggest that the men who helped to form a new government often turned to Beccaria's treatise for guidance (Bessler, 2009).

Schwartz and Wishingrad, writing in the *Buffalo Law Review* (1975), found that there were three American translations of Beccaria which were published in America before the drafting of the Bill of Rights. There is considerable evidence that those three translations were popular at both bookstores and lending libraries in the eighteenth century. It is known that Thomas Jefferson and James Madison were familiar with the writings of Beccaria. Madison, who read many European authors, was a student of Beccaria's work, and he included Beccaria's *On Crimes and Punishments* in the list of recommended books he offered to the Continental Congress (Bessler, 2009).

In 1770, following the Boston Massacre, John Adams, a Boston lawyer and future president of the United States, agreed to defend the British soldiers accused of murdering five colonists. During the subsequent trials, Adams showed that he was familiar with Beccaria's ideas. In fact, in taking on this unpopular cause, Adams eloquently referred to Beccaria in his opening statement on behalf of his British clients (McCullough, 2001).

Dr. Benjamin Rush was a friend of John Adams who lived and practiced in Philadelphia. Like Adams, he was an admirer of Beccaria's work (Bessler, 2014). However, unlike Adams, Rush was against the death penalty. In March 1787, he gave a reading at the home of Benjamin Franklin and during this reading cited Beccaria as an authority in denouncing capital punishment, which Rush saw as an improper punishment (Bessler, 2012).

There were other leaders in colonial America who were reading Beccaria's writings. Among these leading citizens were John Hancock, one of the signers of the Declaration of Independence, as well as William Bradford and Thomas Paine. Bradford, a former Pennsylvania attorney general, wrote in 1793 *An Enquiry How Far the Punishment of Death Is Necessary in Pennsylvania*. This short book reflected many of Beccaria's arguments, in that Bradford not only questioned the necessity of capital punishment but argued that it should never be used—except for offenses such as high treason and murder (Bessler, 2009). Paine, like Benjamin Rush, was an ardent abolitionist, opposing the death penalty for any reason. Beccaria, though, conceded that the death penalty might be useful if it prevented other crimes.

Thomas Jefferson was also fascinated by Beccaria's ideas, often quoting from Beccaria in his *Commonplace Book*. When Jefferson was writing drafts of Virginia's constitution, he proposed banning capital punishment. When Jefferson penned the Declaration of Independence and used the phrase about an "inalienable" right to life, it is clear that Beccaria served as an inspiration for the famous document. When Jefferson served on a committee to expand the death penalty's use during wartime, he also was a member of the Virginia Committee of Revisors for legal reform. In this capacity, he helped draft a bill for Virginia's legislature calling for proportionate punishments, or, in his words, punishments "suited to reason" (Peterson, 1987, p. 125). It was Beccaria who first called for proportionate punishment.

In a draft of his autobiography, written in the later years of his life, Thomas Jefferson reflected on that bill's narrow defeat. He wrote that he rejected the doctrine of *lex talionis*, and he paid homage to *On Crimes and Punishments* for informing his anti–death penalty position. As Jefferson wrote, it was Beccaria, among others, who had convinced him and others of the "unrightfulness and inefficacy of the punishment of crimes by death" (Padover, 1967, p. 42). Jefferson went on to state in his autobiography that the Virginia Committee of Revisors had considered labor on roads, canals, and other public works as appropriate substitutions for capital punishment. But Jefferson opined that the general mood of the country "had not yet advanced" to the point of banning the death penalty (Padover, 1967, p. 42).

In 1816, Jefferson sent a letter to William Wirt, the author of a biography of Patrick Henry. In that letter, Jefferson said, with obvious satisfaction, that Virginia "justly prides itself on having gone thro' the revolution without a single example of capital punishment connected with that" (National Archives, n.d., p. 1).

Thomas Jefferson also revealed his admiration for Beccaria's book in another piece of correspondence. While serving as our third president,

Jefferson, an avid book collector and one of the most well-read men of his time, would write a telling letter in 1807 recommending that the recipient of his letter, one John Norvell, should read Beccaria's work on crimes and punishments. In making this recommendation, Jefferson said he did so "because of the demonstrative manner" in which Beccaria "has treated that branch of the subject" (American History, 2012, p. 1). By singling out *On Crimes and Punishments*, Jefferson made it apparent that he had a certain reverence for Beccaria's work and its condemnation of both torture and state-sanctioned executions.

In Merrill D. Peterson's biography of Thomas Jefferson, it is revealed that Jefferson read Beccaria's book in the original Italian soon after it was published (Peterson, 1987). As indicated, furthermore, he also copied lengthy passages from *On Crimes and Punishments* into his commonplace book, a notebook of his literary and philosophical readings. As an attorney practicing before the General Court in Virginia, he had an opportunity to see some of the problems with the criminal justice system in Virginia. Although as a member of the Committee of Revisors he attempted to revise the criminal law in his home state and have capital punishment abolished for all crimes (except treason and willful murder), he couldn't accomplish this.

But Jefferson did set forth proposals for more humanitarian treatment of offenders. Like Beccaria, he proposed a new classification of crimes for Virginia and then that the punishments be suited to each of the three categories of crime. Beccaria's influence was clear when Jefferson articulated three cardinal principles. First was that punishment is an evil in itself and is justified only insofar as it rehabilitates criminals and prevents future crimes; also, that the death penalty should be the last resort. Second was that punishments more severe than necessary defeat their purpose. Third, crimes are more effectively prevented by the certainty of punishment—not by the severity of punishment (Peterson, 1987). Jefferson's proposed bill, the "Bill on Crimes and Punishments," for a more humanitarian approach to criminal justice in Virginia was defeated twice by the House in the mid-1780s. However, a decade later, some of the features of Jefferson's bill were finally enacted into law.

ARE BECCARIA'S IDEAS STILL RELEVANT TODAY?

The classical view of criminology has never disappeared either in America or in some other countries. Rational choice theory takes many of the classical ideas and makes them perhaps even more relative to today's issues. Rational choice theory is no different from the principles espoused by Beccaria: individuals have free will, and using this free will, they make rational choices to either commit—or refrain from committing—crimes. Rational choice is governed by attempts to increase pleasure and avoid pain. The government has the right and duty to preserve what is in the best interest of most people in a society. And swift, severe, and certain punishment will give the government control over the people's choices and behavior. By threatening and using incarceration and punishment, crimes can be prevented because people will fear getting caught and punished.

Contemporary proponents of rational choice theory follow in Beccaria's footsteps by agreeing that the threat of punishment leads both to specific deterrence and general deterrence. The philosophy of specific deterrence is that by punishing offenders, often with imprisonment, they are less likely to commit new offenses. In general deterrence, the idea is that when some offenders are punished, perhaps severely, it will deter others from committing a similar offense. Although Beccaria did not write in depth about general and specific deterrence, he did write in a general manner about the use of laws and punishment. He stated that if punishment is certain and prompt, the general public and specific criminals will be deterred from committing crimes. In other words, we can see that Beccaria has had a large and lasting impact on the field of criminal justice.

WHY BECCARIA AND *ON CRIMES AND PUNISHMENTS* IS REMEMBERED TODAY

The acclaim that Beccaria received for *On Crimes and Punishments* was not necessarily because what he wrote was new or original. But what it did do was submit in a clear and fairly well-reasoned manner a cry for reform in the administration of justice (Monachesi, 1973). The book advocated changes in the criminal justice system that were generally desired by and supported by public opinion at the time.

And Beccaria's treatise appeared at the very time that countries in Europe—and the colonies in what would become America—were revolting against despotism and absolutism (Monachesi, 1973). Europe, particularly, was ready for this book.

But after it was published in 1764, Cesare Beccaria's literary output abruptly ended. Romantic rumors, perhaps mostly fueled by Beccaria's social awkwardness and his retiring nature, led to speculation, especially in countries other than Italy, that his sparse output of books and writings were somehow due to political suppression. The real reason why there were no subsequent books, of course, was that he lacked the emotional strength and resources to write more treatises.

After his death in 1794, Pietro Verri petitioned the city of Milan to erect a "Monument to the immortal Beccaria" (Paolucci, 1963, p. xvi). That didn't happen. Today, however, he is remembered as a literary champion of the cause of humanity and, for many, as the Father of Criminology.

QUESTIONS FOR DISCUSSION

1. In addition to the examples given in this biography, in what other ways might Beccaria's influence be seen today?
2. Although Beccaria was advocating for prison reform, what are lasting prison reforms for which he could be responsible?
3. Thinking of well-known politicians and legislators, who might be said to be a follower of Beccaria and his ideas?
4. Which arguments that Beccaria makes against the death penalty seem the most effective?

— IMPORTANT TERMS

Academy of fists: Pietro Verri and Alessandro Verri, Beccaria's friends, formed a society that was called the "academy of fists," which was a forum for their advocacy for political, social, and literary reforms.

Enlightenment philosophers: The Enlightenment was the period in the history of Western thought and culture that stretched from about the mid-seventeenth century through the eighteenth century. The Enlightenment philosophers, which included both French and English authors such as Montesquieu, Helvetius, Diderot, Buffon, and Hume, called for revolutions in science, philosophy, society, and politics. Enlightenment ideals included freedom and equality for all based on principles of human reason.

Deterrence: Deterrence is the threat of punishment to influence people to avoid criminal acts.

Classical theory: Classical theory comes from the classical school of thought in criminology, which emphasizes that people have free will and are able to calculate whether they should or shouldn't commit a crime.

Rational choice theory: While fundamentally based on the classical theory of criminology, rational choice theory assumes that the criminal offender's behavior is purposeful and is intended to benefit the offender in some way.

REVIEW QUESTIONS

True or False

1. Cesare Beccaria may well be considered the Father of Criminology.
2. Cesare Beccaria was a member of a revolutionary group called the "academy of fists," which advocated overthrowing the Italian government.
3. Beccaria published his book *On Crimes and Punishments* anonymously because Beccaria was fearful that he was too bold in his recommended reforms and he might get into trouble.
4. Cesare Beccaria is credited with being a classicist, which means, in criminological theory, that he believed people have free will and make rational decisions.

Multiple Choice

5. Beccaria's proposals for punishment were predicated on the idea that people are rational and weigh the pros and cons of committing a criminal act. Therefore, Beccaria believed that if punishment is both swift and severe enough, then

    a. He will commit a criminal behavior.
    b. He will desist from offending.
    c. He will spend a considerable amount of time calculating the benefits and risks.
    d. He will use the insanity defense.

6. *On Crimes and Punishments* created a great deal of both interest and controversy in Europe when it was published because

    a. The concept of due process, as we know it today, literally did not exist.
    b. Torture was never used to elicit confessions.
    c. Punishment was severe, and the death penalty was frequently used as a punishment.
    d. The criminal justice system in Beccaria's time was modern and fair.

7. There is good evidence that many of America's founding fathers carefully read Beccaria's *On Crimes and Punishments* writings and that his work

    a. Had little influence on the founding fathers.
    b. Resulted in America abolishing severe punishment.
    c. Led James Madison to reject Beccaria's ideas on punishment for criminals.
    d. Helped in shaping America's early history and the creation of the Bill of Rights.

8. In writing his autobiography, Thomas Jefferson gave credit to Cesare Beccaria's book for being the inspiration for

    a. Jefferson's antislavery position.
    b. Why Jefferson favored capital punishment.
    c. How Jefferson was opposed to the death penalty.
    d. Jefferson's beliefs about economic matters.

FOR FURTHER READING

Beccaria, C. (1963). *On crimes and punishments.* Englewood Cliffs, NJ: Prentice Hall.

Bessler, J. D. (2014). *The birth of American law: An Italian philosopher and the American Revolution.* Durham, NC: Carolina Academic Press.

REFERENCES

American History. (2012). Thomas Jefferson to John Norvell Washington, June 14, 1807. Available: http://www.let.rug.nl/usa/presidents/thomas-jefferson/letters-of-thomas-jefferson/jefl179.php

Beccaria, C. (1963). *On crimes and punishments.* Englewood Cliffs, NJ: Prentice Hall.

Beirne, P. (1993). *Inventing criminology: Essays on the rise of "Homo Criminalis."* Albany, NY: State University of New York Press.

Bessler, J. D. (2014). *The birth of American law: An Italian philosopher and the American Revolution.* Durham, NC: Carolina Academic Press.

Bessler, J. D. (2012). *Cruel & unusual: The American death penalty and the founders' Eighth Amendment.* Boston, MA: Northeastern University Press.

Bessler, J. D. (2009). Revisiting Beccaria's vision: The Enlightenment, America's death penalty, and the abolition movement. *Northwestern Journal of Law and Social Policy, 4*(2), 195–328.

Maestro, M. T. (1942). *Voltaire and Beccaria as reformers of criminal law.* New York, NY: Columbia University Press.

McCullough, D. (2001). *John Adams.* New York, NY: Simon & Schuster.

Monachesi, E. (1973). Cesare Beccaria. In H. Mannheim (Ed.), *Pioneers in criminology* (2nd ed., pp. 36–50). Montclair, NJ: Patterson Smith.

National Archives. (n.d.). *Thomas Jefferson.* Founders Online. Available: http://founders.archives.gov/documents/Jefferson/03-10-02-0311

Newman, G., & Marongiu, P. (1990). Penological reform and the myth of Beccaria. *Criminology, 28*(2), 325–346.

Padover, S. K. (1967). *The writings of Thomas Jefferson.* Hartford, CT: Easton Press.

Paolucci, H. (1963). In C. Beccaria, *On crimes and punishments* (pp. ix–xxiii). Englewood Cliffs, NJ: Prentice Hall.

Peterson, M. D. (1987). *Thomas Jefferson and the new nation.* Norwalk, CT: Easton Press.

Schwartz, D. A., & Wishingrad, J. (1975). The Eighth Amendment, Beccaria, and Enlightenment: An historical justification for the Weems v. U.S. excessive punishment doctrine. *Buffalo Law Review, 24,* 784–835.

2

JAMES MADISON
Father of American Criminal Justice

If any one person can be said to be the founding father of the American criminal justice system, that person might be James Madison. He wasn't in law enforcement, he never served as a judge or a prosecuting attorney, and he may never even have seen the inside of a prison or a courtroom. Yet, it can be argued that he had an understanding of the United States Constitution and the Bill of Rights that anyone has yet to equal.

Some historians have even claimed that were it not for James Madison, we might not even have a Bill of Rights; certainly it is safe to assert that without Madison, our Bill of Rights would be far different from what it is today.

As a founding father of our country, Madison lays claim—with plenty of good reasons—to being one of the great historical figures in American history. Here are just a few of the reasons why he is a great, albeit sometimes underrated, figure in our history:

- He was a member of the Continental Congress and helped draft the Declaration of Independence;
- He attended and participated in the convention in Philadelphia that produced the U.S. Constitution; as a result, he is hailed by many as the Father of the Constitution;
- He was one of the three authors of the Federalist papers, the historical publications that led to the thirteen original states ratifying the Constitution;
- He served as an adviser to President George Washington;

- He was secretary of state during the presidency of Thomas Jefferson;
- He is mainly responsible for the establishment of the Library of Congress;
- He served eight years as the fourth president of the United States.

But, despite all of these accomplishments, it was as a congressman from Virginia and as a member of the Constitutional Convention of 1787 that he made the contribution to our society that earns him the honorary title of Father of the American criminal justice system.

BIRTH AND EARLY LIFE

James Madison was born in Virginia in the home of his maternal grandmother. His great-grandfather was ship carpenter John Madison, who came to America on a ship from England in 1652. John Madison obtained 600 acres of land and built that land into an estate of 1900 acres—growing and selling tobacco—before he died. His grandson, James Madison Sr., eventually took over the estate, and after marrying seventeen-year-old Nelly Conway, their firstborn child, James Madison Jr., entered the world on March 16, 1751.

The young Madison, one of twelve children (five of whom died in infancy), was probably taught to read and write by his grandmother, Ambrose Madison, who died when James was ten years of age. It was about that time that the family moved into a new brick mansion they named Montpelier. It would be James Madison's home for the next seventy-five years.

In June 1762, just after he turned eleven, young James was enrolled in a boarding school run by Donald Robertson. Regarding the five years he studied in the school, Madison would later say, referring to Robertson, "All that I have been in life I owe largely to that man" (Brant, 1970, p. 7).

After his years with Robertson, his education continued with Thomas Martin, an Anglican minister, and then in his teenage years he attended the College of New Jersey—now Princeton. In college, Madison would study Latin, Greek, mathematics, and philosophy. However, he also studied nations, learning about governments and international relations.

Those particular studies he would continue for most of his life, and he often imported books from Europe in order to learn as much as he could about nations and their governments.

A Portrait of James Madison

https://commons.wikimedia.org/wiki/File:James_Madison.jpg#/media/File:James_Madison.jpg. Copyright in the Public Domain.

Graduating from college in 1771, Madison stayed at college to continue his studies, especially in law. Those months—stretching over a year—of quiet study and reflection after his graduation from the College of New Jersey implanted in him concepts of liberty that helped to guide him throughout his life. But as the break with Great Britain was becoming inevitable, Madison was ready to get involved in politics, and he was elected to the Virginia legislature in his first campaign.

JAMES MADISON'S POLITICAL CAREER

Madison attained his first political office in 1774, when he was twenty-three. That first job was as a member of the Orange County Committee of Safety. The Committee of Safety served Orange County (located in Virginia) by forming militias and ensuring that in the event of revolution, the county would be able to govern itself.

The First Continental Congress started meeting in the summer of 1774. It was short lived, but the Second Continental Congress convened the next summer, and it would last for nearly six years. Madison was elected to serve in the Virginia Convention, which had the job of writing that state's constitution. Together with George Mason, James Madison rewrote the draft that would eventually become Virginia's constitution. He would later use it as a reference and model for the United States Constitution. At age twenty-five, Madison would write the bulk of the Constitution that related to the separation of powers.

Getting back to the political affairs in Virginia and with a constitution written, Virginia assembled its first state government. In late 1776, James Madison was elected to the Virginia House of Delegates. While a member of the House of Delegates, he met Thomas Jefferson, and they worked together on issues pertaining to religious freedom.

After the Revolution, Madison was enlisted to help Thomas Jefferson write the Virginia Statute for Religious Freedom, one of the first documents that established the separation of church and state. This was an ideological underpinning that would become a hallmark of the U.S. Constitution.

In 1778, Madison was defeated in his bid for reelection to the House of Delegates. But he was soon appointed to the eight-member Governor's Committee, which directly advised Virginia's first sitting governor, Patrick Henry. In December 1778, Madison was elected to a three-year term as a delegate to the Continental Congress in Philadelphia. He replaced Jefferson, who was returning to Virginia to serve as governor of the state. Thus, with this election won and headed for Philadelphia, he was ready to assume his first role on the national stage. On that stage in Philadelphia, he would be the youngest delegate.

As a delegate to the Continental Congress, Madison was made part of the committee on rights and government, although the declaration of rights that came out of this committee relied mostly on the writing of George Mason of Virginia. Madison, however, did contribute his ideas that all men are equal and that each should be able to exercise the right of their conscience. All men, Madison declared, are entitled to the free exercise of religion.

In the Continental Congress, he gained a reputation as a man of integrity and wisdom. Serving on various committees during the time that the fledgling nation was negotiating its independence from Great Britain, Madison proved his importance to Congress. He addressed Congress at one point on a plan for national unity, calling on the people of the thirteen colonies to think and act for the good of the nation. Along with Alexander Hamilton, Thomas Jefferson, and George Washington, Madison strongly encouraged the thirteen states to forget self-interest and local bias and

consider what would best bring about a confederation of st.
to a prosperous nation.

Although the work of the Philadelphia Convention was ov
difficult challenges lay ahead. Before the proposed Constitution could be
submitted to the states for ratification, it had to get through the national
legislature. Serving as a member of the Confederation Congress, Madison
was destined to play a key role in that effort. Helping to sidestep crippling
debate and efforts to tinker with the Constitution, Madison saw to it that
the Confederation Congress sent it on to the states for ratification conventions and votes in each state.

Without Madison, who worked tirelessly at the Constitutional
Convention, the Virginia ratifying convention, and the First Congress, the
Bill of Rights—the foundation for individual liberty—might never have
become part of the Constitution.

Although on September 17, 1787, Madison signed his name to the
new Constitution, some others, like George Mason and Virginia governor
Edmund Randolph, refused to sign because it seemingly did not protect
the rights of the citizens and did not include a bill of rights. Their position
was that the Constitution was flawed because it lacked a bill of rights. There
was controversy about this, however, because there were others, such as
Alexander Hamilton, who contended (as Hamilton did in *Federalist 84*)
that a bill of rights would be not only unnecessary in the proposed constitution, but "could well prove dangerous" (Monk, 1995, p. 30).

ADVOCATING FOR RATIFICATION
OF THE CONSTITUTION

As early as the fall of 1787, Madison began hearing alarming reports that
Anti-Federalists—like Patrick Henry and Richard Henry Lee—were warning
citizens in Virginia that the new Constitution would create a government
that betrayed the principles of the Declaration of Independence and
would trample personal liberties.

Richard Henry Lee, one of the most important Anti-Federalists and
perhaps the leading intellectual in their ranks, passionately believed that

the Constitution granted so much power to the new federal government that a bill of rights was necessary to protect citizens from potentially despotic rulers. Specifically, Lee wanted to defend the rights of conscience in a) matters of religion; b) freedom of the press; c) protection against unreasonable searches and seizures; d) the right to trial by jury in civil cases; e) the ban on standing armies unless two-thirds of Congress approves; f) the prohibition of excessive bail or fines and of cruel and unusual punishment; and g) the right of the people to assemble peaceably for the purpose of petitioning legislative bodies (Labunski, 2006).

Madison was elected as a delegate to the Virginia Convention. With the strong opposition to the Constitution, he feared that after the convention voted to allow amendments to the Constitution, other states would also do so, and the number of amendments would quickly multiply as states would submit amendments advancing their own interests. Maybe there would be hundreds that Congress would have to sort through. Madison also knew how difficult another constitutional convention would be, and he wanted to avoid that. Someone needed to step forward to save the new union of states from chaos. But who would that be?

It was none other than a five-foot-six, one-hundred-pound, shy man with a quiet voice, a timid demeanor, and a perpetually upset stomach. That man was James Madison. He and Thomas Jefferson got behind a plan to encourage the Virginia delegates to do what Massachusetts had done: ratify the Constitution with the understanding that amendments could be added later.

By May 23, 1788, eight states had ratified; only one more was needed for the nine required. On June 21, 1788, New Hampshire became the ninth state to ratify the Constitution. With that, the Constitution went into effect, replacing the Articles of Confederation. Still, it was vital that Virginia and New York ratify the Constitution. By the beginning of June 1788, enough state conventions had approved the Constitution to launch the new government. But the largest and most politically powerful state—Virginia—had not.

On June 2, 1788, the Virginia ratifying convention officially began its work. It was attended by 170 delegates and hundreds of spectators, most of whom were there to see and hear many of the leading figures of the revolutionary and founding era debate the Constitution. They met every day from June 2 to June 27, 1788. Edmund Pendleton, a respected Virginia judge and political figure, presided over them.

After voting to debate the Constitution clause by clause, the delegates began a detailed discussion of the Constitution. The orderly approach, however, was soon abandoned, as delegates enlarged the discussion by discussing any part of the Constitution they wished to discuss.

The debate went back and forth with Madison, Patrick Henry, and others debating passionately and logically about the Constitution and the need for a bill of rights. Henry took the position that Virginia should stay out of the Union until the needed amendments were proposed by a second convention or by Congress. Madison said the Constitution should be tried out first and then later amended.

Finally, on June 25, it was time for a vote: They would vote first on the question of whether ratification would be conditional on a bill of rights. By a margin of 88 to 80, the delegates rejected the motion to ratify contingent upon amendments being approved by Congress or a new convention and then being ratified by states.

Next was the vote for the Constitution itself. By a vote of 89 to 79, the delegates approved the Constitution.

New York—the fifth largest state in population, but the most important state in terms of commerce—finally ratified the Constitution in late July, becoming the eleventh state to do so. James Madison and many others were well aware that both Virginia and New York had to join in approving the Constitution—or the new government was doomed.

CREATING A BILL OF RIGHTS

In the Federalist papers, Madison had argued against a bill of rights. In *Federalist 46*, for instance, he implies that a bill of rights was unnecessary because the states could protect citizens from an oppressive federal government (Labunski, 2006). Over time, with the gentle but firm persuasion of Thomas Jefferson and others, Madison softened his opposition to a bill of rights.

After the vote, Federalists kept their word that they would remain at the convention so amendments could be considered. George Wythe, a respected law professor, was named as head of a committee that would prepare a list of amendments that would accompany the ratification resolution. Among those on the twenty-person committee were Patrick Henry, John Marshall, George Mason, and James Madison.

On June 27, 1787, the Wythe committee reported forty amendments, many of which were based on amendments that were put together by a group of Anti-Federalists headed by George Mason earlier in the Virginia Convention. Twenty of those amendments focused mainly on personal rights. The others related to reserving to the states powers not granted to the new government.

Although ratifying the Constitution was a momentary defeat for Patrick Henry and other Anti-Federalists, Henry was not done fighting. He was a prominent and powerful member of Virginia's General Assembly, and thus had a say in whom the General Assembly would choose for the Senate and whether the General Assembly would formally petition Congress for a convention to reconsider the Constitution and a bill of rights. It seemed apparent that Henry would do everything possible to block Madison from becoming a senator or even a representative to the House of Representatives. Madison much preferred the House, as he would be elected by citizens.

However, Madison was suggested as one of three nominations for the U.S. Senate. The other two were selected—not Madison—for the Senate. But the General Assembly reapportioned congressional districts so that Madison would be in a district heavily populated by Anti-Federalists. And his opponent in the election was James Monroe. Still, on February 2, 1789, Madison beat out his friend Monroe. Madison would be in the First Congress.

As Madison made his way to New York, the seat of government then, Madison remembered that he had made a promise to the citizens of his district and state that he would work diligently to support amendments to protect individual liberty.

The new Congress would meet at Federal Hall in Lower Manhattan. On April 1, 1789, enough representatives arrived in New York for a quorum and thus the House could begin its business. Indeed, it had a great deal of business to consider—taxes, criminal laws, establishing executive departments, patents, and the location of the permanent seat of government—among various other tasks.

On May 4, James Madison announced to the House that on May 25 he would introduce a discussion of amendments to the Constitution. In George Washington's first address as the first president, he supported amendments. The May 4 date for discussion was postponed, but on June 8 Madison addressed the House on the subject of amendments. He indicated his resolve to continue to push for amendments until they would be adopted.

The House agreed to debate the topic. Madison took the floor, and in a speech lasting several hours—perhaps one of the most important speeches of his life—outlined his proposal for amendments. His list of amendments included:

- enlarging the size of the House;
- protecting freedom of religion, speech, and the press;
- preserving the right to trial by jury in both civil and criminal cases;
- and prohibiting arbitrary searches, excessive bail, and double jeopardy.

Madison recommended that the list of rights he presented be incorporated into the body of the Constitution and not added at the end. However, there was opposition to this last proposal. For example, Roger Sherman, the congressman from Connecticut, insisted that the amendments not be inserted into the Constitution but be contained in a separate section at the end of the Constitution.

The House tried incorporating what would eventually be the first amendment, and it was seen how awkward this would be. Roger Sherman and several colleagues finally convinced the House, with Madison's grudging acceptance, to place the amendments at the end of the Constitution.

After considerable debate, on June 8 it was decided that the entire House would take up the subject of amendments, but not until July 21, 1789. However, on that date, perhaps to Madison's great frustration, the House debated for hours as to whether the full House or a select committee should take up the matter of the amendments. Finally, the House voted and approved a motion to send the amendments to a select committee. The committee would have eleven members, one from each state. It would begin meeting immediately and report back to the House in one week. Madison was to be Virginia's representative.

A week later, the committee reported back its work. The report was delivered by John Vining of Delaware. The committee accepted most of Madison's recommendations—including his recommendation that amendments be incorporated into the body of the Constitution—but it made several significant changes to his proposed amendments. The committee changed some of Madison's prose, rearranged the order of amendments, and considerably narrowed the guarantees of religious freedom and equal rights of conscience. The committee also eliminated most of Madison's natural-rights preamble, cutting out the assertion that the people have the right to reform or change their government when it becomes antagonistic of their wishes or inadequate in its ability to represent them. The committee replaced some of Madison's words with phrases that would eventually be incorporated into the Bill of Rights. It used the phrase "freedom of speech, and of the press"—language that would become part of the First Amendment. It also changed the words of the "just compensation" clause of the Fifth Amendment; wrote most of what would become the Ninth Amendment, which stated that the people retain rights not enumerated in the Constitution; and approved the principles that would form the Seventh Amendment, providing for jury trials in civil suits.

Furthermore, the committee accepted Madison's recommendation that states, and not just the federal government, be prohibited from infringing the rights of "conscience," freedom of speech and the press, and trial by jury in criminal cases. Madison considered this the most important amendment.

But after Vining presented the report, the House voted to table it until further action.

It would be tabled until August 13, when members of the House, sitting as a committee of the whole, devoted almost all of their attention to the proposed amendments. There was still vigorous discussion about where to place the amendments, and while Madison first stuck to inserting them in the Constitution, he saw he was losing that argument and consented to placing them at the end of the Constitution.

The amendments, which would eventually be combined into one version by the Senate, went through various stages as members of the House offered language they believed would best protect such precious rights. Day after day—for eleven days—the House debated the proposed amendments and changed the language and order of them.

Finally, the House—the committee of the whole—had finished its work. It had rewritten the select committee's language related to the free exercise of religion and the banning of establishments of religion; limited to criminal cases the right against self-incrimination; restored protection against unreasonable searches and seizures, which had been dropped by the committee; and added "or to the people" to Madison's recommendation that powers not delegated to the federal government be reserved to the states.

Overall, the House largely adopted Madison's amendments with relatively minor changes over the eleven days it debated the issues. But before the full House approved the amendments, Madison had to give up the rest of what remained of his preamble, and he reluctantly agreed to Sherman's demand that the amendments be added to the end of the Constitution.

On August 24, after more days of debate, the House forwarded seventeen amendments to the Senate. The House amendments were formally read in the Senate on August 25, 1789. Meeting behind closed doors (which the Senate did until 1794), nothing is known about the debate in the Senate. But after what most surely was heated and intense discussion, the Senate made changes to some amendments while rejecting new ones proposed by several senators. By the time the Senate completed its work on September 14, 1789, it had made twenty-six changes to the House version by tightening language and rearranging some amendments and combining others. They reduced the number from seventeen to twelve.

The most significant decision, though, by the Senate, one that would directly shape the nation's history for 150 years, was the removal of Madison's most favored amendment, the one that prohibited the states from infringing upon the freedom of speech, the press, and religion, and guaranteed trial by jury. Madison might have been disappointed with the changes, but there were others who thought that the Senate had improved the amendments. Now, the House and the Senate had to agree on a compromise set of amendments.

The House was willing to go along with some of the Senate's changes, but it rejected others. On September 21, 1789, the House appointed a conference committee composed of Madison, Sherman, and Vining, who met with their Senate counterparts (Ellsworth, Paterson, and Carroll). Three days later, the House approved the committee's report, and on September 25, the Senate agreed to the House's version. A week later, President Washington submitted the twelve amendments to the states for ratification.

AMENDMENTS SENT TO STATES FOR RATIFICATION

Massachusetts was the first state legislature to take up the proposed amendments. After debate, and even though Governor John Hancock recommended approval of all twelve amendments, the Massachusetts Senate rejected amendments one, two, and twelve and accepted all the rest. Then, by February 2, 1790, both the Massachusetts Senate and House had approved of amendments three through eleven.

As with the ratification of the Constitution, Virginia became the last state to decide whether the Bill of Rights would become part of the Constitution. Once again, it was Anti-Federalists, especially Patrick Henry (who wanted more radical amendments; in particular, one that would forbid the federal government to collect taxes), who lobbied against acceptance of the amendments.

The debate and engineered delays went on for two years until finally it was left up to Virginia to decide for the country if the amendments would go into the Constitution. It would not be until December 5, 1791, that the Virginia House approved all of the amendments. Ten days later, the Virginia Senate would also approve all of the amendments.

THE UNITED STATES HAS A BILL OF RIGHTS

Despite the concerted efforts of Patrick Henry and all of the rest of the Anti-Federalists, James Madison had succeeded in sponsoring the Bill of Rights and preventing the nation from suffering the consequences of a second constitutional convention. The first two amendments put forward by Congress fell short of ratification and were discarded. Thus, we have a Bill of Rights with ten amendments.

Over the more than 225 years since its ratification, the Bill of Rights has assumed greater and greater importance. Originally, the Bill of Rights was mostly intended to limit the powers of the new government. However, since then, it has become fundamental in securing the rights of citizens against the state and the government.

Eventually, the Fourth through the Eighth Amendments were applied to the states—not just to the federal government—through the "due process" clause of the Fourteenth Amendment, which was adopted after the Civil War.

JAMES MADISON AFTER THE BATTLE FOR THE BILL OF RIGHTS

James Madison fell in love with and married Dolley Payne Todd in 1794. They would be together for forty-two years, and she would make her mark as a charming first lady during Madison's two terms as president.

This was after Madison served as secretary of state for eight years under President Thomas Jefferson. During that time, Dolley was considered the unofficial first lady, since Jefferson's wife had died years before. Dolley brought to the relationship a bustling and vivacious personality and a flair for the fashionable (Peterson, 1974). She was everything that her husband was not. In public, James Madison appeared dry and stiff. However, put him in a social setting and he could be—perhaps with no small thanks to the outgoing Dolley—affable, good humored, and always ready with a story or anecdote (Peterson, 1974).

Edward Cole, who would serve as his private secretary, described him as "neat and genteel in his dress," but always wearing a black suit and coat (Peterson, 1974, p. 250). Cole also said that Madison was never seen without his white powdered wig worn low enough on his forehead to cover his baldness. A small man, Madison was about five feet six inches tall in a rather delicate frame. Cole also wrote of him: "... [his] features, and manner were not commanding, but his conversation exceedingly so and few men possessed so rich a flow of language, or so great a fund of amusing anecdotes, which were made the more interesting for their being well-timed and well-told" (Peterson, 1974, p. 251).

After Madison's two terms in the presidency, he and Dolley retired to Montpelier in 1817, where he remained for almost 20 years, rarely venturing away from his house. Their house, which Madison referred to as the farm, was actually a plantation. In the those two decades, the farm was a mecca for visitors, as both Madison and his wife enjoyed entertaining, often having as many as ninety guests at a time.

Although according to some observers he maintained a lively interest in public affairs, Madison considered his primary business as farming. Even though he had more than one hundred slaves on his plantation, he wanted to see slavery abolished. Madison regarded slavery as a moral crime, a curse to society, and a menace to the Union (Peterson, 1974). Before retirement, he thought that the slavery system would collapse as society advanced and became more enlightened. When that didn't happen, he thought a great deal about solutions to the problem. Madison knew that just freeing slaves would not be an adequate solution. However, believing that the two races could never live together in a state of freedom and equality, he finally came to the conclusion that the answer could be found in the idea of colonization.

The concept of colonization, according to Madison's thinking, was to remove blacks to a region beyond what was accepted by or allotted to whites. That might mean, he thought, that blacks might have to be transported to the African coast. The government should finance this in order to compensate both former slaves and the slaveholders.

Aside from his views of colonization, Madison considered the problem of slavery as a piece of unfinished business left over after the Revolution. In fact, he thought that if there was one problem that seriously threatened the United States, it was slavery. However, if slavery was on his mind a lot, so was education, specifically the conquest of ignorance.

In 1785, James Madison had tried and failed to win legislative approval of Thomas Jefferson's comprehensive plan of public education. Still thinking about that many years later, the idea was revived in Virginia in 1818. Although again the idea of creating a public education system for elementary and secondary students, the Virginia legislature did approve of a plan to establish a state university. At one point, Madison proclaimed that a popular government without popular education "is but a prologue to a Farce or a Tragedy, or perhaps both" (Peterson, 1974, p. 379).

Madison and Jefferson together founded the University of Virginia, and it was to be, among many other things, a secular institution. Jefferson would be the university's first rector (a combination of university president and chairman of the board) until he died on July 4, 1824. Madison succeeded him as rector.

James and Dolley lived a serene life in retirement, until his frail body finally failed him on June 28, 1836, when he died quietly at home at age eighty-five. Afterward, Dolley left Montpelier and returned to Washington, where she led an active social life until her own death at age eighty-two in 1849.

A BILL OF RIGHTS WITHOUT MADISON?

Would we have a Bill of Rights today without James Madison? That's difficult to answer. What is certain is that he was a man of extraordinary capabilities who was there at the right time to make sure we did have a

Bill of Rights. These rights have become more important in the last 150 years—perhaps more so even than Madison might have imagined.

It is nearly impossible to think of the American criminal justice system without the Bill of Rights, especially the Fourth, Fifth, Sixth, and Eighth Amendments. These amendments serve as the bedrock of the justice system, a fact that has been reinforced by so many Supreme Court decisions since the 1960s. Was Madison so wise that he knew this would be the case?

Associate Supreme Court justice Ruth Bader Ginsburg seems to think so. She pointed out that Madison recognized that if the Bill of Rights was not to be a mere "parchment barrier" to the will of the majority, the judiciary would have to play a central role (Monk, 1995). And Madison himself said, "If [a Bill of Rights is] incorporated into the Constitution, independent tribunals of justice will consider themselves in a peculiar manner the guardians of those rights; they will be an impenetrable bulwark … naturally led to resist every encroachment upon right" (Monk, 1995, p. v).

Perhaps this prescient wisdom was why Thomas Jefferson referred to James Madison as "the greatest man in the world" (Peterson, 1970, p. 266).

QUESTIONS FOR DISCUSSION

1. What was James Madison's specific role in writing a draft of the Bill of Rights?
2. Could an argument be made that America developed as a nation because of a concern for individual rights?
3. What do you think Thomas Jefferson meant when he wrote in 1778: "Let me add that a bill of rights is what the people are entitled to against every government on earth …?"
4. What did James Madison imply when he wrote to Thomas Jefferson in 1788, "Wherever the real power in a government lies, there is the danger of oppression?"
5. How might our criminal justice system have evolved differently if we had no Bill of Rights?

IMPORTANT TERMS

Continental Congress: The First Continental Congress was made up of delegates from the colonies and met during 1774. In 1775, the Second Continental Congress began meeting right after the Revolutionary War. It declared that America was independent from Britain, and in 1781, ratified the first national constitution, the Articles of Confederation.

Constitutional Convention: The Constitutional Convention took place from May 14 to September 17, 1787, in Philadelphia. The task before the Constitutional Convention was to decide how America was to be governed. George Washington was elected by the delegates to preside over the Constitutional Convention.

Virginia House of Delegates: The Virginia House of Delegates first met in 1619. It is one of two houses in the Virginia General Assembly, the legislative body that governs the state of Virginia.

Virginia Statute for Religious Freedom: The Virginia Statute for Religious Freedom was written by Thomas Jefferson and passed by the Virginia General Assembly in 1786. It is a statement about freedom of conscience and the principle of separation of church and state.

Federalists: In the debates and discussions about the proposed Constitution of the United States, those who supported the Constitution and, in general, were in favor of a relatively strong central government were called Federalists.

The Federalist Papers: Written and published in newspapers during 1787 and 1788, the Federalist Papers were intended to persuade New York voters to ratify the proposed constitution. There were eighty-five essays that comprised the Federal Papers, and although they were all signed "Publius," they were written by James Madison, Alexander Hamilton, and John Jay.

Anti-Federalists: The Anti-Federalists were those who were opposed to the new Constitution of the United States. They argued that the Constitution gave too much power to the government and advocated for a bill of rights in order to protect individual rights.

Bill of Rights: The Bill of Rights was ratified in 1791 and consisted of the first ten amendments to the U.S. Constitution. The purpose of the Bill of Rights was to protect individual liberties and freedoms.

REVIEW QUESTIONS

True or False

1. It is argued in this chapter that James Madison should be considered the Father of the American criminal justice system.
2. James Madison was the youngest man ever to be the president of the United States.
3. Madison helped write the Constitution of the United States.
4. James Madison promised that if the U.S. Constitution was ratified, he would see to it that a bill of rights was enacted.

Multiple Choice

5. Initially, James Madison, as a Federalist, believed that
   a. A bill of rights was absolutely essential.
   b. A bill of rights would protect slaves.
   c. A bill of rights was unnecessary.
   d. A bill of rights should be a separate document from the Constitution.

6. Among the amendments that James Madison proposed to the House of Representatives in 1889 was this one:
   a. The right to a trial by jury should be available to all citizens.
   b. Double jeopardy should be allowed.
   c. All bail should be prohibited.
   d. The number of members in the House of Representatives should be reduced.

7. Eventually, after a great deal of debate in Congress, James Madison agreed that that the amendments making up the Bill of Rights would be
   a. Part of the first clause of the Constitution.
   b. The preamble to the Declaration of Independence.
   c. Buried in the middle of the Constitution.
   d. Added to the end of the Constitution.

8. James Madison was part of a joint House of Representatives Senate conference committee that ultimately submitted this number of amendments to the states for ratification:

   a. Twelve.
   b. Ten.
   c. Eight.
   d. Six.

9. Although he had slaves on his farm, James Madison considered slavery to be

   a. A problem that seriously threatened the Union.
   b. Necessary to the economy.
   c. A fine institution.
   d. A stage in the development of the American farming industry.

FOR FURTHER READING

Brookhiser, R. (2011). *James Madison.* New York, NY: Basic Books.

Cheney, L. (2015). *James Madison: A life reconsidered.* New York, NY: Penguin Books.

Derose, C. (2011). *Founding rivals: Madison vs. Monroe: The Bill of Rights and the election that saved a nation.* Washington, DC: Regnery Publishing, Inc.

Gay, S. H. (2010). *James Madison.* Charlestown, SC: BiblioLife.

Kennedy, A. (2016). *The Madisons.* Cedar Rapids, IA: A. Kennedy.

Ketcham, R. (1990). *James Madison: A biography.* Charlottesville, VA: University of Virginia Press.

Stewart, D. O. (2016). *Madison's gifts: Five partnerships that built America.* New York, NY: Simon & Schuster.

REFERENCES

Brant, I. (1970). *The fourth president: A life of James Madison.* Norwalk, CT: Easton Press.

Labunski, R. (2006). *James Madison and the struggle for the Bill of Rights.* New York, NY: Oxford University Press.

Monk, L. R. (1995). *The Bill of Rights: A user's guide.* Alexandria, VA: Close Up Publishing.

Peterson, M. D. (1970). *Thomas Jefferson and the new nation.* New York, NY: Oxford University Press.

Peterson, M. D. (1974). *James Madison: A biography in his own words.* New York, NY: Newsweek.

3

JAMES Q. WILSON
Fearless Academic and Accidental Criminologist

Perhaps no person is more worthy of a prominent place in a list of significant figures in criminal justice history. Yet, he himself acknowledged that he was a criminologist only by accident, and he never held an academic position in any department of criminal justice. He rarely—if ever—published a paper in a peer-reviewed criminal justice journal. Nor do his theories of criminology usually get taught in criminological theory courses, yet his views on the causes of crime are regarded as influential. Furthermore, he had no practical experience as a law enforcement officer, but he wrote a well-regarded book on policing styles. Although he had no practical experience in the areas of drug abuse or drug laws enforcement, he is in large part responsible for the creation of the Drug Enforcement Agency. Given that he was not a criminologist by training or experience, still he was an adviser on criminal justice to four presidents.

His name is James Q. Wilson, and he was once introduced to a president by Senator Daniel Patrick Moynihan as the "smartest man in America" (Dilulio, 2012, p. 599). It would be foolhardy to dispute that description of him based on his academic achievements and the positions he played in criminal justice, public policy, and political science.

EARLY LIFE AND EDUCATION

James Quinn Wilson was born in Denver, Colorado, on May 27, 1931, but after his family moved when he was young, he grew up in Long Beach, California. His father, Claude, was a salesman, and his mother, Marie, a homemaker. Following high school, he graduated with a BA in political science from the University of Redlands in the San Bernardino Valley. During college, he was the national collegiate debate champion for the years 1951 and 1952. Then he served in the Navy during the Korean War but experienced no combat. Following his stint in the Navy, he pursued graduate degrees at the University of Chicago. There, he earned an MA and a PhD in political science in 1959 ("James Q. Wilson: Biography," 2018).

After finishing his PhD, Wilson continued on at the University of Chicago, teaching political science and also beginning to write his first book. "[His PhD] dissertation was an analysis of the political behavior of African Americans in Chicago during the 1950s and [served as] the basis for his first book, *Negro Politics: The Search for Leadership*" ("Biographical Note," 2013). His next two books, *The Amateur Democrat: Club Politics in Three Cities* (1962) and *City Politics* (1963, coauthored with Edward Banfield), subsequently were published. However, by the time his third book came out, he had moved on to Harvard, first as a lecturer and ultimately as a professor, and there he stayed for twenty-six years. Those first three books addressed the then-brewing conflict in major cities between the professional "machines" and the cause-oriented reformers who sought to replace them (Piereson, 2012). The subjects of these early writings presumably predicted the trajectory of Wilson's career: he intended to be a political scientist writing about city politics.

That was also evident due to the fact that his appointment at Harvard was as a faculty member in the Department of Government, where he stayed during his entire tenure at Harvard. During that tenure, he was appointed Henry Lee Shattuck Professor of Government in 1972 and served as chairman of the department from 1969 to 1973. He was also director of the Joint Center for Urban Studies at both MIT and Harvard from 1963 to 1966.

However, life has a way of intervening in the well-laid plans of most mortals, including James Q. Wilson. In 1966, he was invited to serve as chair of the White House Task Force on Crime (Delisi, 2003). If an interest in crime and criminal justice wasn't already calling him, this experience pointed him in a new direction. In a PBS-TV interview in 2000, Wilson talked about how this came about. He said that when doing his graduate work at the University of Chicago he developed an interest in the study of crime as a by-product of studying cities. After he began teaching at Harvard in the early 1960s, he was trying to understand how the police played a role in the administration of cities. In fact, he said that he tending toward the view of police officers as urban bureaucrats.

During the presidential campaign of 1964, crime had become a decisive issue in American politics because the Republican candidate for president, Barry Goldwater, argued that crime in the streets was a serious problem and his Democratic challenger, Lyndon Johnson, was not likely to be tough on crime. Since Lyndon Johnson was not the sort of man who let a charge against him go unanswered, after he won a decisive victory in the election, he created a national commission on law enforcement and the administration of justice. The idea of the commission was to learn more about the extent of crime and how to reduce it (Petersilia, 2012).Wilson, in this PBS interview, said that a colleague at Harvard Law School found out that Wilson was studying the police and appointed him to a task force on Johnson's crime commission. At the time, Wilson said that he protested to his friend that he didn't know anything about crime. His colleague told him he could learn about crime and Wilson did begin reading about crime.

In reading about crime, Wilson came to the conclusion that much of the existing literature on crime was not very helpful. Wilson believed that much of the information about came was derived from studies of gangs, the childhoods of small groups of boys, and of teenagers living in cities. "And we learned that people commit crimes because other people around them are committing crimes. I [think] that's probably true to some degree, but it doesn't help you control crime" (PBS, 2000, par. 9). Wilson then became part of a group that was looking at data comparing crime rates across states. This group he was working with decided, after reviewing the data that it seemed to make a difference if there were policies in a state that made it likely that people would go to prison for committing a crime. Wilson and his group decided that the likelihood of prison appeared to drive down the crime rate (PBS, 2000).

WORK IN POLICING, CRIME, AND CRIMINOLOGY

In 1968, Wilson's book *Varieties of Police Behavior: The Management of Law and Order in Eight Communities* was published. As he states in his PBS interview (PBS, 2000), he didn't research and write this book because of an interest in criminal justice. Instead, he set out "to investigate some of the core issues associated with understanding the police [as organizations and] how [those] organizations influence the street-level actions of police officers" (Liederbach & Travis, 2008). Furthermore, his interest, at the time, was more related to "the factors that limit organizational control of individual officer behavior, [more particularly,] how the contextual influences of community and political culture contribute to defining certain 'organizational styles' exhibited by local police agencies" (Liederbach & Travis, 2008, p. 447).

In the pursuit of such goals as discovering what differences there were in the ways officers perform their function based on "explicit community decisions" (Wilson, 1970, p. 4), "Wilson identified the primary functions of the local police as law enforcement, order maintenance, and service delivery" (Liederbach & Travis, 2008). These were, according to Wilson, "three distinct operational styles of policing based on the frequency and formality of police-citizen interactions" (Liederbach & Travis, 2008). Although these operational styles were, in a sense, outgrowths of Wilson's search for answers to questions about organizations and local governments, they nonetheless became staples in criminal justice. Liederbach and Travis (2008) describe these organizational styles part of the "common knowledge" of policing (p. 448). Indeed, almost every introduction to criminal justice textbook and American policing textbook provides an overview of these policing styles (Liederbach & Travis, 2008).

After writing *Varieties of Police Behavior*, Wilson was invited to serve as a member of President Lyndon Johnson's Commission on Crime and the Administration of Justice. Out of Johnson's concerns about the rising crime rate, and perhaps because he had been criticized about his approach to crime, the commission Johnson appointed was given the task of identifying how the nation should respond to the crime problem. Ultimately, the commission put out a pioneering report, *The Challenge of Crime in a Free*

Society (1967), which included more than two hundred recommendations for checking crime. Essentially, the comprehensive report concluded that what was needed was a massive government effort to root out the causes of crime, poverty, and racism (The Challenge of Crime in a Free Society, 1967; Petersilia, 2012). Soon after this report was released, Wilson wrote an article in *The Public Interest* that took issue with many of the report's conclusions and proposals. Joan Petersilia, a noted professor, in writing an overview of Wilson's life, commented that Wilson denounced the commission for including recommendations that had little empirical support. In this article in *The Public Interest,* Wilson pointed out that although the commission suggested more monies be directed toward social services, there was no research showing that such programs had any influence on crime. In like manner, Wilson criticized the commission's suggestion that prison sentences should be shortened and that more offenders be diverted from incarceration to probation. Again, Wilson pointed out that there was no evidence that community alternatives were safer for the public than was incarceration (Petersilia, 2012).

That article set a tone and a pattern for the rest of Wilson's career. As Heather Mac Donald put it in a New York Post obituary, "Over the next 45 years, he continued to patiently point out when the emperor had no clothes, to exercise skepticism toward conventional wisdom, and to drive his ground-breaking insights from a close attention to the facts on the ground" (Mac Donald, 2012, p. 1). The pattern, from that point on, was that Wilson devoted considerable time and energy to pondering criminal behavior and criminal trends, as well as various measures to control crime. And he would be called on by presidents to serve on committees and task forces, or to just consult on crime. President Richard Nixon asked Wilson to head up the National Advisory Commission on Drug Abuse Prevention from 1972 to 1973 (Delisi, 2003). After accepting the assignment and learning more about this national advisory committee, Wilson concluded that it was not accomplishing much and suggested to the president that it be abolished. Nixon agreed and shut it down. However, Nixon requested that Wilson appear before Congress and make an appeal for the creation of the Drug Enforcement Administration (DEA). Wilson honored that request from the president by speaking before Congress—and the DEA was created in 1973. At the president's bidding, Wilson served as a consultant to officials of the DEA and as an unofficial adviser to Clarence Kelley, director of the FBI (Delisi, 2003).

It was another book on criminal justice that brought him to the attention of Gerald Ford, who succeeded Nixon as president. *Thinking About Crime*, published in 1975, was Wilson's comprehensive book looking at a multitude of criminal justice issues, and it inspired President Ford to invite Wilson to the White House to discuss the ideas in the book. However, it was this book—*Thinking About Crime*—that propelled James Q. Wilson's name to the forefront among those considered to be conservative thinkers in respect to criminology. In *Thinking About Crime*, Wilson writes that he was frustrated with what he saw as politically motivated, academic nonsense about crime, and his book aimed to apply a "clear and sober understanding of the nature of man" to study crime in a sensible way (Wilson, 1975, p. xi). In this book, he devotes nearly a chapter to the causes of crime while arguing that policy makers commit what he refers to as a "causal fallacy" (p. 51) when they assume that in order to address crime adequately, the ultimate causes of crime must be identified and eliminated. That, he suggests, would be a useless approach to policy making because even if ultimate causes could be found, it is unlikely that the government has the tools to do anything constructive about crime. Furthermore, he adopts the classical criminological perspective by stating that criminal behavior is largely rational and is shaped by the relative risks and rewards that might accrue (Petersilia, 2012). In concluding the book, Wilson wrote that it is a mistake to think about crime in terms of what causes criminal behaviors and then to try to discover ways to eliminate those causes. Instead, he suggests, governments and communities should use scientific approaches to learn what will bring about reductions in "criminal victimizations" (Wilson, 1975, p. 208).

As indicated by assistant professor of sociology at Iowa State University Matt Delisi in 2003, Wilson critiqued mainstream criminology at the time *Thinking About Crime* was published by arguing that society doesn't cause crimes and that efforts to reduce crime through social programs were likely to fail. Further, along the same lines, he suggested that sociologists during that era made pronouncements about crime based not on empirical facts but on ideology. He also contended that white-collar crime was not the equivalent of street crime, and that street crime was more serious (Wilson, 1975). He argued against destigmatizing crime because, in his view, crime is a moral phenomenon and should be stigmatized by society. Finally, Wilson took the position that "wicked people exist" and that "Nothing avails except to set them apart from innocent people" (Wilson, 1975, p. 209). It is these wicked people, Wilson seems to say, who should be controlled (perhaps through capital punishment) and should be the primary focus of the criminal justice system (Delisi, 2003).

BROKEN WINDOWS THEORY

But it wasn't wicked people or the punishment of repeat criminals that was the focus of what has turned out to be the best known of all of Wilson's writing. In 1982, he and George Kelling, who was at the time a research fellow at Harvard's John F. Kennedy School of Government, wrote "Broken Windows" for the *Atlantic Monthly* magazine (now officially named *The Atlantic*). This theory of crime Wilson and Kelling came up with in this article began from a simple premise: that signs of social disorder, such as broken windows in a vacant building, encourage crime because they may be perceived as signals that community norms will not be enforced (Piereson, 2012).

This hypothesis was a challenge to the theory that poverty "causes" crime and that any real efforts to reduce crime must begin with efforts to reduce poverty (Piereson, 2012). Wilson and Kelling argue persuasively in this article that vigorous enforcement of all laws, not just those related to serious offenses, could change a community's environment (Delisi, 2003). Furthermore, in this seminal article, they call for police officers to get out of automobiles and start walking beats again. In his PBS interview in 2000, Wilson discussed how the broken windows theories came about.

He explained that when he was on the board of directors of the Police Foundation, it was suggested by various people that perhaps one answer to street crime was to increase the number of foot patrol officers in our cities. In part, Wilson and others at the Police Foundation saw this as a desire to return to some nostalgic past when patrol officers with billy clubs were walking the streets – instead of driving around in patrol cars and only responding to 9-1-1 calls. Wilson pointed out that many police chiefs were opposed to putting foot patrol officers back on the street; they contended it would make no difference in the crime rate (PBS, 2000).

However, the federal government sponsored a study in Newark, New Jersey, in which they put foot patrol officers back on the street. The Police Foundation, which is a nonpartisan group, was asked to evaluate the outcomes of this experiment. The results were that the police chiefs are right – having foot patrol officers walking the streets had no effect on the crime rate. Yet, the study concluded that it made people in the area where there were officers walking a beat feel much safer. Kelling and Wilson set out to explain this finding. Why did people feel safer, even when the crime rate hadn't changed? (PBS, 2000)

As Wilson and George Kelling, who was a researcher in the Kennedy School of Government at Harvard University, began to try to answer this question, they realized that most people didn't understand what was meant by the crime rate. Instead, they looked at crime in personal terms. More often, the average person is concerned with how safe they are when they go to the grocery store or walk along a street. In addition, as Wilson and Kelling discovered, the level of disorder is just as important to people as actual crime. As Wilson put it in the PBS interview: "By the level of disorder I mean graffiti on the walls, bums drinking alcohol out of paper bags on street corners, prostitutes hanging around, young teenage gangs making noise and wearing loud jackets. These signs of disorder make people apprehensive. And when people get apprehensive they tend to stay indoors. If they stay indoors it means that the streets are free for real crime to takeover" (PBS interview, 2000, par. 23-24).

In the Broken Windows article, they made the argument that if you fix one broken window in a factory building or an abandoned house, the other windows won't be broken. However, if that one broken window goes unfixed, soon all of the windows will be broken (PBS, 2000). People observing a broken window will conclude that no one cares or no one is in charge. Given a certain amount of time, passersby will throw rocks and break other windows. Wilson said that the image of broken windows was used to explain how neighborhoods might decay into disorder and even crime (Wilson, 1996). In their broken windows explanation, they encouraged the police to pay as much attention to public order—by getting rid of prostitutes and gangs on street corners, by painting out the graffiti, by making people feel comfortable around their homes. Wilson and Kelling theorized that by eliminating disorder that this would make people feel safer and it might even drive down the crime rate.

As it has later turned out, Wilson has said, research has suggested that when disorder is dealt with the crime rate does come down. That's because, Wilson concluded, "Good people are on the streets and bad people find it hard to take advantage of them" (PBS, 2000, par. 25).

While the outcome of the application of the broken windows theory is debatable, it has been credited by some (for example, Skogan, 1990; Kelling & Coles, 1996) with remarkable reductions in crime in New York City. When William Bratton was New York City's police commissioner and Rudolph Giuliani was mayor, the police in New York City practiced such relentless social control that they helped to change community norms (Delisi, 2003). Skogan (1990) points out that zero-tolerance policies related to social disorder that were implemented in New York City resulted in a dramatically safer and cleaner city. Wilson himself said in an interview that "A lot of police agencies have responded to this idea of the broken window. Probably the most famous was the U.S. Transit Authority Police, and then later the New York City Police Department. But many cities all over the country have done the same. You find in lots of police departments graffiti campaigns; [you find] campaigns designed to get unlicensed street vendors off the streets, to deal more effectively with the homeless to make sure they have some place to go, to get in the appropriate neighborhoods foot patrol. Although foot patrol is clearly not the key remedy, but in some neighborhoods it makes a difference. This, we think, has helped reduce the level of crime in some neighborhoods. But I say 'we think,' because the police departments that have done these things have also done a lot of other things ... So we can't say that the broken window strategy has driven down the crime rate in the cities that have tried it, but it is part of the package, and it is not making things worse" (PBS, 2000).

CRIME AND HUMAN NATURE

Of the twenty-six books written, coauthored, or edited by Wilson, he believed his greatest contribution to criminology was the book he wrote with his close colleague at Harvard, Richard Herrnstein (Petersilia, 2012). Joan Petersilia, also a colleague of Wilson's, wrote that Wilson said he wrote *Crime and Human Nature: The Definitive Study of the Causes of Crime* (1985), "which required painstaking and comprehensive research over several years, to learn for himself about crime causation" (Petersilia, 2012). In fact, he once told a reporter that "I often write books about problems for which I can't think of a solution. The reason I write the book is not because I know what I want to say to the public. I write the book in order to figure out for myself what I think about the subject" (Newton, 2007).

However, *Crime and Human Nature*, which concerns Wilson's search for answers about the causes of crime, raises the question about whether crime results from environmental factors, particularly poverty, or individual choice. *Crime and Human Nature* was a controversial book because "Wilson and Herrnstein concluded that a propensity toward crime had some biological roots (e.g., gender, age, race, intelligence) [that] were inherited" (Petersilia, 2012). This kind of conclusion was, if anything, a sensitive issue, and their conclusion fired up a debate over the "nature versus nurture" controversy in criminal behavior. Although Joan Petersilia has written that she disagreed with her friend's position, still she admired him for being a fearless academic when it came to taking positions he believed in and thought the evidence supported (Petersilia, 2012).

Brandon Welsh, in the School of Criminology and Criminal Justice at Northeastern University, and David Farrington, in the Institute of Criminology at the University of Cambridge, wrote that they consider *Crime and Human Nature* to be an extremely important book in the history of criminological thought (Welsh & Farrington, 2013). One of the reasons for this point of view is that when the book was published in the mid-1980s, most criminologists clearly preferred sociological explanations for how people behaved. That is, they tended to see structural or societal forces as strongly influencing the behavior—especially the criminal behavior—of individuals. As Delisi put in 2011, "The psychology of individuals, and certainly the inner-working of their brains, were believed to be irrelevant to crime and criminology" (Delisi, 2011, p. 1016). What Wilson and Herrnstein's book did was to open up dialogue—and research—on biological and psychological criminology and the developmental/life-course paradigm (Welsh & Farrington, 2013).

The theory of criminology advanced by Wilson and Herrnstein in *Crime and Human Nature* was simple and straightforward. While recognizing there are myriad forces that have an influence over behavior, when it comes right down to it: "At any given moment, a person can choose between committing a crime and not committing it" (Wilson & Herrnstein, 1985, p. 44). Furthermore, like prior classical theorists, they saw human behavioral choices as mostly controlled by rewards and punishments. Additionally, if there was any recommendation for public policy in this book and in their theory, it was this: "We know that crime, like all human behavior, has causes, and that science has made progress—and will make more progress—in identifying them. But the very process by which we learn to avoid crime requires that the courts act as if crime were wholly the result of free choice" (Wilson & Herrnstein, 1985, pp. 528–529).

Throughout the 1980s, Wilson perhaps had more contact—and maybe more influence—with the Reagan administration than any other criminologist. "In 1982, he was appointed to the Justice Program Study Group of the MacArthur Foundation" (Welsh & Farrington, 2013). This group came to the conclusion that crime and justice research needed more ambitious longitudinal studies (Welsh & Farrington, 2013). This group also commissioned the book coauthored by Wilson (along with Farrington and Ohlin) *Understanding and Controlling Crime: Toward a New Research Strategy* (1986). This book recommended several longitudinal studies of children and youth at different life stages, but these studies were never implemented (Welsh & Farrington, 2013). "Instead, the MacArthur Foundation joined forces with the National Institute of Justice to [fund] the Program on Human Development and Criminal Behavior, which ran from 1987 to 1989" (Welsh & Farrington, 2013). Wilson was involved in this program, serving on the Research Advisory Board.

"Between 1983 and 1985, Wilson was a member of the prestigious and influential National Academy of Sciences Panel on Criminal Career Research. He also organized executive sessions at Harvard University, funded by the Office of Juvenile Justice and Delinquency Prevention" (Welsh & Farrington, 2013). These sessions led to the book From Children to Citizens: Families, Schools and Delinquency (Wilson & Loury, 1987). Wilson also served the Reagan administration as an adviser on foreign intelligence, overlooking international activities of the Central Intelligence Agency.

He retired from Harvard in 1987 and moved to California, where he became professor of management and public policy at the University of California at Los Angles. After retiring from UCLA in 1998, he became professor emeritus of management at ULCA. He moved on to a post at Pepperdine University in 1998, staying until 2009 as Ronald Reagan Professor of Public Policy.

"In the 1990s, Wilson coedited two anthologies of criminological research: a volume on drugs and crime with [Michael] Tonry (Tonry & Wilson, 1990), and an overview of criminological research with Petersilia titled Crime (Wilson & Petersilia, 1995)" (Delisi, 2003).

"Wilson also served on the RAND Corporation's Board of Trustees, [and] it was in this capacity that he played an [important] role in [RAND's] pioneering research initiatives on early childhood development and the prevention of [criminal] offending" (Welsh & Farrington, 2013).

After leaving Pepperdine in 2009, his final position was as distinguished scholar at Boston College.

WILSON'S WORK ON CHARACTER AND MORAL PHILOSOPHY

Throughout much of the last two decades of his life, James Q. Wilson thought and wrote about moral philosophy, particularly the foundations of human nature (Delisi, 2003). Starting in 1991 with his book *On Character*, he presented a series of essays that are further reflections of ideas that first appeared in *Crime and Human Nature*. In *On Character*, he argues that to have good character, one needs to have developed a sense of empathy and self-control ("Summary," 1995). But in addition to extolling the importance of empathy and self-control, he also writes about crime, families, communities, and schooling. In the book, Wilson demonstrates a great concern about society and, indeed, the survival of society. Acknowledging that humans have an inborn "moral sense," he believes that we have an obligation to each other to develop that moral sense if we really care about each other ("Summary," 1995).

Wilson further explores the issues he raised in *On Character* two years later in the book *The Moral Sense* (1993). In this book, Wilson seeks to bring together some traditional ideas with a number of important empirical research findings into the sources of human behavior over the last half of the twentieth century. Drawing on evidence "from diverse scientific disciplines—including animal behavior, anthropology, evolutionary theory, biology, endocrinology, brain science, genetics, education, and psychology—[he concludes] that our basic sense of right and wrong actually [has] a biological and behavioral origin" ("Summary," 1997). He makes the argument that the "moral sense" arises from the infant's innate sociability, though it must also be nurtured by parental influence ("Summary," 1997).

This series of books culminated in *Moral Judgment: Does the Abuse Excuse Threaten Our Legal System?* in 1997. Wilson raises serious questions about forces in our society that threaten to undermine our moral sense. He points a critical finger at our judicial system, which he believes has compromised its obligation to discriminate between right and wrong. Bringing together highly publicized court verdicts, he makes a case for reexamining the ethical drift of contemporary jurisprudence. The headlines produced by the infamous court cases suggest to Wilson that our judicial system has a limited capacity to resolve even the gravest moral issues: judging guilt or innocence in capital cases. In a sense, Wilson sends a strongly worded message to criminal justice administrators: Invest more in old-fashioned common sense and less in beliefs that social circumstances should influence justice (Delisi, 2003). And he issues a warning: "… a law that permits compassion also permits revenge" (Wilson, 1997, p. 112).

Starting with *Crime and Human Nature* and gradually gaining momentum throughout his succeeding books, Wilson makes it clear that he considers the family to be the most important institution—and the one responsible for cultivating and inculcating morality (Delisi, 2003). In one of his last books (*The Marriage Problem*, 2002), Wilson advocates for the two-parent family. The two-parent family, he argues, helps "instill the importance of education, employment, personal responsibility, and propriety in children" (Delisi, 2003). Wilson strongly suggests that the solution to crime and other social problems is the two-parent family.

WILSON AND DEMOCRACY

Remembering that he was always a political scientist and professor of government first, it is not surprising that Wilson frequently returned to the fundamental theme of democracy in America. He was constantly interested in where American democracy has succeeded and where it's going wrong, as well as how it can be strengthened (Petersilia, 2012).

He wrote a popular textbook on American government (*American Government: Institutions and Policies*), which at this writing is in its fourteenth edition. His final two books, both edited, were titled *American Politics, Then and Now* (2010) and *Understanding America: The Anatomy of an Exceptional Nation* (2008).

WILSON AS AN UNABASHED CONSERVATIVE

James Piereson, a conservative scholar and senior fellow at the Manhattan Institute for Policy Research, suggests that Wilson was a conservative who followed the views of Alexis de Tocqueville. That is, Wilson was always concerned about how American democracy could preserve itself and how it could be compatible with civilization.

James Q. Wilson came into his share of criticism throughout his career. Since he took unpopular positions, this was to be expected. He was viewed as a "neoconservative" (Rozansky and Lerner, 2012) whose work was an attack on mainstream (here, read liberal) criminology (Cullen & Gilbert, 1982). The political left saw him as being too conservative, advocating punishment, and being the modern spokesperson of the crime-control movement (Siegel & Worrall, 2012). He didn't shy away from talking about aspects of criminology and society that others avoided. One example is his explorations of African Americans and violent crime (Wilson, 1997). As a result of such writings, he was accused of promoting "scientific racism" (Jones, 2005, p. 13). However, as Matt Delisi points out, many, if not most, of Wilson's more controversial positions and statements have been backed up by empirical data (Delisi, 2003). Delisi raises the question as to why a "rightist political orientation or a commonsense sensibility" is so threatening to some criminologists (2003, p. 671). Wilson, Delisi contends, has been willing to confront some not-so-pretty criminological realities; for instance, by being willing to call wicked people *wicked* (Delisi, 2003). Wilson seemingly was undaunted by the criticism. He told Mark Jones in an interview that he believed his unpopularity with the political left may have stemmed from his steadfast and unchanging belief in punishment (Jones, 2005). Wilson responded to jibes from the left by stating that mainstream America believes that moral concepts such as punishment have a place in the criminal justice system, although social leftists who tend to dominate colleges and universities do not share this belief (Jones, 2005, p. 13).

Joan Petersilia, who is currently the Adelbert H. Sweet Professor of Law at Stanford Law School, as well as the faculty codirector of the Stanford Criminal Justice Center, wrote in 2012 that while she didn't always agree with Wilson when he explained crime, she did highly respect his ability to stick to his thinking. She said that he maintained his own opinion, even when his views were offensive to others. Petersilia referred to him as a fearless academic who took positions he believed in and thought research supported (Petersilia, 2012).

As Petersilia, who coauthored books and articles with Wilson, points out, "whether you agreed with [Wilson's] positions or not, there was no denying that his writings were a force to be reckoned with on such diverse topics as the death penalty, gun control, drugs, juvenile justice, crime prevention, deterrence, prisons, [morality, marriage,] and policing" (Petersilia, 2012).

LIFE OUTSIDE OF ACADEMIA

John Dilulio, who knew James Q. Wilson as a colleague and friend for the last thirty-two years of Wilson's life, comments that despite Wilson's prolific public and professional pursuits, he spent quality time with both his wife and two children. He always attended his children's special events and took them on many trips abroad (Dilulio, 2012).

Dilulio described him as a model neighbor and community member. For instance, he says that Wilson coached a youth soccer team, even though his own children didn't play on the team, and he served on a local library board (Dilulio, 2012).

Wilson loved scuba diving and was a professional instructor. He enjoyed underwater photography, at which he excelled. He and his wife, Roberta, his high school sweetheart, wrote a book together: *Watching Fishes: Life and Behavior on Coral Reefs* (1985). He loved fast cars. And he was "insanely devoted" to the Boston Red Sox (Dilulio, 2012, p. 560).

Dilulio also remembers Wilson as an amazingly dedicated undergraduate and graduate student classroom teacher, who enjoyed being a thesis supervisor, a dissertation adviser, colleague, coauthor, or editor (Dilulio, 2012). Welsh and Farrington (2013) describe him as quiet, modest, and unassuming in his personal interactions, as an inspiring man with fierce intellectual honesty, not afraid to take unpopular positions in his public speeches. And Petersilia adds that throughout all of the accolades and criticisms, Wilson remained steadfast and centered (Petersilia, 2012).

> He was mild mannered and reserved, bordering on shy. He was thoughtful, never quick to opine. He had high expectations of everyone. He possessed a formidable memory and an encyclopedic knowledge of philosophy, government, and many areas of the social sciences. He never stopped asking hard questions, believing we still didn't have sufficient answers to the most pressing problems of our time. (Petersilia, 2012)

Petersilia concludes that it was almost impossible to find anyone who ever worked with Wilson or got to know him who ever had an unkind word to say about him (Petersilia, 2012).

THE FINAL ACCOLADES

John Dilulio describes him as a "real genius and a laudable giant" (Dilulio, 2012, p. 559), and his final posts and achievements bear this out. At the time of his appointment at Pepperdine, Wilson was the president of the American Political Science Association. The association presented to Wilson a Lifetime Achievement Award in 2001.

> [Wilson served on] the President's Council on Bioethics from 2002 to 2005, [...] the boards of the New England Electric System, Protection One, State Farm Mutual Insurance, the RAND Corporation, and the Pardee RAND Graduate School.Pardee RAND Graduate School. He chaired the Council of Academic Advisors of the American Enterprise Institute.American Enterprise Institute. [...] From 2009 until his death, he was Distinguished Scholar in the Department of

Political ScienceDepartment of Political Science and Senior Fellow at the Clough Center for the Study of Constitutional DemocracyClough Center for the Study of Constitutional Democracy at Boston College. [...] In 2003, Wilson was awarded the Presidential Medal of Freedom, the nation's highest civilian award. ("Biographical Note," 2013)

He was the rare academic who won a Presidential Medal of Freedom, and when President George W. Bush presented him with the medal, he said, "Whatever his subject, James Q. Wilson writes with intellectual rigor, with moral clarity, to the appreciation of a wide and growing audience." He received the Bradley Prize from the Lynde and Harry Bradley Foundation in 2007, and during his lifetime he was awarded honorary degrees from seven universities, including Harvard University. ("Biographical Note," 2013).

"Over the last several years [of his life], he gallantly battled aggressive leukemia and other health problems." (Dilulio, 2012). He died at age eighty on March 2, 2012. His obituary was front-page news for the *New York Times* and other leading newspapers.

QUESTIONS FOR DISCUSSION

1. Can a good argument be made that the "broken windows" theory has been shown to effectively reduce crime?
2. James Q. Wilson liked to think that he came up with "commonsense" solutions to problems in criminology. Do you agree? Why or why not?
3. What did Wilson mean in his book *Thinking of Crime* when he said that some people are wicked?
4. Could Wilson be said to be a classical theorist?

IMPORTANT TERMS

Broken windows theory: James Q. Wilson and George Kelling in 1982 came up with the broken windows theory. This theory said that even minor offenses and disorders ought to be responded to by the police. If one offense or disorder (for instance, one window gets broken in a building) is let go, then other offenses and disorders will take place (all of the windows in a building will get broken).

Classical theory: In criminology, classical theory refers to the theory that individuals commit crime by making rational decisions about whether or not to engage in an offending behavior.

Policing styles: Wilson, along with others, has said that each police officer must decide what style of police officer he or she will be. Wilson identified the primary functions or styles of policing as the watchman, the legalistic officer, and the service provider.

FOR FURTHER READING

Wilson, J.Q. (1970). *Amateur Democrat: Club politics in three cities.* Chicago, IL: University of Chicago Press.

Wilson, J.Q. (1970). *Varieties of police behavior: The management of law and order in eight communities.* New York, NY: Atheneum.

Wilson, J.Q. (1975). *Thinking about crime.* New York, NY: Basic Books.

Wilson, J.Q. (1991). *On character.* Washington, DC: AEI Press.

Wilson, J.Q. (1993). *The moral sense.* New York, NY: Free Press.

Wilson, J.Q. (1997). *Moral judgment: Does the abuse excuse threaten our legal system?* New York, NY: Basic Books.

Wilson, J.Q. (2002). *The marriage problem: How our culture has weakened families.* New York, NY: Harper Collins.

Wilson, J.Q., & Kelling, G. (1982, April). Broken windows. *Atlantic Monthly.*

Wilson, J.Q., & Loury, G. C. (Eds.). (1987). *Children to citizens: Families, schools and delinquency prevention, Vol. III.* New York NY: Springer Publishing.

REVIEW QUESTIONS

True or False

1. James Q. Wilson may be best known as the coauthor of "Broken Windows."

2. James Q. Wilson was proud that he avoided "commonsense" solutions to problems in criminology.

3. The major concept in Wilson's book *Thinking of Crime* is that people make choices about whether or not to engage in criminal behavior.

4. Early in his career, Wilson thought he would be a political scientist writing about city politics.

5. Wilson wrote *Varieties of Police Behavior: The Management of Law and Order in Eight Communities* because of his great interest in criminal justice.

Multiple Choice

6. It was the book *Thinking About Crime* that established James Q. Wilson as the nation's leading

   a. Liberal criminologist writing about public policy.
   b. Conservative on crime policy.
   c. Liberal sociologist who was anti-police.
   d. Conservative political scientist concerned about police brutality.

7. In *Thinking About Crime*, Wilson said that he was frustrated with what he perceived as politically motivated, academic nonsense about crime and his book sought to

   a. Apply a "clear and sober understanding of the nature of man" to study crime sensibly.
   b. Promote social bond theory.
   c. Establish that crime is caused by poverty and inadequate housing.
   d. Find out why wicked people ought to be placed on probation.

8. In *Thinking About Crime*, Wilson took the position that "wicked people exist" and that it is these wicked people who should be

   a. Controlled through prison sentences.
   b. Better understood.
   c. Executed by firing squad.
   d. The primary focus of sociology classes.

9. In the broken windows theory, Wilson and Kelling argue that vigorous enforcement of all laws, not just those related to serious offenses, could

   a. Reduce the number of criminal offenses.
   b. Stop white-collar crime.
   c. Change a community's environment.
   d. Improve parenting.

10. *Crime and Human Nature* was a controversial book because Wilson and Herrnstein concluded that

    a. A propensity toward crime had sociological roots.
    b. Some criminals were mentally ill.
    c. A propensity toward crime had biological roots.
    d. Some criminals lacked self-control.

11. The theory of criminology advanced by Wilson and Herrnstein in *Crime and Human Nature* recognized that while there are myriad forces that have an influence over behavior, when it comes right down to it:

    a. "At any given moment, a person can choose between committing a crime and not committing it."
    b. "All offenders had broken windows to begin their criminal career."
    c. "Human behavior is controlled by forces over which few people have control."
    d. "If people wanted to avoid crime, they would go to church."

12. In his 1997 book *Moral Judgment: Does the Abuse Excuse Threaten our Legal System?* Wilson raises serious questions about the criminal justice system and its ability to

    a. Determine guilt or innocence.
    b. Select a jury of one's peers.
    c. Force people to obey the moral code.
    d. See the good in even the wickedest person.

REFERENCES

Biographical Note. (2013). *James Q. Wilson Collection: 1949-2012*. Santa Monica, CA: Pardee RAND Graduate School. Retrieved from: https://www.prgs.edu/content/dam/prgs/documents/CP760.pdf

Cullen, F.T. and Gilbert, K.E. (1982). *Reaffirming rehabilitation*. Cincinnati, OH: Anderson.

Delisi, M. (2011). James Q. Wilson and Richard J. *Herrnstein's Crime and Human Nature*. In F.T. Cullen & P. Wilcox (Eds.), Encyclopedia of criminological theory, Vol. 2, (pp. 1014–1018). Thousand Oaks, CA: Sage.

Delisi, M. (2003). Conservatism and common sense: The criminological career of James Q. Wilson. *Justice Quarterly* 20(3): 661–674.

Dilulio, J.J. (2012). James Q. Wilson. *Political Science and Politics*, 45 (3), pp. 559 – 561.

James Q. Wilson: Biography. (2018) Retrieved from: http://contemporarythinkers.org/jq-wilson/biography/

Jones, M. (2005). *Criminal justice pioneers in U.S. history*. Boston, MA: Pearson Education, Inc.

Kelling, G. L. and Coles, C.M. (1996). *Fixing broken windows: Restoring order and reducing crimes in our communities*. New York: Touchstone.

Liederbach, J., & Travis, L.F. (2008). Wilson redux: Another look at Varieties of Police Behavior. *Police Quarterly* 11(4): 447–467.

Mac Donald, H. (2012, March 12). The power of policing. *New York Post*. Retrieved from: http://nypost.com/2012/03/05/the-power-of-policing/

Newton, J. (2007, June 3). James Q. Wilson: The power of his written word. *Los Angeles Times*. Retrieved from: http://www.latimes.com/la-op-newton-3jun03-story.html

PBS. (2000). The first measured century: James Q. Wilson Interview. PBS-TV. Retrieved from: http://www.pbs.org/fmc/interviews/jwilson.htm [Producers: John C. Sorensen, John Mernit, and Vincent Cannato]

Petersilia, J. (2012, March 19). Remembering James Q. Wilson. *The Crime Report*.

Piereson, J. (2012, April). James Q. Wilson, 1931–2012. *New Criterion*, pp. 37–39.

President's Commission on Law Enforcement and the Administration of Justice (1967). *The challenge of crime in a free society*. Washington, DC: US Government Printing Office.

Rozansky, J. and Lerner, J. (2012). The political science of James Q. Wilson. *The New Atlantis*, No. 35, pp. 84 – 98.

Siegel, L.J., & Worrall, J.L. (2012). *Introduction to criminal justice* (13th ed.). Belmont, CA: Cengage.

Skogan, W.G. (1990). *Disorder and decline: Crime and the spiral of urban decay in American neighborhoods*. New York, NY: Free Press.

Summary. (1995). [Summary of the book *On Character*, by J.Q. Wilson]. Retrieved from: https://books.google.com/books/about/On_Character.html?id=Qd9L2kQoxr0C

Summary (1997) [Summary of the book *Moral Sense* by J.Q. Wilson]. Retrieved from: https://books.google.com/books/about/The_Moral_Sense.html?id=kgrrbYtYq2MC

Tonry, M., & Wilson, J.Q. (1990). *Drugs and crime*. Chicago, IL: University of Chicago Press.

Welsh, B.C., & Farrington, D.P. (2013). Preventing crime is hard work: Early intervention, developmental criminology, and the enduring legacy of James Q. Wilson. *Journal of Criminal Justice 41*, 448–451.

Wilson, J.Q. (1996). Foreword. In G.L. Kelling and C.M. *Coles Fixing broken windows: Restoring order and reducing crimes in our communities*. p. xii- xvi. New York: Touchstone.

Wilson, J.Q. (2002). *The marriage problem: How our culture has weakened families*. New York, NY: Harper Collins.

Wilson, J.Q. (1997). *Moral judgment: Does the abuse excuse threaten our legal system?* New York, NY: Basic Books.

Wilson, J.Q. (1993). *The moral sense*. New York, NY: Free Press.

Wilson, J.Q. (1991). *On character*. Washington, DC: AEI Press.

Wilson, J.Q. (1975). *Thinking about crime*. New York, NY: Basic Books.

Wilson, J.Q. (1970). *Varieties of police behavior: The management of law and order in eight communities*. New York, NY: Atheneum.

Wilson, J.Q., Farrington, D.P., and Ohlin, L.E. (1986). *Understanding and controlling crime: Toward a new research strategy*. New York: Springer.

Wilson, J.Q. and Herrnstein, R.J. (1985). *Crime and human nature*. New York: Simon and Schuster.

Wilson, J.Q., & Kelling, G. (April, 1982). Broken windows. *Atlantic Monthly*.

Wilson, J.Q., & Loury, G.C. (Eds.). *Children to citizens: Families, schools and delinquency prevention*, Vol. III. New York, NY: Springer Publishing.

Wilson, J.Q., & Petersilia, J. (Eds.). (1995). *Crime: Public policies for crime control*. New York, NY: ICS Press.

TRAVIS HIRSCHI
The Father of Social Bond Theory

Travis Hirschi is a notable contemporary criminologist who is highly regarded for several reasons. Not only has his work had an extraordinary impact on the field of criminology, but he is one of the only criminologists who advanced not one, but two important and influential theories of theoretical criminology.

Although he himself has dismissed the biographies of important theorists as being essentially meaningless (Laub, 2002), still, there is no denying the impact his life has had on his career as a leading sociologist and criminologist.

Travis Hirschi was born on April 15, 1935, in Rockville, Utah. He was the fifth of eight children born to Warren G. and Orra Hirschi. His father, Warren, was a transit man on highway survey crews in Utah and Idaho. Travis Hirschi has described his mother, Orra, as a women's liberationist who, although she only had an eighth grade education, was educated beyond her years in school (Laub, 2002). Despite neither of his parents being well educated, Hirschi has said that it was always assumed he would go to college.

Following high school, he entered the University of Utah, where he expected he would end up being a civil engineer. After all, he had spent several summers working with a highway engineering crew. Married while in college, his wife, Anna, with whom he brought up three children, raised strong objections to him majoring in engineering, and he selected sociology with the idea that he would be an academic. As an undergraduate student, he actually majored in both sociology and history.

As it turned out, at the University of Utah, Hirschi was exposed to the work and ideas of scholars who would be major influences throughout his whole career. One of those influences was Arthur Beeley, one of his professors. Beeley was a positivist who believed that everyone's behavior is determined by what happens before the behavior. In addition, and in a related way, Beeley expressed the view that punishments used by the criminal justice system were rather silly, outmoded traditions (Laub, 2002). Beeley helped Hirschi become acquainted with the basic assumptions and tenets of social control history and theory (Schreck, 2014). The second major influence was Émile Durkheim. As a graduate student working on a master's degree in sociology and education at the University of Utah, Hirschi read Durkheim's book *Suicide*, which emphasized how society regulates a person's impulses and that those outside of society were basically free to do whatever they wanted to do (Schreck, 2014). Hirschi told John Laub in an interview that "Before I read 'Suicide,' I had no idea what sociology was about. I read 'Suicide' and said aha! ... to my mind, that was the beginning of my involvement in control theory" (Laub, 2002, p. xiv).

Before Hirschi could be further involved in exploring control theory, he was drafted into the Army in 1958. After completing basic training, he was assigned to Fort Meyer, Virginia, and to a research unit in close-by Washington, D.C. This research unit analyzed survey data from soldiers, and one particular aspect of the survey data was to track the morale of U.S. Army troops. For two years, Hirschi worked as a data analyst for the Army (Laub, 2002). But when his stint with the Army was finished, he enrolled in the University of California at Berkeley to begin a PhD in sociology. From the beginning of his studies, his intent was to examine crime (Laub, 2002).

At UC Berkeley, Hirschi became acquainted with many of the leading sociologists of the day, all of whom were on the faculty there. These outstanding sociologists included Kingsley Davis, Irving Piliavin, David Matza, Hanan Selvin, and Erving Goffman. But it was in Goffman's courses that Travis Hirschi became intimately familiar with Robert Merton's strain theory. By studying strain theory, he came to see strain theory's internal logic as well as its limitations (Schreck, 2014).

It was also in Goffman's classes that Hirschi learned more about social control theory and how the theory had been all but discarded over the first half of the 20th century, although he also came to realize that the neglect of this theory had little to do with its internal validity. To Hirschi, social control theory had important theoretical and research implications (Schreck, 2014).

Another professor who influenced Hirschi's development was Hanan C. Selvin. Appointed as a research assistant at UC Berkeley, Hirschi had the job of reviewing and critiquing what was known about delinquency statistics at that time. That led him to delinquency theories and the work of Jackson Toby, Albert Reiss, and F. Ivan Nye (Schreck, 2014). But the research Hirschi conducted on delinquency led to his book—a collaboration between Selvin and him titled *Delinquency Research: An Appraisal of Analytic Methods* (1967).

As the research and writing of this book was going on, Hirschi would also be trying to narrow down his dissertation topic. Charles Y. Glock, the director of the Survey Research Center at UC Berkeley, agreed to be Hirschi's dissertation adviser. Glock, in turn, arranged for him to meet and work with Alan B. Wilson, the director of the Richmond Youth Project, which was just getting started (Laub, 2002). Hirschi started out working with Wilson and the project as a volunteer, but when the deputy director of the project left the university, Hirschi filled that spot. He got a chance to add some questionnaire items that interested him, and when the research was finished, he had the data he needed to write his dissertation (Schreck, 2014).

However, in 1967, Hirschi left UC Berkeley for a position at the University of Washington–Seattle in the department of sociology. But he was still working on his dissertation and in addition had a full teaching load. Finally, he was able to finish the dissertation, which he titled "Infraction as Action." He showed the final draft to his friend, the sociologist Rodney Stark. Stark, though, passed it on to Grant Barnes, an editor at the University of California Press. Within a couple of days, Barnes called Travis Hirschi and told him he would like to publish the dissertation as a book. Hirschi agreed, and the book that resulted was *Causes of Delinquency*, which came out in 1969. In the meantime, he and Selvin, who coauthored the 1967 book *Delinquency Research: An Appraisal of Analytic Methods*, shared the C. Wright Mills award given out by the Society for the Study of Social Problems (Laub, 2002).

CAUSES OF DELINQUENCY AND SOCIAL CONTROL THEORY

Although Travis Hirschi didn't create social control theory (nor was he the first to present it as a criminological theory), his theory of social bonding may well be the most influential social control theory (Tibbetts & Hemmens, 2010). No other social control theory has been so studied, cited, researched, and critiqued as the theory Hirschi presented in his book *Causes of Delinquency*.

As was indicated above, Hirschi was profoundly influenced by his reading of Durkheim's book *Suicide*. To develop his own theory, Hirschi took the Durkheim assumption that we are all animals and "thus naturally capable of committing criminal acts" (Hirschi, 1969, p. 31). However, while we are all capable of being criminal offenders, very few of us end up being criminals. Hirschi asks the essential question of why not. His answer is that most humans can be adequately socialized to become tightly bonded to society's conventions—family, school, and community. And the stronger our bonds to conventional society, the less likely we are to engage in illegal activities.

In general, control theories seek to explain *not* why people commit crime, but why people *do not* engage in criminal activities. Hirschi's theory, advanced in *Causes of Delinquency*, points to social bonds as the critical element determining who is a criminal and who is not. Hirschi sees the delinquent as the person who lacks intimate attachments, commitments to society, and moral beliefs. These are the bonds that tie people to live within the law. As Taylor (2001) points out, "A person is free to commit delinquent acts because his ties to the conventional order have somehow been broken" (p. 372). On the other hand, when the ties are strong, an individual is not free to act outside of the standard rules and conventions.

According to Hirschi's theory, social bonds are made up of four elements: 1. Attachment; 2. Commitment; 3. Involvement; and 4. Moral belief.

Attachment has to do with the affectionate bonds between an individual and the important people in his or her life, such as parents or siblings. It is through attachment that people acquire and internalize conventional values. Similar to what Freud first said, Hirschi believed that strong attachments early in life are crucial to the development of social bonds (Tibbetts & Hemmens, 2010). Without attachments, though, the other elements in social bonding are not possible. Commitment, one of those other elements, has to do with the investment a person has in conventional society. If there is no commitment to society and its values, then there is no reason for a person to avoid criminal behavior. Involvement is another element, and it relates to how much time is spent in conventional activities. If an individual spends considerable time in conventional activities, there is much less time available—and perhaps less interest—for illegal activities. Finally, the last of Hirschi's four elements is beliefs. This has to do with morality and the laws and rules of society. A person who has a set of moral values is less likely to engage in activities that run counter to their values and beliefs. Hirschi wrote that "… the less a person believes he should obey the rules, the more likely he is to violate them" (Hirschi, 1969, p. 26).

As John Laub makes clear in his book *The Craft of Criminology* (2002), Hirschi perhaps has done more than any other delinquency theorist in terms of bringing the family and family relations into the discussion. Loeber and Stouthamer-Loeber (1986) reviewed the family variables that are related to juvenile delinquency. Their review indicates that such variables as poor family functioning and inadequate child-rearing practices play a role in delinquency. But that doesn't mean that most theories pay homage to these important variables. In fact, just the opposite is true, especially sociological theories (Laub, 2002). Hirschi's social control theory changes that.

While the social bond theory has been decidedly influential in the field of criminology, it has not been accepted by everyone, nor has it been accepted uncritically. One fundamental complaint about Hirschi's social bond theory, and about control theories in general, is that these theories do not provide a motivation for offending—only for not offending (Smith, 1995). So, while social bond theory may explain why most people refrain from offending, it does little to elucidate why, after an individual begins offending, they keep offending or why their behavior may escalate (Tibbetts & Hemmens, 2010). As it turns out, Travis Hirschi was aware of this criticism and addressed it in *Causes of Delinquency* (1969) when he wrote, "The question 'Why do they do it?' is simply not the question the theory is designed to answer" (p. 34).

As Tibbetts and Hemmens (2010) acknowledge, the theory has been tested by many researchers and, for the most part, been supported (p. 463). However, Tibbetts and Hemmens go on to list other criticisms of the theory. For instance, a prominent criticism is that the components of the social bond may predict criminal behavior only if they are defined in a certain way. For example, Tibbetts and Hemmens indicate, with respect to the involvement element of the bond, studies suggest that not all conventional activities are the same in terms of preventing delinquency (p. 463). Two conventional activities that research indicates tend to inhibit delinquency are academic and religious activities (Tibbetts & Hemmens, 2010, p. 463). On the other hand, such conventional activities as dating and playing sports tend to bring with them an increased risk of delinquent behavior.

Another criticism of Hirschi's theory has to do with attachment and how attachments relate to crime. Although it is generally agreed that attachments are important, whether a strong attachment reduces criminal behavior depends on to whom one is attached. For instance, studies have shown that attachment to delinquent peers is a predictor of criminal behavior (Tibbetts & Hemmens, 2010).

Following the publication of *Causes of Delinquency* and the ensuing criticism, Hirschi spent a considerable amount of time responding to the criticism and defending his social control theory. He told John Laub (2002) that he was virtually the only social control theorist coming to its defense, even though he acknowledged that social control theory was certainly not original with him. Furthermore, he told Laub that he defended his theory because he believed it was superior to alternative theories (p. xxvi). But despite the criticism, Hirschi's social bonding theory is still one of the most accepted theories of criminal behavior.

COLLABORATION WITH MICHAEL GOTTFREDSON: A GENERAL THEORY OF CRIME

Two years after *Causes of Delinquency* came out, Travis Hirschi left the University of Washington to become professor of sociology and chair at the University of California at Davis. It was there that he met Michael Gottfredson, who was an undergraduate student in sociology. But Gottfredson went on to do his graduate work at the State University of New York at Albany. Nonetheless, they began working together, and their collaboration resulted in a number of works, including *Measuring of Delinquency*, one of Hirschi's most famous papers and a critique of the theorizing and research on the age-crime curve (Schreck, 2014). The age-crime curve is a staple in criminology and posits that across all societies, predatory street crimes, including robbery, rape, burglary, larceny, and murder, tend to peak during the teenage years and drop off sharply after the teen years (Tibbetts & Hemmens, 2010). The paper, titled "Age and the Explanation of Crime" (1983), stated Hirschi and Gottfredson's age invariance thesis (it should be noted that although Hindelang was involved in the early stages of this paper, he dropped out because he was dying from a brain tumor). This thesis asserts that the effect of age on criminal behaviors does not vary across social and cultural conditions and that it applies to all demographic groups (Hirschi & Gottfredson, 1994). As they explain it, crime increases with age until the mid- to late teens and then declines rapidly and continuously throughout the rest of life (Hirschi & Gottfredson, 1994). The age invariance thesis tends to disregard the impact of external social control factors, such as marriage or employment, on an individual's propensity to commit crime (Taylor, 2001). But to Hirschi and Gottfredson, the age invariance thesis explains much in criminal justice. For instance, they believed that this effect explains why the treatment of offenders is usually unsuccessful and why experiments involving random arrests show no effect on recidivism (Hirschi & Gottfredson, 1994). Together, Gottfredson and Hirschi continued to develop their age invariance ideas throughout the 1980s, and this work culminated in *A General Theory of Crime* in 1990.

The essence of *A General Theory of Crime* is a proposed theory that the nature of criminality has to do with low self-control. This theory seems to stem from the classical view of criminology in that the authors posit that "all human conduct can be understood as the self-interested pursuit of pleasure or the avoidance of pain" (1990, p. 5).

Adopting the viewpoint from the classical theory of criminology, Hirschi and Gottfredson suggest that the pursuit of pleasure and the avoidance of pain is a concept that has been neglected because, to their way of thinking, criminal acts are an expression of "fundamental human tendencies" that have straightforward and profound implications (Hirschi & Gottfredson, 1990, p. 5). On the other hand, they have various problems with the positivist school of thought that superseded the classical school. The positivist approach was to see crime as related to determinism; and that crime was caused by factors outside of the control of the offender (Hirschi & Gottfredson, 1990). However, after thorough review of several positivistic viewpoints, the authors reject them all, suggesting that positivistic social science does not end up with conceptual schemes or theories (p. 82). So, they go back to the classical approach, stating that classical theory is a theory of social or external control (p. 87); it only lacks an "explicit idea of self-control" (p. 87). And that's what Hirschi and Gottfredson offer—a concept of self-control as a way of explaining that criminal acts provide immediate gratification of desire for individuals who have a "here and now orientation"; in other words, individuals with low self-control (p. 89).

To Hirschi and Gottfredson, low self-control is an individual-level attribute that causes crime at all ages, especially when combined with appropriate opportunities and attractive targets (Taylor, 2001). The General Theory of Crime (GTC) asserts that individuals are born predisposed toward selfishness and self-centeredness, and that any effective child-rearing and socialization can produce a child with self-control (Tibbetts & Hemmens, 2010). It also includes the key ideas that the relationship between crime and age is invariant; that any individual differences in the tendency to commit crime can be understood in a person's level of self-control; that self-control not only accounts for all types of crime, but also other kinds of behavior (such as drinking and gambling); that differences in self-control between individuals has to do with the child-rearing practices to which they were exposed; and that crime declines with age for every person (Laub, 2002).

Hirschi drew on parenting and family relations for his social bonding theory, and he and Gottfredson do so again here as they state that without effective and competent parenting involving appropriate socialization that leads to self-control, the child will follow his or her natural tendencies and grow into a selfish predator (Tibbetts & Hemmens, 2010). So, an individual who fails to receive adequate parenting and thus not learn self-control will tend to be impulsive, insensitive, and physical (rather than more cerebral); a risk taker who is short-sighted and non-verbal; in short, a person who will be inclined to engage in criminal behaviors (Taylor, 2001). The GTC also assumes that self-control must be established by age 10. If not, then the person is always likely to lack self-control.

One of the problems for others, but perhaps not so much of a problem for Hirschi himself, is the fact that he has two theories of criminology. For others, a central question becomes: How can the two theories be reconciled? An additional question might be: Does one theory—either social control theory or self-control theory—play a greater, more dominant role in criminological theory? That question was put to Hirschi by John Laub (2002). Hirschi's answer:

> I think that the fairest way to say it is this: To the extent the age curve is invariant, self-control theory trumps social control theory. To the extent that it can be shown that there is variation that can be explained, social control theory trumps self-control. In that sense, it is a purely empirical question. We are arguing today because we don't have adequate data. In principal, we should be able to resolve this because

there should be no ideological component in either position. I don't see any. We should be able to say social control is right or self-control is right. (p. xxxi)

Similar to Hirschi's social bonding theory, self-control theory attributes the formation of controls as coming from the socialization process. However, the self-control theory may be very attractive as a criminological explanation because it identifies only one primary factor as causing criminality. While low self-control may seem like a simplistic explanation for criminal behavior, it implies a series of personality traits and behaviors as indicated above: risk taking, impulsivity, lack of future perspective, and a quick temper.

The General Theory of Crime has led to a significant amount of debate and research—perhaps as much or more than Hirschi's social bonding theory or any other theory in criminology (Tibbetts & Hemmens, 2010). Research has suggested that low self-control may be due to emotional dispositions. That is, some people may be predisposed toward pleasure seeking and toward avoiding pain and negative emotions (Tibbetts & Hemmens, 2010). Furthermore, other research indicates that there may be physiological aspects of low self-control. Some studies show that chronic offenders have greater arousal toward danger and risk taking (Tibbetts & Hemmens, 2010). Other studies show that chronic gamblers tend to receive a physiological "jolt" from gambling activities. In summary, there may be various research studies suggesting that self-control comes about not just from the socialization process in early life, but may come about in more complicated ways. Nonetheless, public policy implications of self-control theory are that programs to help improve the competency of parents may be important in improving self-control in individuals, thus reducing their risk taking and impulsive behavior.

THE END OF HIS ACADEMIC CAREER

Travis Hirschi left the State University of New York at Albany in 1981 to become professor at the University of Arizona. He remained at the university in Tucson until he retired in 1997, after which he became Regent Professor Emeritus at the same university. Michael Gottfredson left the State University of New York at Albany in 1981 to become part of the faculty in the Department of Sociology at the University of Illinois–Urbana, but in 1985, he left to join Hirschi at the University of Arizona–Tucson.

During his career, Hirschi authored or coauthored four books, wrote more than 30 journal articles, contributed nearly 30 book chapters or book forewords, and penned many book reviews and review essays. Continuing to write up to his death in January 2017, his last published article was titled *The Criminal Career Perspective as an Explanation of Crime and a Guide to Crime Control Policy: The View From General Theories of Crime*, coauthored with Michael Gottfredson and published in the *Journal of Research in Crime and Delinquency* in 2016.

In 2002 in *The Craft of Criminology: Selected Papers: Travis Hirschi*, John Laub wrote that the trademark of Hirschi's work since the 1960s is "profound theoretical insights coupled with rigorous research methods" (p. xli). And Laub suggests that perhaps more than any other scholar, Hirschi's work has dominated intellectual discussion and created the research agenda for the field of criminology (Laub, 2002).

If success is based on the influence of ideas and theories and the amount of attention paid to a scholar's work, then by all accounts, Travis Hirschi might be said to have been highly successful. But what is Hirschi's abiding legacy? Schreck in 2014 observed that Hirschi not only had a tremendous impact on the field of criminology but his work has been noteworthy for advancing and defending ideas that were not fashionable at the time he advanced them (p. 2). That he continued to write about and defend both social bonding theory and self-control theory up to the time of his death indicates the continuing strong intellectual interest in his theories in the criminological field. His work has resulted in dozens of research projects as well as dozens of dissertations (Laub, 2002).

In 2002, John Laub asked Travis Hirschi what he saw as his legacy to the field of criminology. His response was both measured and humble:

> I guess I am pleased to see the success of control theory, however it is defined. But I am not sure how much credit to take for that. I have made the comment before and I still think it has some validity that control theory was more vital before than after "Causes of Delinquency." The ideas were there, had been for a long time, and will be around for a long time to come.... But as far as my own contribution, I don't know. I had fun. I have greatly enjoyed criminology.... But the legacy question, I am uncomfortable with that. Clearly, if you want to have a legacy in the field the best way is through students, through a program of graduate education.... If I could count Michael Gottfredson and John Laub and Robert Sampson and Chester Britt and Barbara Costello as my students, I'd give myself high marks indeed. (Laub, 2002, pp. xl, xli)

QUESTIONS FOR DISCUSSION

1. Travis Hirschi's major influences seem to be related primarily to his college professors. Which professor seems to have had the greatest impact on the theories he would later develop?
2. Does Hirschi's social control theory, presented in *Causes of Delinquency* in 1969, still hold up today as a useful explanation of why young people become delinquent? Why or why not?
3. Could an individual be strongly attached to his or her parents and still commit crimes? Why or why not?
4. If you accept the age-invariance thesis, what would be the best approach to dealing with offenders?
5. Which is a better theory explaining criminal behavior: social control theory or self-control theory? Give reasons for your answer.

IMPORTANT TERMS

Age-crime curve: The age-crime curve refers to the well-established trend: the prevalence of offending tends to increase from late childhood, peak in the teenage years (from ages 15 to 19), and then decline in the early twenties.

Age-inversion thesis: Hirschi and Gottfredson contend that the relationship between age and crime for various populations follows a similar pattern characterized by a single peak occurring fairly early in the life cycle (usually in the late teens for most offenses), with steady declines thereafter.

Attachment: Attachment has to do with close connections to others. When people are closely attached to others, they worry about others' opinions of them. Children conform to society's norms in order to gain approval (and prevent disapproval) from family and friends.

Beliefs: Beliefs, in Hirschi's social bond theory, has to do with an agreement on common values in society. Viewing social values as beliefs, an individual will likely conform to those beliefs.

Commitment: Commitment refers to the investments we make in the community. The more invested a person is in his or her community, the more they have to lose from committing a crime.

Control theories: A group of theories that try to explain criminal behavior by suggesting that people are born with propensities to offend, but they can be controlled by factors in their upbringing, such as socialization, discipline, and being taught self-control.

Criminology: Criminology is the scientific study of crime, including the causes of crime.

General Theory of Crime: The theory presented by Travis Hirschi and Michael Gottfredson in 1990; it proposes that the explanation of crime has to do with low self-control.

Involvement: In Hirschi's social bond theory, involvement has to do with participation in socially legitimate activities, which tends to lessen a person's likelihood of criminal behavior.

Positivism: A school of criminology which sees the root cause of crime as factors outside of the control of the offender.

Positivists: Criminologists who subscribe to the school of positivism.

Social bonding theory: A control theory proposed by Travis Hirschi in 1969. This theory begins with the assumption that individuals are predisposed to commit crime, but the social bonds formed by individuals help prevent or reduce criminal offending.

Strain theories: A group of theories in criminology that emphasize frustration at not being able to achieve or obtain socially accepted goals. This strain or frustration may lead some individuals to criminal offending.

FOR FURTHER READING

Durkheim, É. (1966). *Suicide: A study in sociology.* New York, NY: Free Press.

Hirschi, T., & Gottfredson, M. (1994). *The generality of deviance.* New Brunswick, NJ: Transaction Books.

Hirschi, T., & Selvin, H. (1967). *Delinquency research: An appraisal of analytic methods.* New York, NY: Free Press.

REVIEW QUESTIONS

True or False

1. The theory proposed by Travis Hirschi in *Causes of Delinquency* is a form of control theory.
2. The social bonding theory in Hirschi's *Causes of Delinquency* has been accepted without any criticism by criminologists.
3. The age-inversion thesis states that age and crime are closely connected.
4. The General Theory of Crime has to do with self-control.

Multiple Choice

5. In Hirschi's social control theory of delinquency causation, the family plays a crucial role because
   a. It is within the family that socialization takes place.
   b. Children need to learn how to play appropriately.
   c. Young children need to imitate their siblings.
   d. Parents use severe punishment to teach children right from wrong.

6. Hirschi writes in *Causes of Delinquency* that the question is not "Why do they do it?" in discussing causes of delinquent behavior. He suggests, however, that the more important question should be:

   a. "What makes them become criminals?"
   b. "How does religion play a significant role in prevention?"
   c. "Why can't they do it?"
   d. "Why don't they do it?"

7. The General Theory of Crime asserts that unless there is competent and effective parenting, children will not

   a. Learn to be independent.
   b. Be successful in the business world.
   c. Develop self-control.
   d. Become overly attached to their mother.

8. Self-control theory, as a theory of criminology, seems to be attractive to many people because

   a. It answers all questions about the causes of criminal offending.
   b. It implies that there is one easily understood theory of criminal behavior.
   c. It blames parents for the criminal behavior of their children.
   d. It helps explain every type of crime.

REFERENCES

Hirschi, T. (1969). *Causes of delinquency.* Oakland, CA: University of California Press.

Hirschi, T., & Gottfredson, M. (1983). Age and the explanation of crime. *American Journal of Sociology, 89,* 552–584.

Hirschi, T., & Gottfredson, M. (1990). *A general theory of crime.* Stanford, CA: Stanford University Press.

Hirschi, T., & Gottfredson, M. (1994). *The generality of deviance.* New Brunswick, NJ: Transaction Books.

Hirschi, T., & Gottfredson, M. (2016). The criminal career perspective as an explanation of crime and a guide to crime control policy: The view from general theories of crime. *Journal of Research in Crime and Delinquency, 53*(3), 406–419.

Laub, J. (Ed.). (2002). *The craft of criminology: The selected papers of Travis Hirschi.* New Brunswick, NJ: Transaction Books.

Loeber, R., & Stouthamer-Loeber, M. (1986). Family factors as correlates and predictors of juvenile conduct problems and delinquency. *Crime and Justice, 7,* 29–149.

Schreck, C. J. (2014). Hirschi, Travis. *Encyclopedia of theoretical criminology* [Online]. Retrieved from http://onlinelibrary.wiley.com/doi/10.1002/9781118517390.wbetc133/full

Smith, D. (1995). *Criminology for social work.* London, United Kingdom: Palgrave Macmillan.

Taylor, C. (2001). The relationship between social and self-control: Tracing Hirschi's criminological career. *Theoretical Criminology, 5*(3), 369–388.

Tibbetts, S. G., & Hemmens, C. (2010). *Criminological theory: A text/reader.* Thousand Oaks, CA: Sage.

CREDIT

Travis Hirschi; ed. John Laub, "Selection," *The Craft of Criminology,* pp. xxxi, xl, xli. Copyright © 2002 by Taylor & Francis Group. Reprinted with permission.

5

AUGUST VOLLMER
The Father of American Policing

He was the dominant authority in policing in the first half of the 20th century. He was a police chief, a policing innovator, the first academic criminologist, and the most influential voice in both national and international policing. All of these accolades help explain why August Vollmer is known as the Father of American Policing.

Vollmer, born in New Orleans, Louisiana, in 1876, was a self-educated man who went beyond theory to bring about practical changes in policing. He was a man who stood up for what he believed and was a strong leader in reforming his own police department, but, with a strong national reputation, encouraged reform throughout the United States. He rebelled against the corruption and brutality in policing that was prevalent in the nineteenth and early twentieth centuries, while preaching respect for suspects, the accused, and every other citizen. In many ways, August Vollmer was ahead of his time; yet, in many ways, he was also right for his time as he became a voice of reason, of dignity, and of forging a professional police officer who would be a model citizen and a dedicated public servant.

But August Vollmer's early life certainly gave no indication of what would come later. If anything, it was a rather ordinary childhood and adolescence, and he never thought about becoming a policeman. If he had a career goal, it was to be a stenographer. But that came after a childhood marked by the early death of his father and a portion of his childhood living in Germany.

Shortly after his birth to John and Philippine Vollmer, the family moved from New Orleans to San Francisco. Little is known about John Vollmer, although one incident reveals the influence he had on his oldest son, August. In May, 1884 when young August was just eight years old, he showed up at home beaten and bloodied after a fight with another boy. When John Vollmer came home and learned about the fight and found out that August had run away from the altercation, he was angry with his wife, Philippine, and not very happy with his son. John took his son to a local gymnasium so he could be taught to box and be better able to defend himself in the future. As it turned out, though, it would be the last lesson John would teach August. Three months later, John Vollmer died of a heart attack. However, a few months after that, August was challenged by another boy. Instead of running away, he used his new boxing skills and bested the other boy this time.

For August, his adopted sister Josie, his younger brother Edward, and his mother, life changed after his father died. Philippine took over the grocery store that John had run, but after two years of trying to make a go of it, she decided to sell the store. She then made the decision to pack up her family and go to Germany to be close to her family. So, at age ten, August was living in Germany, attending a German school, and learning to speak German.

After two years in Germany, Philippine made another decision—to return to the United States and go back to New Orleans. August was sent to New Orleans Academy, a vocational school, where, with encouragement from the academy's principal, John Wilson, August decided he wanted to become a stenographer. He studied shorthand, typing, and bookkeeping.

But Philippine was not happy with New Orleans as a place to raise her children. At the time, she saw New Orleans as riddled with corruption, crime, and dangerous gangs. Once again, she packed up their belongings, and the family took the train west to San Francisco, where Philippine had a few friends. Renting an apartment on O'Farrell Street, August, fresh from his course work at the New Orleans Academy, went out looking for a job as a stenographer. Although no one seemed interested in a thirteen-year-old stenographer, he was able to land a job as an assistant shipping clerk and messenger at W. and J. Sloane and Company, Household Furnishings.

But once again, Philippine had a new idea. She decided to have a house built in Berkeley, the small college town across the bay from San Francisco. During the year that the construction was taking place, August continued to work for W. and J. Sloane and Company. His teenage sister Josie ran away from home, never to be heard from again by the family. But in 1891, August, his brother, and mother moved to their new house on Bonita Street in North Berkeley. And soon thereafter, Philippine acquired a job as a practicing nurse.

August was finally hired as a stenographer for a company called E.H. Driggs in San Francisco. Although it meant a daily commute from Berkeley to San Francisco, the energetic young man didn't mind at all. In fact, he enjoyed his life. He often hiked in the hills in the area after work, learned to play the guitar, and sailed in an old boat he bought, named the *Ruby*. He also had taken an interest in girls. One girl he was interested in was Pat Fell, a young woman he met at a church social. But they didn't date very long; apparently Pat wasn't impressed with August.

In 1895, at age nineteen, August and a friend, Ted Patterson, opened a coal and feed store in Berkeley. Vollmer didn't mind the hard work that went along with starting a business, and in a few years the coal and feed store was thriving. While he was helping to grow his new business, he found time to help to organize a volunteer fire department in North Berkeley. Within two years, he was awarded the town's Fireman Medal for his role in establishing the fire department. His business, his role in civic endeavors, and the friendships he made reflected the life of a young man who was settling in as a member of the community. But then the United States declared war on Spain in 1898. August Vollmer decided immediately that he couldn't stand by in Berkeley while Americans were fighting a war. He quickly arranged to sell his half of the business to his partner Ted Patterson and went to San Francisco to enlist. After six weeks of military training, he boarded a ship and was headed to Manila in the Philippines.

Vollmer was assigned to the Third Artillery, Company G, which participated in the capture of Manila from the Spanish. Then, during the next several months, he and his company were involved in twenty-four battles and engagements. But when the insurgency ended in August 1899, he boarded another ship to cross the Pacific to return home. There, receiving a hero's welcome along with other returning veterans of the Spanish-American War, Vollmer was ready to go back to work. He quickly accepted a job delivering groceries until he heard about openings at the post office; he took and passed the exam to become a mailman in Berkeley.

Being a mail carrier was a great job for August because he was friendly, personable, and liked getting to know people in Berkeley. He was content to keep on delivering the mail, but his friends and acquaintances suggested he run for marshal against the town marshal who had, according to many citizens and politicians of Berkeley, allowed gambling and other vices to flourish there. His friends thought that August, an Army hero and an upright, moral individual, wouldn't stand for the drugs, the gambling, and the prostitution. Besides that, he was also celebrated in the local newspapers for his heroic actions in stopping a runaway railroad car that would have resulted in serious injury to other people.

Persuaded, Vollmer allowed his name to be submitted as a candidate for town marshal. He was first endorsed by the *Berkeley Advocate*, one of the local newspapers. In an editorial, the *Berkeley Advocate* wrote: "The man is a Berkeley product and known of Berkeley men. He is ambitious to make a record for himself and the record will be good" (Carte & Carte, 1975, p. 17). And the *Berkeley Daily Gazette* also endorsed him: "Gus Vollmer is a man of mental acumen and sagacity, and his service in the Army has particularly fitted him for the job of tracking down and apprehending criminals.... He has the physical strength to cope with a criminal, and besides he has the necessary grit and courage" (Carte & Carte, 1975, pp. 18–19). He handily defeated the incumbent and took office in 1905. He was determined to prove he was the right choice to clean up Berkeley.

HIS CAREER IN POLICING BEGINS

Refusing to be influenced by anyone who could benefit by allowing vice to persist unchecked, Vollmer and his small police force initiated raids on opium dens and brothels. This would be his first attempt to not only rid a city of its unhealthy vices but to contend with political corruption.

Conducting raids and avoiding political pressures, he managed to get the vice problems under control. Vollmer then petitioned the town council for more staff. Three officers, he argued, were an insufficient police force to run a town that had had an influx of immigrants from the near destruction of San Francisco following the great earthquake of April 1906. The citizens who migrated to Berkeley soon pushed the population to nearly 50,000. The town council was sympathetic to Vollmer's problems, and the police force was increased to twelve officers. But besides adding to the force, Vollmer centralized the record system, started a police

August Vollmer in 1929

Underwood & Underwood, https://commons.wikimedia.org/wiki/File:August_Vollmer_cph.3b17374.jpg. Copyright in the Public Domain.

training school, and initiated a dog-catching service. With a growing reputation, he was elected president of the California Police Chiefs Association—despite the fact that he was not a police chief. However, this would only be the first of many positions he would hold with police, criminal justice, and community organizations.

With its growing population, Berkeley adopted a new charter in 1909, and it became a city. The elected position of town marshal was switched to that of appointed police chief. The new city council was happy with August Vollmer's performance, and he was appointed chief of police, a job he would hold for the next 21 years.

Although he had little education and no formal training to be either a police officer or a chief of police, August Vollmer was intelligent and was always on the lookout for ideas and innovations that would enhance the quality of police services in his adopted city. Early on as chief, he formalized foot patrol beats to get his officers out on the sidewalks and in touch with the citizens. To increase the mobility of his officers, Vollmer became the first police chief in the country to introduce bicycle patrols. As the automobile became more commonplace, he had his patrol officers patrolling the streets in cars by 1915. Visiting Los Angeles and noticing the effectiveness of traffic lights, he brought the idea north to Berkeley and instituted traffic lights in his city. When he saw that San Francisco was using callboxes for policemen, he adopted the idea in Berkeley; it was a way to improve response time and keep track of his officers, who were required to call in to headquarters regularly.

Vollmer also was interested in the "hard sciences" and how they could be used in policing. He was one of the first police chiefs to recognize that nearly every phase of policing was complex and that not only was training of officers required, but so was using technology. This recognition resulted in his establishing a forensics laboratory to assist his police force in solving crimes. That came about in 1916 when he began an association with Dr. Albert Schneider, a professor in the pharmacy school at the University of California. Schneider had been doing work in forensic medicine, and this intrigued Vollmer. Initially, Schneider agreed to give lectures in the police school, but within a year, he had joined the Berkeley Police Department as a full-time criminologist. That led to Schneider and Vollmer establishing the first scientific crime laboratory, which, of course, during the course of the 20th century became the backbone of police investigations. But it all started with Vollmer's first laboratory.

When Chief Vollmer heard about the Modus Operandi System in France and other countries of Europe, he was quick to understand the implications of this system as an investigative tool. The concept of *modus operandi* asked the question: how does the individual criminal typically operate? In fact, translated from Latin, *modus operandi* (MO) means the method of operation. Vollmer readily understood that the police in the United States usually focused on the crime but rarely on the criminal. By understanding the way certain criminals went about their business, Vollmer believed, the police could figure out who committed the crimes based on how those crimes were carried out. He became the first American police administrator to adopt the MO system, which was first devised by the English constable L.W. Atcherley (Carte & Carte, 1975).

Likewise, he was also interested in scientific lie detection. While many other people worked on developing a polygraph or lie detector, including

Cesare Lombroso, William Marston, and Leonard Keeler, it was a young scientist by the name of John Larson, an employee of the Berkeley Police Department, along with Vollmer and his assistant, Clarence D. Lee, who are usually credited with the invention of a lie detector to aid in police interrogations.

In addition to these interests and advances, August Vollmer firmly believed that educated and intelligent men would make better police officers. He was also well aware that because police officers were not trained that this situation helped to perpetuate the perception of a police officer as the "dumb cop." In many cities, police officers got their job not through any talent or skill, but through political patronage. Vollmer set out to change that. He himself, although not college educated, was a voracious reader but as early as 1908 was advocating for hiring college-educated men. By 1917, through his relationship with the faculty at the University of California at Berkeley, he created the Berkeley Police School, the first formal training for police officers in America.

But before the training, he wanted educated employees. So, in 1916, he placed an advertisement in the *Daily Collegian*, the student newspaper at the University of California. In this ad, he urged young men to "Learn a new profession. Serve on the Berkeley Police Force while you go to college" (Leonard, 1964, p. 137). That ad generated one hundred responses from college students. But how to weed out the best from the rest? That question led to the development of a comprehensive police entrance examination. With the assistance of Dr. Jau Don Ball, a psychiatrist, Vollmer put together a battery of psychological tests to select the best applicants. Vollmer was very clear about who he was looking for. He desired men of "high intelligence, sound nerves, good physique, sterling character, fast reaction time, good memory, and the ability to make accurate observations and correct decisions (Leonard, 1964, p. 137). He also began using the polygraph to screen police candidates—a practice still used today by the FBI and other law enforcement agencies.

With the success of the first newspaper advertisement, Vollmer continued to recruit new officers in the same manner. Over the years, hundreds of college students applied for positions in the Berkeley Police Department. Some of his most notable "college cops" included Walter Gordon, the department's first black officer; John Larson, the future inventor of the polygraph; and V.A. Leonard, who became a well-known writer and criminal justice educator (and author of *Police of the 20th Century* in 1964). But there were others. Many of Vollmer's protégés became police administrators, like O.W. Wilson, who was the chief in Wichita, Kansas, before being appointed superintendent of the Chicago Police Department. Others became forensic scientists, lawyers, military leaders, and politicians. By the late 1940s, at least twenty-five police chiefs around the country had served under August Vollmer (Fisher, 2015).

Although a police innovator, August Vollmer was also a decent—and demanding—police chief. Through his writings, his teachings, and through the example he himself set, he made the best possible case for the "new policing" (Carte & Carte, 1975, p. 3). He insisted that his officers accept no gifts and do no special favors for any citizen. Furthermore, he demanded that no juveniles be put in jail, and he was opposed to any use of force. There was to be no excessive force, no torture, and no intimidation by his officers.

Vollmer's high standards for his officers included strict prohibitions against force and brutality, especially against prisoners. One of his officers in Berkeley said that August Vollmer told his men that no Berkeley police officer was to ever strike any person, particularly a prisoner, except in extreme self-defense. And then, should that happen, the officer said, Vollmer's policy was that by taking that action, that officer had just turned in his resignation (Carte & Carte, 1975). His opposition to brutality and intimidation was so important to him that the chief had a habit of visiting the police jail every morning and talking to prisoners asking how they had been treated.

Vollmer's model of the professional police officer centered around the concept of an idealized police officer who was a skilled and dedicated crime fighter. This model police officer would be rigorously trained to perform a difficult job. If officers were to be aggressive, it was to be aggressive in using science and technology in all phases of policing. In addition, Vollmer's officers should be deeply involved in the community they served.

In fact, he envisioned that police officers would become an integral part of the community. Chief Vollmer not only preached this philosophy; he practiced it. During his tenure as police chief, Vollmer practiced his belief that the police had an obligation to be involved with the community. He served as president of the Society for the Prevention of Cruelty to Animals, was an active worker in the Berkeley Charitable Organization, served as a member of the State Recreation Inquiry Commission, was vice president of the California Mental Hygiene Society, was a member of the board of directors of the Alameda County Health Center, and the founder of the Los Angeles Child Guidance Clinic (MacNamara, 1977).

The police officer's job, Vollmer declared, was to form alliances in the community that would lead to strategies to deal with the "pre-delinquent" youngster, while at the same time working to alleviate the social and psychological causes of later delinquency and crime. His view of his idealized crime-fighting police officer was suggested in his 1919 article titled "The Policeman as a Social Worker." In this article, he described his view of the officer as the ultimate crime fighter who understood crime and worked to prevent its occurrence. In order to bring about this kind of police officer, he realized that the officer must be intelligent, educated, and trained. That meant, essentially, elevating the role and status of police officers to make them law enforcement professionals. If this could be accomplished, Vollmer thought, then the police officer would secure the people's confidence, sympathy, respect, and cooperation.

Vollmer's philosophy was passed on to new recruits in the Berkeley Police Department in the remarks he addressed to his newly hired officers: "Better still you can prevent people from doing wrong; That's the mission of a policeman ... I'll admire you more if in the first year you don't make a single arrest. I'm not judging you on arrests. I'm judging you on how many people you keep from doing something wrong" (Carte & Carte, 1975, p. 45).

In 1922, when August Vollmer was president of the International Association of Chiefs of Police, he addressed the annual convention held that year in San Francisco. His address was titled "Aims and Ideals of the

Police." In this address, he outlined a number of reforms he wanted to see in policing, which included:

1. The increased use of policewomen, especially in the "vast field of pre-delinquency." (Carte & Carte, 1975, p. 56)
2. Police schools for training purposes.
3. Modern equipment, such as signal devices, wireless telephones, automobiles, and laboratory apparatus.
4. Greater emphasis on crime prevention, which he described as "our principal function." (Carte & Carte, 1975, p. 57)
5. The police contributing to the solving of the problem of unnecessary delay and the miscarriage of justice in criminal trials.
6. Uniform national and even international laws, uniform classification of crimes, and simplified court procedures.
7. Police investigators abandoning "trial-and-error" methods of crime solving in favor of more efficient scientific techniques. (Carte & Carte, 1975, p. 57)
8. Centralization and improved methods of maintaining police records.
9. Universities should be urged to devote more time to the study of "human behavior, its bearing upon political and social problems, and for the training of practical criminologists, jurists, prosecutors, police-men, and policewomen." (Carte & Carte, 1975, p. 57)

In this list, it is easy to see that Vollmer was a police chief well ahead of his time in advocating for professional police officers, for changing police departments, and, in fact, reforming the criminal justice system.

THE WICKERSHAM REPORT

The Wickersham Commission is the popular name for the National Commission on Law Observance and Enforcement, which was appointed by President Herbert Hoover in 1929. The commission, which derived its name from its chairperson, former U.S. attorney general

George Wickersham, conducted the first comprehensive national study of crime and law enforcement in U.S. history. Its findings, which were published in fourteen volumes in 1931 and 1932, covered every aspect of the criminal justice system, including the causes of crime, police and prosecutorial procedures, and the importance of probation and parole.

Hoover established the commission to address several important issues. With the passage of the Eighteenth Amendment, Prohibition began in 1920, making illegal the manufacture and sale of alcoholic beverages. By 1929, illegal sale of alcohol by organized crime had become a national problem. President Hoover charged Wickersham's commission with studying the problem of crime.

Among the many professionals and distinguished people who were part of the Wickersham Commission was August Vollmer, who was appointed to direct the police section of the Wickersham Report. Vollmer was assisted in his research by David G. Monroe and Earle W. Garrett, both of whom were in the Department of Political Science at the University of Chicago. Their final report articulated standards and goals in policing that if read today would still remain valid. The police report section authored by Vollmer spoke of the low standards of policing and the disconnect between the police and the public: "Law enforcement agents are usually held in contempt, and law enforcement is one of our national jokes." As a result, Vollmer made recommendations at the end of the report that echoed the recommendations he would continually make, both before and after the Wickersham Report: Remove the police from politics; make chiefs of police independent of politics; maintain high recruitment and training standards for police officers; establish good working conditions for the police; maintain good communication and records systems; establish active crime prevention units. On the state level, he recommended that each state establish a police organization that would consist of bureaus of criminal investigation and information (Carte & Carte, 1975).

POLICING AND EDUCATION

August Vollmer was the first person to blend policing and education. Despite his own very limited formal education, he was a life-long learner who advocated for better trained and better educated police officers.

But beyond advocating for more highly educated police officers, he devised the idea of a school to train officers. As previously indicated, in 1908, he began the Berkeley Police School, which became the first formal training for police officers in America. At first, he encountered opposition from his own officers in Berkeley because they had to attend his school on their own time, but that didn't deter Vollmer.

Using professors from the University of California, he had his officers taking classes in first aid, police methods, public health and sanitation, photography, and basic law. One of the professors who taught some of these classes was Dr. Albert Schneider, the pharmacy school professor, who helped establish the initial scientific crime lab.

Around 1916, Vollmer began a series of summer session courses at the University of California. These courses were designed for both college students and police officers. These summer courses covered such topics as methods of police investigation, medical examinations of crimes, juvenile delinquency, and other topics. The summer courses continued every year (except 1927) until 1932, when the university offered similar classes during the regular school year.

In 1929, August Vollmer was appointed the first professor of police administration at the University of Chicago, and in 1931, he became a professor at the University of California at Berkeley. Both as a police chief and as a professor, he strongly influenced other California universities and colleges to institute courses in criminology. Ultimately, the police courses that began in the summer of 1916 developed into a School of Criminology. Now, hundreds of colleges offer degrees in criminology and criminal justice.

NATIONAL INFLUENCE

Nationally, Vollmer worked through such forums as the International Association of Chiefs of Police, serving as president in 1922. He served as a police consultant, often conducting surveys and making recommendations for change in cities like Kansas City, Los Angeles, Chicago, Minneapolis, Gary, Portland, and San Diego. Based on his intimate knowledge of what went on in police departments around the country, he could—with direct and personal knowledge—condemn the corruption and ineffectiveness that prevailed in most American police departments while continually urging professionalization of the police function, removal of political influence from routine police operations, and the adoption of modern technological methods.

The Berkeley Police Department also served as the training ground for new Alameda County deputy district attorneys, and it was in this connection that Vollmer came to know Earl Warren, who received his early experience as a prosecuting attorney in Berkeley. Warren, who went on to become both the attorney general and the governor of California and subsequently the chief justice of the United States Supreme Court, has said that Vollmer excited his interest in a host of problems relating to law enforcement and the need for improvement. When Warren was a district attorney in Alameda County and began the "gangbusting" raids against gambling that brought him fame throughout California, he used Berkeley policemen and equipment to supplement his own small staff and locked up his prisoners in the Berkeley jail. Vollmer's department had already developed the techniques of investigation and photography that Warren needed to gather evidence that would hold up in the courts, which were often unsympathetic. In later years, Warren and Vollmer worked together to set up police education programs in the state colleges and to develop state law enforcement agencies.

His national prestige was constantly enhanced by his writings in journals and magazines beginning in 1917. However, he gained further recognition when he published his first book (*Crime and the State Police*), coauthored with Alfred E. Parker in 1935. The main themes of this book were Vollmer's advocacy for state policing and the centralization of police facilities. This was followed the next year by his book *The Police and Modern Society*. This book presented his views on the police role and the organization and structure required to support effective police roles. Again, as in the previous book, he lobbied for a single state police force and the doing away with the complex variety of police agencies that existed then—and continues to exist today. In the 1940s, he wrote other books, such as *The Criminal* (1949), which was Vollmer's attempt to explain the causation of criminal behavior and reflect on much of what he learned in his career. He suggested in this book on criminological theory that there could never be one cause of crime, but that to understand criminal behavior, you had to be aware of biology, psychology, sociology, pathology, and law. In the end, he concluded that much more research was needed to better understand criminal behavior.

THE MAN AND HIS PERSONAL LIFE

Donal E.J. MacNamara, who was professor of corrections administration at John Jay College of the City University of New York, worked for a brief time with Vollmer. MacNamara wrote a biography of Vollmer, which was published as a chapter in 1977 in the book *Pioneers in Policing*. In a brief personal epilogue to this biography, MacNamara describes how he viewed August Vollmer. "[He was] erect, roughly handsome, somewhat shy, but very positive, energetic, and inveterately curious," MacNamara wrote (MacNamara, 1977, p. 190). He went on to say that he was "intolerant of fools and knaves, quick to recognize poseurs and manipulators, Vollmer had endless patience and time for those who shared his dedication to the police profession" (p. 190).

If this biography gives the impression that he neglected his personal life and avoided romantic relationships, let me dispel that. Although he had dated Pat Fell until she broke off their relationship, Vollmer continued to date. In the summer of 1911, he married Lydia Sturdevant, a young woman he met in San Francisco around the same time he was dating Pat Fell. Sturdevant was a well-respected soprano with the Milan (Italy) Opera Company. However, her career and the different directions of their lives caused stress in their marriage, and they divorced by 1920. But the next year he ran into Pat Fell after not seeing her for several years. They began dating again, and they ended up getting married in 1924.

This relationship was much more compatible, and Pat was more involved with his busy professional life. Since much of Vollmer's life required travel and stays in different places for sometimes weeks or months at a time, she always traveled with him. Thus, she was with him when he spent two years in Chicago, consulted with the Hawaiian Police Department, and surveyed the Havana Police Department.

After Vollmer retired from his job as chief of the Berkeley Police Department in 1932, he and his wife visited Scotland Yard in England, spent time at the Sûreté in France, and inspected dozens of other European police departments. After their trip around the world, he continued to be in demand as a consultant, lecturer, and professor.

August and Pat had no children, and in 1948, Pat died. Seven years later, in 1955, at the age of seventy-nine, Vollmer ended his life by shooting himself with his service revolver. He had had vision problems for several years and was suffering from both Parkinson's disease and cancer. Gene Carte and Elaine Carte (1975), who studied Vollmer's work and career at the University of California and who developed an oral history of his work and his influence on others, concluded that based on his letters to others that he did not want to become a burden on anyone else. Before pulling the trigger, he called the Berkeley Police Department to report his own suicide. In his will, he left his papers, including a voluminous collection of letters and an extensive criminal justice library, to the University of California at Berkeley. His archives are now located at the university's Bancroft Library.

HIS LEGACY

This brief biography of August Vollmer highlights his many innovations and firsts in the field of policing, and it can be said without much doubt that what he left behind is truly remarkable. However, in summary, it is good to remember these singular accomplishments:

1. He started college and university criminal justice, criminology, and police studies departments;

2. Helped to found what would become the American Society of Criminology, thereby guiding the field of criminology to focus on sociological theories;
3. Led the reform of policing into an era of professional policing;
4. Developed the first scientific criminal investigation laboratory, recognizing the importance science would have in solving crimes;
5. Constructed the ideal of the professional police officer, who would use his intelligence and skill to exercise self-control and deescalate volatile situations;
6. Modeled the ultimate police officer and police administrator, who never stopped learning, was unceasingly innovating, and always respected the rights of others;
7. Promoted the image of a police officer as ethical, honest, dedicated, and intelligent.
8. Advocated for the police to not only be relentless crime fighters, but to also, and perhaps more importantly, be citizens highly involved in their community and to be as devoted to preventing crime as to arresting the guilty perpetrator.

All of his many accomplishments and innovations transformed policing, making it into a proud profession, while ensuring his own last recognition as the Father of American Policing.

QUESTIONS FOR DISCUSSION

1. Which of August Vollmer's many innovations would you consider the most important? Why?
2. It can be argued that in many ways August Vollmer was ahead of his time. What ideas did he promote that perhaps have not yet been fully realized?
3. Which of Vollmer's ideas or visions were rejected or have not been well accepted? Give reasons for your answer.
4. Where would policing be today if it were not for August Vollmer?

IMPORTANT TERMS

International Association of Chiefs of Police (IACP): An international law enforcement organization, it was founded in 1893. August Vollmer was the president of the IACP in 1922.

Modus operandi: A Latin term which translates as the method of operation. In police work, it is used to determine a pattern by a particular criminal offender in the commission of his or her crime.

Polygraph/lie detector: A lie detector or polygraph is a device for measuring physiological reactions that are presumably related to stress, which, in turn, may indicate whether an individual is telling the truth or lying.

Scientific crime laboratory: A laboratory set up to study and analyze aspects of crime, such as fingerprints, blood type, bullet comparison, and DNA.

Wickersham Report: The Wickersham Report was the report that followed the national study of crime and law enforcement by the National Commission on Law Observance and Enforcement. The commission was appointed by President Herbert Hoover in 1929, and the findings were published in fourteen volumes in 1931 and 1932. August Vollmer directed the police section of the Wickersham Report.

FOR FURTHER READING

National Commission on Law Observance and Enforcement, Report on Police. (1931). Washington, DC: U.S. Government Printing Office.

Oliver, W. M. (2008). August Vollmer. In J. B. Baumgarner (Ed.), *Icons of crime fighting: Relentless pursuers of justice, Vol. 1* (pp. 83–116). Westport, CT: Greenwood Press.

Vollmer, A. (1936). *The police and modern society.* Berkley, CA: University of California Press.

Vollmer, A., & Parker, A. E. (1935). *Crime and the state police.* Berkeley, CA: University of California Press.

REVIEW QUESTIONS

True or False

1. August Vollmer is remembered as the Father of American Policing.

2. August Vollmer's first position in law enforcement was as chief of police.
3. August Vollmer served as Berkeley's chief of police for 21 years.

Multiple Choice

4. August Vollmer recognized early in his career as chief of police that
   a. Police officers needed to be educated.
   b. Science was important to policing.
   c. Ongoing training of police officers was essential.
   d. All of the above.

5. Although August Vollmer was a tough and demanding police chief, he was adamantly opposed to
   a. Police officers learning new skills.
   b. Officers using force and violence in encounters with citizens.
   c. Treating suspects with kindness.
   d. Police officers being promoted.

6. It can be argued that August Vollmer was a forerunner in the area of
   a. Decentralized policing.
   b. The "tough-on-crime" approach.
   c. Political oversight of police operations.
   d. Community policing.

7. One reform August Vollmer called for in policing throughout his career was that there should be a greater emphasis on
   a. Crime prevention.
   b. The police officer as strictly a crime fighter.
   c. The tough love approach to dealing with wayward juveniles.
   d. Police investigators using the trial-and-error method of solving crimes.

8. One of August Vollmer's recommendations that has never really gained much support was
   a. That there should be civilian review boards to supervise police departments.
   b. That there should be diversity in police departments.

    c.   That there should be one strong state police bureau in each state.

    d.   That there should be more women hired as police officers.

9. One of August Vollmer's lasting legacies is his pioneering work in establishing

    a.   Jails for juvenile offenders.

    b.   The Federal Bureau of Investigation.

    c.   The third-degree approach in interrogations.

    d.   University criminal justice departments.

REFERENCES

Carte, G. E., & Carte, E. H. (1975). *Police reform in the United States: The era of August Vollmer.* Berkeley, CA: University of California Press.

Fisher, J. (2015). August Vollmer: The forgotten father of community policing. *Jim Fisher true crime.* Retrieved October 24, 2016, from http://jimfishertruecrime.blogspot.com/2012/09/august-vollmer-forgotten-father-of.html

Leonard, V. A. (1964). *The police of the 20th century.* Brooklyn, NY: Foundation Press, Inc.

MacNamara, D. E. J. (1977). August Vollmer: The vision of police professionalism. In P. J. Stead (Ed.), *Pioneers in policing* (pp. 178–190). Montclair, NJ: Patterson Smith Publishing.

6

J. EDGAR HOOVER
The Powerful Paradox

The name on the FBI Building on Pennsylvania Avenue in Washington, D.C., is virtually synonymous with the Federal Bureau of Investigation. But if that law enforcement agency was far from the flawless agency he convinced the public that it was, still, there is no doubt that J. Edgar Hoover built the FBI into a remarkable law enforcement entity.

During his lifetime, he wielded such enormous power as director of the FBI that he brooked no criticism—either of himself or his beloved "Bureau." In order to suppress criticism and maintain his control, Hoover was willing to do anything to carry out what he, in some twisted way, believed was necessary. That "anything" included illegal wiretaps, bribery, intimidation, burglaries, thefts, and blackmail. Author Anthony Summer writes that he lived like an "oriental potentate," milking FBI funds and facilities for his own private profit and pleasure. Wealthy friends gave him lavish gifts and treated him to trips and vacations as well as investment tips. He in return protected them from criminal investigations. Tim Weiner, author of *Enemies: A History of the FBI*, refers to Hoover as a masterful manipulator of public opinion and says that he practiced political warfare and secret statecraft in pursuit of national security, but at the expense of civil liberties and morality.

Still, J. Edgar Hoover was not quite the monster that he was portrayed as in the two decades after his death. Instead, Summers regards Hoover as the paradox of our time and describes him as "a man with a crippled psyche, capable of great evil, [who] became the trusted symbol of all that was safe and good" (Summers, 1993, p. 14).

To get a balanced, objective portrait of the man who was director of the FBI for 48 years, it is necessary to follow his life from his childhood in Washington, D.C., through his rise to power and to his unexpected death in 1972. Although little of a critical and objective nature was written about him during his seventy-seven years, since his death there has been an outpouring of dozens of detailed biographies and histories that reveal both the man and the myth.

EARLY LIFE

He was born on January 1, 1895, the third of three children to his mother, Annie Hoover, and his father, Dickerson Hoover. His father was the head of the printing division of the U.S. Coast and Geodetic Survey, and by all accounts, Dickerson Hoover was a quiet and kindly man who suffered from depression and mental illness. His mother was the disciplinarian, who instilled in young John Edgar a scrupulous regard for law and a zealous sense of duty and morality. She was religious, and her children attended church with her.

Hoover graduated from Central High School in Washington, D.C., in 1913. At Central, he was a good student, who had a love of sports and was an outstanding member of the debate team, despite having a stuttering problem which he overcame by reading aloud. He participated in the Cadet Corps, becoming a captain of one of the Cadet Corps companies at his school. However, he was regarded as a loner who read the Bible, studied diligently, and graduated with honors—after which he was offered a scholarship to the University of Virginia. However, he decided to stay at home in Washington, D.C., and attend George Washington University while working as a clerk in the Library of Congress. Living at home, he graduated with honors with a law degree in 1916 and a year later obtained a master's degree in law.

HIS CAREER BEGINS

His first job after law school was as a law clerk in the Justice Department. Just a few months later, he was assigned to aid John Lord O'Brien, the newly named special assistant to the attorney general for war work. Hoover's job under O'Brien was the registering of more than 1 million enemy aliens.

With the United Stated entering World War I in the spring of 1917, there was talk over the next few years by homegrown Socialists and domestic Communists of overthrowing the American government. As a result, a new General Intelligence Division was formed within the Justice Department. In 1919, Hoover, who by this time decided his name should be J. Edgar Hoover, was given the position of director of this division. His main job was to determine the scope of subversive activities and to come up with methods to prosecute those involved in efforts to overthrow the government. Approaching everything in his life with vigor and persistence, he threw himself into this new job with his typical zeal and righteous enthusiasm. Consequently, he soon became an indefatigable opponent of the Communist ideology—a position he would maintain for the remainder of his life. Later, as director of the FBI, he would see a Communist plot behind nearly every political protest and sometimes even behind what amounted to mild dissent. However, in his first two positions, registering enemy aliens and ferreting out subversives, he developed an index system that served him well throughout his career.

By 1921, Harry M. Daugherty was the new attorney general of the United States, and Daugherty soon moved Hoover into the job of assistant director of the Bureau of Investigation.

THE BUREAU OF INVESTIGATION

The Bureau of Investigation was created in 1908, but before that year, the Justice Department had no organized force of investigators to gather evidence. Instead, the Justice Department relied either on private detectives or detectives borrowed from the Secret Service. During the administration of President Theodore Roosevelt, there was a more vigorous application of older laws and an increase in new laws that began to tax the Justice Department's ability to detect crime. Each year, the Justice Department was asking for the loan of more detectives from the Secret Service, but that agency just didn't have enough operatives to spare. By 1906, Congress was beginning to question this arrangement.

In that year—1906—the chairman of the Congressional Appropriations Committee asked the Justice Department why they didn't hire their own investigators. Although nothing was decided then, Congress kept an eye on the situation. When U.S. Attorney General Charles Bonaparte was appointed attorney general in 1907, he quickly recognized that the practice of using Secret Service investigators was a problem, and he asked Congress for a squad of investigators. Congress first canceled the ability of the Justice Department to borrow investigators from the Secret Service but did not authorize a force of investigators within the Justice Department. The next year, Attorney General Bonaparte realized that a reorganization of the Justice Department to address the impending loss of access to the Secret Service operatives was necessary. Without much publicity, Bonaparte put together a group of about ten investigators hired as Justice Department special agents. On July 26, 1908, Bonaparte ordered Department of Justice attorneys to refer most investigative matters to the chief examiner, Stanley W. Finch, who would determine if there were special agents under his direction available to investigate the case.

As it turned out, no one criticized Bonaparte's force of special agents, and many congressmen approved what Bonaparte did. And by 1909, Bonaparte's force would gain firm legislative sanction when Congress awarded appropriations for the investigative unit. With George Wickersham as the new attorney general in 1909, Wickersham issued an order formally bringing the Bureau of Investigation into existence. Within two years, Congress had tripled the size of this force and greatly broadened its investigative authority.

However, by the early 1920s, the Bureau of Investigation was a corrupt and inefficient unit. It was badly tarnished by the Teapot Dome scandal and other scandals during the administration of President Warren G. Harding. Harry M. Daugherty was sent packing from his job as attorney general and the new attorney general, Harlan Fiske, looking to clean house, appointed Hoover as acting director of the Bureau of Investigation in May 1925. By December, he was made the permanent director with a priority to clean up the Bureau of Investigation. That priority fit right in with the personality and temperament of J. Edgar Hoover.

Seemingly relishing the urgent task he was given, Hoover started cleaning house at the Bureau of Investigation by firing every man whose character was at all suspect. Then, he hired new agents who were intelligent and educated. Following that, he forbade agents from engaging in any extralegal activities. Hoover next concentrated on making the Bureau an organization devoted to criminal investigation. In addition, he initiated an inspection system over all field operations, and he assigned a special agent in charge to each field office. In order to help ensure that agents were exemplary employees, he established strict rules of conduct for every employee, and these rules applied both on and off the job. Among the rules were those that required sober and discreet behavior, avoidance of politics, an unimpeachable personal life, and conservative dress (Murphy, 1977).

Hoover's ambition was to not only mold the Bureau of Investigation into an elite criminal investigation entity, but he also sought to broaden its scope of activities. To that end, he readily took over the compiling and publicizing of the Uniform Crime Reports from the International Association of Chiefs of Police in 1930. Two years later, he established the Bureau's forensic laboratory and made its services free of charge to local and state police departments throughout the country. In 1935, after Hoover changed the name of the department to the Federal Bureau of Investigation, he set up the National Academy. This academy would begin providing local and state law enforcement personnel with advanced training in various aspects of law enforcement.

CAPTURING PUBLIC ENEMIES

J. Edgar Hoover loved publicity and always took advantage of every opportunity to use the news media and the spotlight to portray himself and the FBI in the most positive light. As Bryan Burroughs points out in his book *Public Enemies*, Hoover created the "crime wave" of the 1930s and then made sure that he (and the FBI) got headlines for capturing or killing the most notorious criminals of the day, including John Dillinger, Baby Face Nelson, Pretty Boy Floyd, the Barker-Karpis Gang, Machine Gun Kelly, and Bonnie and Clyde. Furthermore, not only did he promote and capitalize on the publicity surrounding the demise of these criminals, but he released constant press releases, assisted in making motion pictures about G-men (the popular name for government men or federal law enforcement agents), and helped develop both a radio program and a comic strip—all of which served to enhance and embellish the reputation of the FBI and himself. He contrived to have photos taken of himself, sometimes holding a gun and sometimes standing over a dead gangster, making it look like Hoover himself had effected the capturing or killing of the desperadoes. Hoover's main goals were to convince the American people—and Congress—that "FBI" was interchangeable with "crime fighting" so that he and the FBI could reap the rewards of sterling reputations and he could annually return to Congress to request additional funding.

Edgar J. Hoover

Marion S. Trikosko, https://www.loc.gov/item/2004672754/. Copyright in the Public Domain.

THE DEVELOPMENT OF THE FBI

At times, it seems almost impossible to talk about the FBI without talking about J. Edgar Hoover and his personality, as well as his personal life style. However, it is important to strike a balance between his personal foibles and how he developed the FBI into a unique law enforcement and U.S. security organization. In discussing the development of the FBI, there are several areas that need to be highlighted:

1. Personnel and management practices;
2. Investigative practices;
3. Law enforcement liaison and training;
4. National security;
5. Division 8/UCR.

Personnel and Management Practices

Firing incompetent and corrupt agents after taking over as director of the Bureau of Investigation, Hoover endeavored to remove the hiring of FBI agents from the previously employed patronage system. He set strict standards for hiring, and he made sure that men were hired based on their qualifications, not on whom they knew. Furthermore, to reduce the lure of corruption, he increased salaries and fringe benefits for agents to see to it that they were paid more than police officers in other law enforcement agencies.

Hoover's special agents had to fit a certain FBI template: white males with a clean-cut appearance and neatly trimmed hair. They had to dress in a certain way, with every special agent wearing a dark suit and match-ing ties and socks. They all had to have successfully completed a law or accounting degree from a college or university. Additionally, they were re-quired to have three years' experience in law enforcement. Hoover looked for a strict work ethic in each of his special agents. They were expected to work overtime and to turn in meticulous progress reports on cases. Furthermore, he demanded that every special agent report all suspicious behavior of other agents.

As this suggests, Hoover ran a tight ship, and discipline was strictly controlled. Every person who worked for the FBI was expected to conduct themselves with dignity and decorum—even when off duty. When agents were disciplined, there was no appeal process, with Hoover handling almost all discipline issues himself (Johnson & Wolfe, 2003). Hoover expected the same kind of loyalty he had to the Bureau from every person, whether a special agent or part of the clerical staff. Advancement, like appointment, was unrelated to political influence. Personnel procedures did not fall under the normal federal civil service system, so Hoover could maintain broad discretion in terms of whom he hired, who got promotions (or demotions), or who got fired.

Investigative Practices

Under Hoover, the FBI gained a well-earned reputation for investigative work that was thorough, persistent, and results oriented (Johnson & Wolfe, 2003). Their investigative practices led to a public perception that the FBI always got their man—no matter how much time or resources were needed.

Helping to initiate and cement that reputation was the training that FBI special agents received and the innovations brought about by Hoover at the FBI. Agents were trained to use the most advanced scientific techniques in order to successfully solve crimes. When Hoover opened the FBI laboratory in 1932, it was the first crime lab. Hoover wanted his special agents to use the best possible technology and to apply the newest concepts in science. The FBI's crime laboratory quickly became the most advanced in the world, and it was, according to Anthony Summers, the key to the expansion of Hoover's empire (Summers, 1993). Certainly, what the FBI's forensic lab (along with the fingerprint operation) did was to transform the FBI from a small federal agency with limited jurisdiction to a vital facility upon which all other law enforcement agencies depended (Summers, 1993). In short, the FBI Laboratory became the leading forensic and identification facility in the nation.

In the FBI Crime Lab, meticulous intelligence files were maintained, both in regard to criminal activity and in the counterintelligence field. These files were carefully cross-indexed, and they came to provide a treasure trove of information regarding individuals who had come to the FBI's attention.

One of Hoover's goals after becoming director of the Bureau of Investigation was to have "universal fingerprinting." It was his notion that the prints of every citizen—innocent as well as the guilty—should be recorded. After setting up a fingerprint department as early as 1924 (which ultimately became the Identification Division), the fingerprint collection grew so large that at one point, it occupied a six-story building. When Hoover died, the vast Identification Division contained the prints of 159 million people (Summers, 1993).

Hoover's legacy can be seen today as the FBI's largest division, Criminal Justice Information Services (CJIS). It was created in 1992 to merge several smaller departments into one large information services division, and today is located in Clarksburg, West Virginia. This division includes the National Crime Information Center, Integrated Automated Fingerprint Identification System, National Instant Criminal Background Check System, the Uniform Crime Reporting program, and the National Incident-Based Reporting System.

In addition to investigative procedures, the FBI became a leading law enforcement agency in extending procedural rights and guarantees to suspects. Before the U.S. Supreme Court under Earl Warren began to enumerate the protections guaranteed to accused individuals, the FBI had implemented those rules in its operations manuals (Johnson & Wolfe, 2003).

Law Enforcement Liaison and Training

The FBI's National Academy, the FBI Crime Lab, and the Fingerprint Identification Bureau, all developed in the 1930s, have played a pivotal role in training state and local police officers, as well as providing invaluable support to law enforcement officers nationwide. That the FBI has done all of this with distinction for decades attests to the vision of J. Edgar Hoover and his remarkable ability to shape a dream into a successful reality.

Hoover always promoted the ideal of the police officer in the street fighting crime. As a crime fighter, Hoover's ideal of a police officer was a strong, brave man who engaged in hot pursuits, had gun battles with criminals, and was involved in aggressive patrols (Murphy, 1977). However, given the events of the 1960s, Hoover was forced to change his thinking somewhat about police officers.

Hoover's conception of the officer as crime fighter was a rather traditional and superficial view at the time that many experts in the field were beginning to see that law enforcement had a role in maintaining the peace, easing community tension, discouraging crime at the source, and increasing police services to the community (Murphy, 1977). This kind of thinking was spearheaded by the International Association of Chiefs of Police (IACP), which in the 1960s was no longer blindly following J. Edgar Hoover's lead. Instead, the IACP became involved in surveying police departments, developing new training courses, offering technical assistance, and touting other aspects of progressive policing (Murphy, 1977). Hoover wanted to maintain control over all police training, but the IACP had other ideas.

Hoover established the National Academy in 1935 for the training of state and local law enforcement officers. This was revolutionary because prior to this, police officer training tended to be limited to big-city police departments. But carefully selecting candidates from police departments around the country to attend the national academy, the FBI began offering training in the latest investigative techniques, instruction in the use of the latest equipment, and lectures on the topics of police science deemed essential to true law enforcement professionals (Gentry, 1991).

However, by making this training available, the National Academy created a valuable network of cooperative colleagues with a common affiliation. By setting up training programs for police officers from around the United States, Hoover developed an influence over the police which had not previously existed. Thus, he played a major role in shaping police attitudes toward themselves, toward criminals, and toward the rest of the criminal justice system (Murphy, 1977).

When law enforcement officers finish the ten-week training at the National Academy, located in Quantico, Virginia, they are asked to join the National Academy Association. This organization is committed to raising the standards of professionalism in law enforcement by developing higher levels of competency, cooperation, and integrity (Raptopoulos & Walker, 2008). When the National Academy conducted its first classes in 1935, twenty-three officers participated. Today, the National Academy alone has 17,000 members.

National Security

Following Hoover's graduation from George Washington Law School, he got a job with the Justice Department as a law clerk. Within a few months, he was placed in charge of the Enemy Alien Registration section. His job, along with the fourteen people who worked under him, was, in general, to keep America safe from foreign threats. However, specifically, his section sorted through the mounds of reports and threats to try to figure out who might be a legitimate threat.

Hoover's department developed and grew, and eventually, they started sending out undercover agents to investigate organizations that waged protests against the war effort. But this was only the beginning of Hoover's career-long focus on catching both domestic and foreign "radicals" who were opposed to the United States' involvement in wars and disagreed with America's current policies (Raptopoulos & Walker, 2008).

Going back to August 1, 1919, an event happened on that day that added impetus to Hoover's career. On that date, a terrorist ring exploded a bomb outside the home of the U.S. Attorney General A. Mitchell Palmer. Palmer wasn't hurt, but part of his home was destroyed. This terrorist attack, along with the general "Red scare" that was sweeping the nation at the time, fueled fears of a Communist invasion, and prompted Attorney General Palmer to appoint Hoover as the head of the General Intelligence Division in the Justice Department.

His new job involved studying subversion in the United States and recommending ways and means to contain it. All special agents from the Bureau of Investigation were now to report to J. Edgar Hoover. Already, at this stage of his life and career, Hoover condemned communism and viewed it as morally and ethically wrong. At the same time, Palmer was conducting raids around the country to round up people who were attending Communist Labor Party meetings or other people who might be sympathetic to both communism and Russia. Hoover was assigned to help with the prosecution of Emma Goldman and Alexander Berkman, two of the most notorious of the many thousands of people who were arrested in Palmer's raids. With Hoover's help, both Goldman and Berkman were deported back to Russia in late 1919.

In his work in the General Intelligence Division, Hoover developed a huge index card system as a means of cataloging individuals and organizations considered radical. Within a couple of years, he had a filing system containing almost half a million names (Raptopoulos & Walker, 2008).

In 1921, with a new U.S. president and a subsequent change of attorney general, Hoover became the assistant director of the Bureau of Investigation. His priority was no longer to root out Communists and radicals; instead, it was to focus on federal crime investigations and to keep Americans safe from its "public enemies." However, it was also critical for Hoover to avoid being tarnished by the corruption in Warren Harding's government. It wasn't until World War II that counterespionage activities again dominated either Hoover's or the FBI's agenda. President Franklin D. Roosevelt placed Hoover in charge of counterespionage in the United States. Hoover responded by creating the Special Intelligence Service (SIS) to coordinate the FBI's counterespionage investigations.

In the mid-1930s, President Roosevelt asked Hoover to develop a broad picture of the Communist and Fascist movements in the United States (Kessler, 2002). However, Hoover told the president that the FBI lacked authority to pursue such an investigation. By law, the FBI was supposed to investigate only violations of criminal laws. But Hoover knew a loophole. The FBI could carry out any investigation requested by the State Department (Kessler, 2002). The next day (August 25, 1936), Roosevelt and Hoover met with the secretary of state, Cordell Hull. Hull told Hoover to proceed to investigate the Communists and the Fascists.

Thus, Roosevelt established a broad new avenue of FBI investigations that had no basis in law. But when Germany invaded Poland on September 1, 1939, Hoover urged Attorney General Frank Murphy to ask the president to issue a statement to all police officials in the United States that they were to turn in to the FBI any and all information pertaining to espionage, counterespionage, sabotage, and neutrality regulations. Roosevelt actually stated that the FBI would be in charge of investigating subversive activities, which included espionage, counterespionage, sabotage, and neutrality regulations. Hoover's goal was that it be made clear that when it came to the security of the country, the FBI was in charge (Kessler, 2002).

However, as Kessler points out, "Moralist that he was, Hoover never understood the difference between criticism of the government and illegal conduct aimed at subverting the government" (Kessler, 2002, p. 55). In fact, he took it a step further. Whenever there was any criticism of his own tactics following this granting of authority, Hoover's stock reply was that criticism and controversy were inspired by Communists who wanted to smear the FBI and destroy the Bureau (Kessler, 2002).

Then, in March 1947, following revelations of spying by Soviet agents in the United States amid growing allegations of Communist influence in the federal government, President Harry S. Truman ordered the FBI and the Civil Service Commission to conduct loyalty investigations of federal employees. During the subsequent four years of investigation, the FBI was instrumental in the convictions of eleven leading members of the American Communist Party for conspiring to overthrow the government.

Hoover emerged from these investigations as a leading figure in the anti-communism forces in the United States (Murphy, 1977). While he steadfastly maintained that the FBI was apolitical, Hoover's personal political position was that of a staunch and dogmatic anti-communist. By the early 1950s, Hoover's friendship with Wisconsin senator Joseph McCarthy, along with his many magazine articles and books (such as *Masters of Deceit* and *A Study of Communism*), displayed his public opposition to communism. He maintained both publicly and privately that communism posed the greatest threat to the American way of life (Murphy, 1977).

Division 8 and the Crime Records Division

Although Hoover claimed that the FBI had no public relations office, the Crime Records Division (Division 8) in part functioned like a public

relations department (Raptopoulos & Walker, 2008). Agents in this department wrote and sent out press releases, but they also regularly leaked
stories and information that Hoover wanted to show up in the media
(Raptopoulos & Walker, 2008).

However, there were only certain newspapers and certain reporters
or journalists who got leaked information. Hoover liked the *Chicago
Tribune*, for instance, but he didn't like the *New York Times*. Papers such
as the *New York Times*, Hoover decided, were anti-Bureau and therefore
should not be privy to information coming from the FBI (Raptopoulos &
Walker, 2008).

In addition to compiling and distributing the Uniform Crime Report,
which the Bureau took over from the International Association of Chiefs
of Police in the early 1930s, Division 8 had multiple functions. One of

Visit of Attorney General and Director of FBI. President Kennedy, J.Edgar
Hoover, Robert F. Kennedy. White House, Oval Office.

https://commons.wikimedia.org/wiki/File:Visit_of_Attorney_General_and_Director_of_FBI._President_
Kennedy,_J.Edgar_Hoover,_Robert_F._Kennedy._White_House..._-_NARA_-_194173.jpg. Copyright in the
Public Domain.

those functions had to do with public messages that had almost nothing to do with law enforcement, but everything to do with what Hoover was preaching. That could include messages about moral degeneration, disrespectful young people, moral decay, anarchists, the "jackals of the media," and various other things that might be on Hoover's mind (Summers, 1993, p. 51).

Other functions of Division 8 included the writing of books that would come out in Hoover's name. He got the credit—and undoubtedly the royalties—for his books, such as *Masters of Deceit* (Summers, 1993). Since most of his books did very well because of his very positive public reputation as the steadfast director of the greatest law enforcement agency in the nation (and maybe the world), the royalties often on a single book would be thousands of dollars.

J. EDGAR HOOVER AS A DIRECTOR AND AS A MAN

As indicated in this chapter, J. Edgar Hoover was a paradox as a man, a despot as a director, and a national figure who aimed to keep his reputation unsullied while also building his image as the nation's top cop. However, Curt Gentry says this about him: "One of the deepest and darkest secrets of all the FBI's secrets was that America's number one law enforcement officer was himself a crook" (Gentry, 1991, p. 449).

There were many ways that Hoover either broke the law or violated ethical standards that he expected others to follow. First, he either ordered or sanctioned illegal break-ins, in which his agents burglarized buildings when Hoover was interested in getting information he could use or to install illegal wiretaps. Second, he used the information he gathered, often unconstitutionally, to blackmail people, especially government officials—up to and including presidents. Third, he dipped into FBI funds for his personal use, and when he had special agents write books for him on government time, he personally pocketed the royalties.

In many ways, he was an insecure and petty man who envied other people who got the limelight. And he was not able to put aside his racial attitudes and prejudices to properly run the FBI, which was evident during the era of the civil rights movement. As a result, Hoover and the FBI did not have an enviable record in terms of protecting the civil rights of citizens in the 1950s, 1960s, and 1970s.

One reason for this, aside from his personal prejudices, was that Hoover allowed presidents to use the Bureau to persecute pacifists and civil rights activists (Weiner, 2012). Another reason was that the FBI often targeted the heroes of the civil rights movement, just as much, if not more, than the knights of the white supremacy organization, the Ku Klux Klan (KKK) (Weiner, 2012). Finally, unable to see beyond his moralistic and long-held beliefs about dissenters and radicals, Hoover linked the Communist Party to the campaign for civil rights (Hack, 2004).

There is no doubt that the 1960s was a controversial decade for the FBI, just as it was for the rest of the country. Although Hoover saw FBI special agents as crime fighters, he also wanted them to be involved in national security. However, when it became clear that as a national law enforcement agency the FBI could not avoid becoming involved in civil rights violations and even the protests against the war in Vietnam, it was difficult both for Hoover and the FBI to adjust to the new world they had to confront. Some critics said that the FBI failed to protect those in the South who sought to exercise their civil rights guaranteed by federal law, and at the same time, it was evident to many people that the FBI tried to suppress legitimate dissent. In addition, Hoover developed an intense dislike for Martin Luther King Jr., whom he constantly investigated (Raptopoulos & Walker, 2008).

As a result of all these factors in the 1960s, both Hoover and the Bureau saw their reputations diminished by their roles in dealing with the civil rights movement and the Vietnam War protests (Raptopoulos & Walker, 2008).

In 1956, Attorney General Herbert Brownell intended to ask Congress for a new civil rights law in order to establish an independent Civil Rights Commission, to grant the Civil Rights Section of the Justice Department full status as a division, and for the power to bring suits in federal courts to enforce voting rights. However, J. Edgar Hoover spoke against such a law. He said that there was too much explosive resentment in the South, which he blamed on the U.S. Supreme Court's school desegregation decisions.

He said the NAACP and other civil rights groups were preaching "racial hatred" and they had been targeted by the Communist Party for infiltration. Hoover said emphatically that there was no need for such legislation—and no such legislation was passed (Gentry, 1991). Throughout the time that the civil rights movement was going on, Hoover used counterintelligence programs (coined COINTELPRO). The aim of each COINTELPRO was to disrupt, disorganize, and neutralize specific chosen targets. One COINTELPRO was directed at the Communist Party, but others were directed at the civil rights movement (Gentry, 1991).

As early as 1957, Hoover had ordered his agents to begin monitoring the activities of Martin Luther King Jr. and the Southern Christian Leadership Conference (SCLC) (Gentry, 1991). In 1959, on his own and without opening a security investigation, Hoover ordered FBI agents to burglarize the SCLC offices. It was the first of twenty known break-ins between that date and 1964 (Gentry, 1991). Some of these break-ins had one purpose: to obtain information about King; however, during these break-ins, wiretaps and surveillance bugs were installed.

In 1962, Hoover sent a report to Attorney General Robert Kennedy claiming that King and his civil rights movement were tainted by "godless communism" (Gentry, 1991, p. 501). Hoover did this, even though his special agents regularly reported they could find no evidence of Communist influence on King or the SCLC (Gentry, 1991). This was just further evidence of Hoover's growing obsession with destroying King (Gentry, 1991). As part of this campaign to discredit and destroy King, Hoover sent derogatory reports about him to any colleges that were considering awarding the civil rights leader an honorary degree. Hoover went so far as to attempt to discredit King when he went to Stockholm to accept the Nobel Peace Prize (Gentry, 1991). In 1965, Hoover referred to Martin Luther King Jr. as "the most notorious liar in the country" (Holden, 2008, p. 1129). Finally, Hoover maintained a secret file on King, which he used, on one occasion, to attempt to break up King's marriage (Summers, 1993).

CRITICISM OF HOOVER

J. Edgar Hoover was able to maintain his outstanding national reputation as an incorruptible law enforcement icon up to the 1960s. He often was able to accomplish this by suppressing any criticism that was anticipated. However, with the problems he encountered in his positions on Martin Luther King Jr. and the civil rights movement, his opposition to the protests against the war, and his rabid anti-Communist stance, there was no stemming the tide of criticism that began to seep out in the turbulent 1960s. And after his death in 1972, articles and books could be written and published without fear of Hoover's retaliation. In addition to the criticism that was leveled at him related to his alignment with Senator McCarthy during the 1950s and his investigations of King in the 1960s, other critiques poured forth in the 1970s.

For instance, his stance regarding organized crime began to be more fully explored and brought to the public's attention. Throughout the 1940s and 1950s, Hoover virtually denied that organized crime existed. When reports of mob bosses' meetings surfaced, Hoover could no longer turn a blind eye to the problem of organized crime in America. Also, despite his influence in policing, he tended to ignore problems in that arena. According to Patrick Murphy, who was chief of police over several years in both New York and Detroit, Hoover did not assume a role of progressive leadership in the United States. That inhibited real progress toward mature, wise, and effective policing (Murphy, 1977).

Furthermore, it became clear in the 1960s that his position—that the FBI, in particular, and law enforcement, in general, was all about crime fighting—was an anachronism. Hoover was, as many people began to realize, behind the times, too set in his traditional and conservative views of policing, and too preoccupied with Communist subversion to recognize that law enforcement had to expand its role to include community relations and accept that policing had to be about diversity and acceptance. Refusing to accept women and African Americans as special agents handicapped the FBI, just as it was a detriment to law enforcement on a local level.

HOOVER'S DEATH

The usual age of retirement for government employees came—and went—and Hoover hung on to the directorship of the FBI. Many presidents wanted to replace him, but his power was too enormous for any administration to seriously contemplate such an action. At one point, he announced that he would retire at age eighty, which would have been in 1975. However, on the morning of May 2, 1972, when he was seventy-seven, he was found on his bedroom floor by his housekeeper and his chauffer. His private physician was called and listed his cause of death as a heart attack brought on by high blood pressure.

President Richard Nixon was undoubtedly relieved that he didn't have to try to force him to retire. But Nixon had Hoover's body lie in state in the Capitol Rotunda, where an estimated 25,000 people filed by his casket. President Nixon, who was an admirer of Hoover's from the early days of Hoover's anti-Communist crusades, delivered the eulogy at the funeral services at Washington's National Presbyterian Church. "The United States is a better country because this good man lived his long life among us," Nixon said in his remarks (Lovegrove & Orwig, 1989).

It was disingenuous, of course, for President Nixon to make those and similar remarks at Hoover's funeral, because he knew better. And for many years after his death, each administration, along with Congress, was involved in bringing about reforms to improve the conduct and image of the FBI (Jeffreys-Jones, 2007). But even before his death, Congress put in a clause in the Omnibus Crime Control Act of 1968, requiring Senate confirmation of any nominee for FBI director. In addition, a 1976 law imposed a ten-year maximum term for every succeeding FBI director.

However, J. Edgar Hoover was a paradox of a man who made the FBI an outstanding law enforcement agency that has survived the excesses of the Hoover administration and today remains a paragon among government agencies. In many ways, it can be said that the FBI created by Hoover and nurtured by him was, in a very real sense, the alter ego of the man—at least while he was living, and perhaps for a good many years afterward. The FBI mirrored the strengths, the pride, the prejudices, and the weaknesses of J. Edgar Hoover himself.

QUESTIONS FOR DISCUSSION

1. What were your perceptions of J. Edgar Hoover before reading this biography? How did those perceptions change after reading about him?
2. After reading both this biography of Hoover and the previous chapter on August Vollmer, how do you imagine they got along? Could you picture them as friends?
3. What would you argue was Hoover's single greatest accomplishment?
4. What are the pros and cons of the limitation Congress imposed on the FBI restricting any FBI director to a maximum of ten years in the position?
5. In your opinion, what is the public perception of the FBI today?

IMPORTANT TERMS

Bureau of Investigation: The initial department within the Justice Department that would be created in 1908. It would ultimately become the FBI in 1935.

COINTELPRO: COINTELPRO was a term that referred to a series of covert operations conducted by Hoover and the FBI with the aim of watching, infiltrating, discrediting, and disrupting U.S. political organizations.

Criminal Justice Information Services: Growing out of the Bureau of Investigation's Identification Division, created by Hoover in the 1920s, the Criminal Justice Information Services (CJIS) is the largest division in the FBI. Its programs brought together the National Crime Information Center (NCIC), Uniform Crime Reporting (UCR), and Fingerprint Identification into one building and division.

FBI Crime Lab: A laboratory set up in 1932 to scientifically study various aspects of crime, the lab's services are available to all local and state police departments. Today, it goes by the name of the FBI Scientific Crime Detection Laboratory.

The National Academy: An FBI program begun in the 1930s and offering training programs for law enforcement personnel across the country.

Uniform Crime Report: An annual report submitted to the public from the FBI, compiled from reports that come from more than 17,000 police departments across the country. This comprehensive report gives detailed information about crime in America.

FOR FURTHER READING

Cook, F. J. (1964). *The FBI nobody knows.* New York, NY: Macmillan Company.

Hoover, J. E. (1958). *Masters of deceit: The story of Communism in America and how to fight it.* New York, NY: Holt, Rinehart and Winston.

Jeffreys, D. (1995). *The Bureau: Inside the modern FBI.* New York, NY: Houghton Mifflin Company.

Kessler, R. (1993). *The FBI: Inside the world's most powerful law enforcement agency.* New York, NY: Pocket Books.

REVIEW QUESTIONS

True or False

1. J. Edgar Hoover served as director of the Bureau of Investigation and the FBI for a total of 48 years.
2. Hoover never worked in law enforcement prior to being appointed to the Bureau of Investigation.
3. The FBI is no longer concerned with national security.

Multiple Choice

4. Early in his career, J. Edgar Hoover was

    a. Sympathetic to the Communist Party.
    b. Developing an aversion to communism.
    c. More a liberal than a conservative.
    d. A believer that socialism was inevitable in the United States.

5. The ideal special agent during Hoover's years as director of the FBI was

    a. A person—either male or female—who had a criminal justice degree from an accredited university.
    b. A person capable of using force in dealing with criminal suspects.
    c. A white male who was college educated.
    d. A woman with a law enforcement background.

6. For the most part, the FBI investigates cases that
   a. Are too complicated for state and local police departments.
   b. Are related to kidnapping or serial murders.
   c. Represent security breaches.
   d. Are violations of federal laws.

7. It can be said that Hoover never seemed to focus the FBI's attention on
   a. Crime prevention.
   b. Crime fighting.
   c. Anti-communism.
   d. Forensic science.

8. The FBI's record of protecting the civil rights of American citizens during the era of the civil rights movement can best be described as
   a. Dismal.
   b. Exceptional, and beyond reproach.
   c. Aggressive and staunchly pro–civil rights.
   d. Providing outstanding leadership.

9. Among J. Edgar Hoover's innovations was
   a. The FBI Crime Lab.
   b. The National Academy.
   c. The IAFIS fingerprint system.
   d. All of the above.

REFERENCES

Burroughs, B. (2004). *Public enemies: America's greatest crime wave and the birth of the FBI, 1933–34*. New York, NY: Penguin Press.

Gentry, C. (1991). *J. Edgar Hoover: The man and the secrets*. New York, NY: W. W. Norton.

Hack, R. (2004). *Puppetmaster: The secret life of J. Edgar Hoover*. Beverly Hills, CA: New Millennium Press.

Holden, H. M. (2008). *FBI: 100 years: An unofficial history*. Minneapolis, MN: Zenith Press.

Jeffreys-Jones, R. (2007). *The FBI: A history*. New Haven, CT: Yale University Press.

Johnson, H. A., & Wolfe, N. T. (2003). *History of criminal justice* (3rd ed.). Cincinnati, OH: Anderson Publishing.

Kessler, R. (2002). *Bureau: The secret history of the FBI*. New York, NY: St. Martin's Press.

Lovegrove, R., & Orwig, T. (1989). *The FBI*. New York, NY: Exeter Books.

Murphy, P. V. (1977). John Edgar Hoover. In P. J. Stead (Ed.), *Pioneers in policing* (pp. 262–279). Montclair, NJ: Paterson Smith.

Raptopoulos, K., & Walker, J. T. (2008). J. Edgar Hoover and the FBI. In J. Baumgarner (Ed.), *Icons of crime fighting: Relentless pursuers of justice* (pp. 117–142). Westport, CT: Greenwood Press.

Summers, A. (1993). *Official and confidential: The secret life of J. Edgar Hoover*. New York, NY: G. P. Putnam.

Weiner, T. (2012). *Enemies: A history of the FBI*. New York, NY: Random House.

7

JACK MAPLE
Solving Crime Through Technology

In 1991, Jack Maple was a New York City Police Department cop who worked in the New York City Transit Department looking for crooks in the subway tunnels deep under the city. But after work, he would sit at his table along the wall in Elaine's, the now-defunct trendy restaurant bar at 1703 Second Avenue in Manhattan, and think about how there were more than 2,200 murders in New York City each year. All the politicians and urban experts thought the situation was hopeless; New York City was a city doomed to sink into oblivion, weighted down by a staggering amount of violent crime.

But while everyone else had given up on crime, Jack Maple had not. He bragged to friends at Elaine's that he could cut crime in half in New York City. To everyone, it sounded like the booze talking. Besides, who was Jack Maple? He was just that short, fat, transit cop who dressed in a Homburg hat, wore bow ties, had a full black beard, and spent more money on suits and shoes than he made.

Even though no one took him seriously, everyone was wrong. In less than three years as New York's deputy police commissioner for crime-control strategies, he made his boast come true.

How did he do it?

The simple answer was that he pioneered a way of reducing crime by challenging the old ways things were done in law enforcement. Certainly, he was not afraid to question authority or established procedures. But perhaps the best way of explaining his accomplishments was his invention of COMPSTAT.

WHO WAS JACK MAPLE?

John Edward Maple was born on September 23, 1952, and grew up in the Richmond Hill section of Queens in New York. His father was a postal worker and his mother a nurse's aide. After going to Catholic schools, he attended Brooklyn Tech, an elite school for math and science nerds. He failed various classes and described himself as being mainly a truant who preferred spending his time at the Museum of Natural History (Remnick, 1997). Since he didn't graduate from Brooklyn Tech, for all intents and purposes, he was a high school dropout. But he would later get a high school degree from the Fort Greene Night School.

His father, a veteran of World War II's Battle of the Bulge, knew his son was on the road to becoming a loser. When Jack was in about the seventh grade, his father took him to Grand Central Terminal to see coffins returning from Vietnam. "Kid," he said to young Jack, "if you don't make something of yourself, you're going to die in Vietnam" (Remnick, 1977, p. 104). When he was sixteen, his father had him take every civil service test that came along. Jack ended up passing one of those civil service exams in 1970, and at age eighteen, he became a transit trainee for the New York Police Department. Prior to joining the force as a transit officer, he had worked unloading UPS trucks and for a time was a pageboy at the glamorous 21 Club on 52nd Street in Manhattan.

Working as a transit officer, or in the vernacular of the force, being a "cave cop," meant that he was a patrolman on subway platforms. His job was to stop people from jumping turnstiles and robbing people in the subterranean netherworld of New York. He might not have ever taken anything seriously before, but he took this job seriously and began racking up arrests. Over time, being too good at his job got him in hot water with his supervisors; arrests meant paperwork, and often his supervisors didn't want the extra burden of paperwork. That led to him getting transferred frequently, but that didn't stop him. He was a transit officer, and his job was to stop crime. If that meant making arrests, then that's what he would keep doing.

When he had completed his transit training, he became a full officer at age twenty-one. In his book *Crime Fighter*, Maple says that from the first day as a transit cop, he was thrilled. "I loved the crime-fighting part of the job," he wrote (Maple & Mitchell, 1999, p. 11). And by the time he made lieutenant in transit, he had established a reputation by running decoy squads in the subway. His decoy squads were responsible for arresting hundreds of teenage muggers (Remnick, 1997). It was sometimes dangerous work, but Maple loved the danger and the long hours. He also felt compelled to make arrests aboveground—something that transit patrolmen were discouraged from doing. The rules didn't particularly affect Jack Maple's behavior. Neither did the danger of his job. His willingness to work hard, ignore danger, and even walk away from being hit on the head by a man wielding an iron pipe earned him the honor of becoming the youngest detective in the transit department at twenty-seven. And he kept chasing suspects out of the subways and arresting them on the streets, irking bosses who resented the extra paperwork.

During his years as a "mole" working in the caves, Jack Maple began to develop his own theories about crime and policing. For instance, he frequently told friends that until the entire police force got out of its rut and until police officers got out of their patrol cars and started *fighting* crime instead of responding to 911 calls, the crime rate would continue to climb (Remnick, 1997). It was while he was a transit cop that he started compiling his "Charts of the Future."

CHARTS OF THE FUTURE

Concerned about doing something other than just arresting people during or after the commission of a subway crime, Maple began mapping strategies to fight crime. He drew maps of the subway system by hand and papered his walls at home with these crude maps.

He called those maps the Charts of the Future. Using 55 feet of wall space, he mapped every train station in New York City and every train (Dussault, 1999). Once the maps were pinned up on his walls, he used crayons to mark every violent crime, robbery, and grand larceny that occurred and indicated which were solved and which unsolved. Eventually, he graduated to using colored pins.

When William Bratton was named chief of the transit police in 1990, Bratton quickly learned of Jack Maple. Bratton was particularly impressed with the crime-mapping system that Maple had developed. Working together and employing the Charts of the Future, between 1990 and 1992, Bratton and Maple were able to cut felonies in the caves by 27 percent and robberies by a third (Remnick, 1997).

Then, in 1994, Bratton was appointed by Mayor Rudolph Giuliani to head the New York Police Department. In a surprising move, the new commissioner of the NYPD promoted Jack Maple to be his second-in-command. In his new position, Maple introduced his new computerized Charts of the Future. For the first time, precinct commanders were held accountable for crimes in their area (Dussault, 1999). And for the first time that anyone could remember, crime in New York City began to decline.

But this was also the birth of COMPSTAT. COMPSTAT (or COMSTAT; it goes by both names) as it was developed by Maple was a process by which crime statistics are collected, computerized, mapped, and disseminated rapidly. In this process, police officers in supervisory positions are held responsible for the crime in their areas. In addition, all crimes, including the "quality-of-life" infractions like loitering or public intoxication, are pursued aggressively. The COMPSTAT program not only led to dramatic crime reductions in New York City but became the talk of police departments around the country.

In the short time that Maple and Bratton ran the NYPD, Maple, in his role as New York's deputy police commissioner for crime-control strategies, wiped out decades of accepted wisdom about police work, crime fighting, and responsible government. His COMPSTAT process, which brought accountability to the NYPD, went on to be used by more than a third of the country's big-city police departments (Maple & Mitchell, 1999).

STRATEGIES AND COMPSTAT

When Maple came in as deputy police commissioner, he worried that while the NYPD had strategies to combat various urban problems, there was no process in place to ensure that those strategies, which were designed to address such things as guns, drugs, violence, and auto crimes, for instance, would get carried out. Thinking about it over drinks at night, Maple slowly began to sketch out a solution. Soon, he had come up with principles that he believed should become the guideposts as the NYPD began to redefine their objectives, methods, and outcomes. The four principles he developed were:

1. Accurate, timely intelligence;
2. Rapid deployment;
3. Effective tactics;
4. Relentless follow-up and assessment (Maple & Mitchell, 1999).

The relentless follow-up and assessment principle led to the establishment of weekly meetings, in which Maple and other top brass in the NYPD met with various commanders about crime maps for their areas. Jack Maple wasn't concerned that a commander's precinct numbers might be going up; what did bother him was when commanders had no clue as to why certain kinds of crimes were going up or had no plan to address the problem (Maple & Mitchell, 1999).

The entire process soon came to be known as COMPSTAT or COMSTAT. No one can remember for sure, but the name either came from "computer statistics" or "comparative statistics" (Maple & Mitchell, 1999). But it was clear that the meetings between the police executives and the commanders were extremely important. In the meetings, which became twice-weekly conferences, commanders were put on the spot to report on the up-to-the-minute crime statistics for their area and explain exactly what strategies were in place to deal with criminal events, patterns, or problems. In addition, it was not just about putting strategies in place; it was also about making sure police officers and departments within the

NYPD were doing a better job of sharing intelligence that was being gathered.

But Maple soon figured out that his Charts of the Future were invaluable in other ways. Maps, he determined, were ideal for focusing attention on the greatest concentrations of crime. He also saw that a crime map literally forces anyone looking at it to ask a vital question: What are the underlying causes of this crime problem we're looking at? And that's where highlighting possible correlations between crimes or types of crime came into play (Maple & Mitchell, 1999). His maps, he constantly preached, were methods to figure out the best way of satisfying principle number two: rapid deployment. In other words, when you map the crimes, you should put the cops where the dots are at; or as Maple said it: "Put cops on dots" (Maple & Mitchell, 1999, p. 128).

When Bratton and Maple took over the NYPD in 1993, there were 1,946 murders, 5,933 shootings, and 86,000 robberies in New York City that year. In the two years of their leadership of the NYPD, Bratton and Maple saw murders drop by half and felony crime decrease by 39 percent (Maple & Mitchell, 1999). And in the years since then, violent crimes and murders have continued to drop in New York City. From a city with over 2,200 murders annually in the 1980s, the number of killings was 419 in 2015, and estimates for 2016 were even lower (FBI, 2016).

When the mayor of New York City decided to go with another NYPD commissioner in 1995, Bratton and Maple both left for other pursuits. Jack Maple was invited to go to New Orleans to help out the Crescent City with its high violent crime rate. He readily agreed, and when he was sworn in on October 13, 1994, the New Orleans Police Department was solving about 38 percent of the murders that took place in the city (Remnick, 1997). This was well below the national average for solving murders. Furthermore, the city had only 1,300 police officers—about half the number that other cities of comparable size had. And the NOPD was one of the most poorly paid police forces in the country. The Department of Justice had described NOPD as one of the most brutal in the country (Remnick, 1997). And, on top of everything, Maple soon learned that there was an astonishing level of corruption within the police department.

Soon after arriving in New Orleans, Maple submitted a fifty-five-page report of recommendations for changes at the NOPD. One of those recommendations was to institute the COMPSTAT model, which was quickly implemented. Then, he worked on restructuring the command, with the goal of ridding the department of the most corrupt and brutal cops (Maple & Mitchell, 1999). Although it was a struggle to overcome the pervasive culture of the NOPD, when the department followed his model, the results in reducing violent crime were even more dramatic than those in New York. New Orleans saw one of the greatest crime declines in 1996 of any city in the nation. There were sharp decreases in murder, rapes, robberies, and assaults. Those numbers continued going down in 1997 and 1998 (Maple & Mitchell, 1999; Dussault, 1999).

The flamboyant Jack Maple told Raymond Dussault (1999) in an interview for *Government Technology* that he could achieve the same results anywhere. He boasted that he could go into any city in the world and he would put up $100,000 of his own money against anyone else's money and strategies that Maple's strategies would reduce crime dramatically.

A MAN AHEAD OF HIS TIME

Jack Maple worked out strategies in the transit division that he had a grand chance to carry out in a large city where violent crime was rampant. His Charts of the Future and his four principles worked. COMPSTAT and the weekly meetings with commanders paid huge dividends. While reaping the rewards of his innovations, he developed a great deal of faith and trust in the fourth of his four principles: Relentless follow-up and assessment.

Part of the relentless follow-up, Maple explained, was a process that after making an arrest, detectives must be committed to the strategy of debriefing every offender they arrested (Maple & Mitchell, 1999). Since the detectives had maps at their disposal, those maps reflected accurate and timely intelligence. But after an arrest was made, they needed to not only solve a particular crime, but to see if that one crime could be linked to other crimes that were previously mapped (Maple & Mitchell, 1999).

It was just another aspect of looking at intelligence—information that is gathered—as the key to every aspect of fighting crime. Debriefing arrestees was vitally important, according to Maple. From every interrogation, he wanted his detectives to come away with

- Incriminating statements about the crime in question;
- Incriminating statements about other crimes the suspect may have been involved in;
- The identities and whereabouts of his or her accomplices;
- Physical evidence that might strengthen the case against the suspect;
- Information about other crimes or other contraband (such as drugs, guns, or stolen property) that the suspect knows about (Maple & Mitchell, 1999, p. 69).

Maple's reasoning was sound: "The bad guys know who the other bad guys are and what they're up to" (Maple & Mitchell, 1999, p. 69). He also believed that since society had computers, it was the police who should be putting these to good use to solve crimes.

Jack Maple talked about how he saw computers being used in police work during an interview for *Government Technology* (Dussault, 1999). Maple said that a detective should be able to use computers to find out any important information about the person they are interviewing. Shouldn't you be able to find out how many times he has been a witness, how many times he was a complainant? Was he ever in a car accident? Has he ever been a perpetrator? These are things you would want to know, Maple emphasized. In 1999, Maple conceded that there was no police department with the capability of doing that. But, he said, the technology is available to do that (Dussault, 1999).

Today we know what Jack Maple was talking about—and envisioning—in 1999 as crime and intelligence analysis. The NYPD was the first city police department to create a real-time crime center (Grana & Windell, 2017).

But now, many city police departments have computerized crime centers manned by tactical crime analysts constantly mining for intelligence, trying to discover hot spots of crime and crime patterns (Grana & Windell, 2017).

Although he didn't live long enough to see his vision of the future realized, his dreams have come true.

QUALITY-OF-LIFE ISSUES

Jack Maple believed that one of the most important things he and Bratton did in New York was what he referred to as quality-of-life enforcement. In his book *Crime Fighter*, Maple put it this way:

> ...[T]he NYPD had been demonstrating that assertive enforcement of quality-of-life laws, like those against public urinating, public drinking, loud radios, turnstile jumping, and truancy, can knock down more serious crime problems if each resulting stop or arrest is treated as an opportunity, potentially, to lock up a fugitive or shake out new intel about various unsolved crimes.... Quality-of-life enforcement works to reduce crime because it allows the cops to catch crooks when the crooks are off-duty, like hitting the [enemy's] planes while they're still on the ground.... (Maple & Mitchell, 1999, pp. 151, 155)

AN EARLY DEATH

The idea for enforcing quality-of-life infractions was given a name in 1982 when James Q. Wilson and George Kelling wrote a highly influential article in the *Atlantic Monthly* about "broken windows" (Wilson & Kelling, 1982). The central theme that Wilson and Kelling expounded was that if minor incidents of disorder were dealt with, that would prevent more serious incidents in the future. But Maple didn't buy this theory. His thinking was that if enforcement of minor disorders and infractions were to make a difference in terms of crime reduction, it had to be supported by a larger strategy. He referred to the broader strategy as "quality-of-life Plus" (Maple & Mitchell, 1999, p. 155). He came up with the "plus" part of the strategy, and that was to be selective about who was arrested (they should be people in areas of the highest crime concentration); any suspect arrested must be the subject of a computer check to find out if they are on parole or probation, or if there is an outstanding warrant for their arrest; and there must be a thorough interrogation of every individual arrested (Maple & Mitchell, 1999).

Maple explained his theory further by noting that when you stop someone and find that there is a warrant or the person is on parole, they should be taken to the station for what he called debriefing by detectives. He compared this debriefing like pulling a loose thread on a sweater. He said that the police can unravel a major crime from these quality-of-life crimes (Dussault, 1999).

Jack Maple suffered from colon cancer, and this took his life in 2000. In a 2001 article in *New York Magazine*, Craig Horowitz, a writer who knew Maple throughout the 1990s and wrote several articles about him, described Maple as not changing much over the years, despite being stricken with cancer. Horowitz says that Maple was funny, cranky, and irrepressible up to the day he died. He also saw Maple as facing his cancer in a courageous way (Horowitz, 2001).

Horowitz recalls talking with Maple in his cramped office at police headquarters in 1995. They were drinking coffee, Maple's was an espresso, and discussing why crime was falling in New York City. Maple refuted all of the possible theories that Horowitz could tick off. He seemed offended that the police department was not given credit for the declining crime rate. He claimed that all police departments were different, but the New York City Police Department was really different. Maple compared them to the mighty New York Yankees baseball team of 1927 (Horowitz, 2003).

Douglas Martin, obituary writer for the *New York Times*, wrote:

> ..."Jack was one of the truly great innovators in law enforcement who helped to make New York City the safest large city in America," said Mayor Rudolph W. Giuliani, who recently visited him ... Mr. Maple was architect of the department's Compstat program, through which crime statistics are examined weekly at rigorous meetings of top officials and precinct commanders ... the system allowed the police to act against crime, rather than just react. Though Compstat may sound like common sense, Mr. William Bratton said that it marked a radical departure. "The best-kept secret in the United States is how ineffective police have been in fighting crime," he said. One reason Compstat worked was that it allowed top officials to question lower-level commanders directly. "Jack Maple cleaned out the whole middle level of bureaucracy," said Richard Emery, a civil rights lawyer. (Martin, 2001, p. 1)

COMPSTAT won an award from the Ford Foundation as an innovation in American government and was adopted in dozens of other cities, including New Orleans, Newark, and Baltimore (Dussault, 1999). Although Jack Maple kept his family life private, he was married to his third wife, Brigid O'Connor, when he died. During his marriages, he had a daughter, Jacqueline, and two sons, Brendan and Breen.

The television police series *The District*, which ran from 2000 to 2004, was developed from a concept presented by Jack Maple. The lead character in this series was modeled after Maple.

Craig Horowitz referred to him as the most creative cop in history (Horowitz, 2001). And William Bratton called him the smartest man on crime matters he ever met (Martin, 2001).

QUESTIONS FOR DISCUSSION

1. In what ways did Jack Maple change policing?
2. How could quality-of-life enforcement lead to civil rights violations?
3. How was Jack Maple responsible for modernizing policing?

IMPORTANT TERMS AND NAMES

Broken windows: A theory proposed by James Q. Wilson and George Kelling in 1982 that used broken windows as a metaphor for disorder in neighborhoods and communities. The theory suggests that if broken windows and other signs of disorder are allowed to exist, then this sends a signal to criminals that crime is tolerated.

Charts of the Future: This is a name that Jack Maple came up with to describe the maps he developed to track crime.

COMPSTAT: COMPSTAT or COMSTAT, a name that apparently came from computer statistics, is a police performance management system that was instituted in the New York Police Department to reduce crime and achieve other police department goals, such as information sharing, responsibility, and accountability.

Intel or Intelligence: This means the information gathered to solve a crime problem.

Quality-of-life issues: Quality-of-life issues is a term that has been used in criminal justice to refer to behaviors and minor crimes that affect the well-being and sense of satisfaction by citizens. Behaviors such as public drinking, public urination, graffiti, and littering send a signal that disorder, and even crime, are tolerated.

The 1927 Yankees: Jack Maple referred to the collaboration between William Bratton and himself as the 1927 Yankees. The New York Yankees of 1927 are considered one of the best baseball teams ever in the Major Leagues. The 1927 lineup, which had the nickname of "Murderers' Row," included babe Ruth and Lou Gehrig.

Transit officers: Transit officers are the police officers in the NYPD who patrol the subway system.

William Bratton: William Bratton became the head of the NYPD's transit department in 1990 and then after that served two different terms as the police commissioner of the NYPD. Working with Jack Maple, Bratton reduced crime significantly both in New York City's transit system and throughout the city. He would also serve as the chief of police in Boston and in Los Angeles.

FOR FURTHER READING

Dussault, R. (1999, March 31). Jack Maple: Betting on intelligence. *Government Technology.* Retrieved from http://www.govtech.com/magazines/gt/Jack-Maple-Betting-on-Intelligence.html

Maple, J., & Mitchell, C. (1999). *Crime fighter: Putting the bad guys out of business.* New York, NY: Doubleday.

REVIEW QUESTIONS

True or False

1. Jack Maple could be called the Father of 21st-century policing.
2. Jack Maple was a corrupt NYPD cop.
3. It is perhaps true that Jack Maple single-handedly discovered the crime-fighting potential of computers.
4. A transit officer is an NYPD police officer who patrols the city's buses.

Multiple Choice

5. Jack Maple's Charts of the Future were
   - a. Charts listing minor crimes.
   - b. Maps that helped to track crime.
   - c. Decorative maps that served no useful police function.
   - d. Charts that showed the NYPD chain of command.

6. When the Charts of the Future were first put to use in New York City's transit department, it was found that
   - a. The city needed fewer police officers patrolling the subways.
   - b. Felonies and robberies were reduced by 30 percent.
   - c. The subways were running on time.
   - d. Crime was reduced by 95 percent.

7. Jack Maple developed four principles for redefining the objectives, methods, and outcomes of the NYPD; one of those principles was
   - a. Relentless follow-up and assessment.
   - b. Stop and frisk young people of color.
   - c. Keep police officers in police cars.
   - d. Ignore intelligence gathering.

8. COMPSTAT refers to
   - a. Weekly meetings to discuss police strategies to increase salaries for police officers.
   - b. Computerized statistics related to human resource problems.
   - c. Tracking of the movement of police officers.
   - d. Regular meetings of police personnel to discuss crime problems and strategies to manage those problems.

9. Jack Maple believed that every arrested suspect should be
   - a. Jailed for ninety days.
   - b. Debriefed in a careful interrogation.
   - c. Released with a warning.
   - d. Placed immediately in a lineup for possible identification by crime victims.

REFERENCES

Dussault, R. (1999, March 31). Jack Maple: Betting on intelligence. *Government Technology.* Retrieved from http://www.govtech.com/magazines/gt/Jack-Maple-Betting-on-Intelligence.html

FBI. (2016). *Crime in the U.S.* Retrieved from https://ucr.fbi.gov/crime-in-the-u.s/2015/crime-in-the-u.s.-2015/tables/table-8/table-8-state-pieces/table_8_offenses_known_to_law_enforcement_new_york_by_city_2015.xls

Grana, G., & Windell, J. (2017). *Crime and intelligence analysis.* Boca Raton, FL: CRC Press.

Horowitz, C. (2001, August 13). Remembering Jack Maple. *New York Magazine.* Retrieved from http://nymag.com/nymetro/news/crimelaw/features/5087/

Horowitz, C. (2003, April 7). Jack Stat. *New York Magazine.* Retrieved from http://nymag.com/nymetro/news/anniversary/35th/n_8551/

Maple, J., & Mitchell, C. (1999). *Crime fighter: Putting the bad guys out of business.* New York, NY: Doubleday.

Martin, D. (2001, August 6). Jack Maple, 48, a designer of city crime control strategies. *New York Times.* Retrieved from http://www.nytimes.com/2001/08/06/nyregion/jack-maple-48-a-designer-of-city-crime-control-strategies.html

Remnick, D. (1997, February 24). A reporter at large: The crime buster. *New Yorker,* 94–109.

Wilson, J. Q., & Kelling, G. (1982). Broken windows. *Atlantic Monthly.* Retrieved from https://www.theatlantic.com/magazine/archive/1982/03/broken-windows/304465/

LUCY LOUISA FLOWER
The Mother of the Juvenile Court

No one person was responsible for establishing the world's first juvenile court in Chicago at the end of the nineteenth century. Yet, as you will see in this chapter, a good case can be made that Lucy Flower should be called the mother of the juvenile court.

It is true that Lucy Flower didn't act alone in working to bring about a court for children. Nor was she the only woman who was concerned about poor and delinquent children. But teaming up with Julia Lathrop, a social worker in Chicago, the two women were a formidable duo, together developing a vision of a court for children, and then attaining the necessary political clout to ensure that a bill was passed by the Illinois legislature to create a juvenile court.

She was born May 10, 1837, in Boston, Massachusetts, but soon after her birth she was orphaned and later adopted at a young age by Samuel Elliott Coues and his second wife, Charlotte Haven Ladd (Hoeveler, 1971). Samuel Coues was a prosperous Portsmouth, New Hampshire, merchant and a reformer who numbered among his friends Charles Sumner, William Lloyd Garrison, and Elihu Burritt (Hoeveler, 1971). Charlotte Haven Ladd Coues grew up in New Hampshire and was the niece of William Ladd, founder of the American Peace Society.

Thus, Lucy Coues had the good fortune to grow up in a well-to-do family, with parents who were inclined toward social reform. She was one of eight children, and she attended Portsmouth schools until 1853, at which time her father accepted a Patent Office appointment from his friend, President Franklin Pierce, and the family moved to Washington, D.C. Lucy then attended Parker Collegiate Institute in Brooklyn for one year starting in 1856, but family illness the next year prevented her from continuing in this school.

Her first job, in 1859, was as a drafter in the U.S. Patent Office, but this was not a very satisfactory experience for her (Hoeveler, 1971). Later that same year, she moved to Madison, Wisconsin, taking a job as a teacher at Madison High School. In 1860, she became the first assistant in the high school and also took a position at the Preparatory Department of the University of Wisconsin (Farwell, 1924). After the Madison School District shut down because of financial problems, Lucy was allowed the use of the Madison High School building where, during the 1862–1863 school year, she operated a private school.

She was married to James Monroe Flower, a young, rising Madison lawyer, on September 4, 1862. They subsequently had three children—Elliott, who became a journalist and novelist; Harriet Dean, who, after marrying, wrote a biography of her mother; and Louis Bertram, who died in 1916. The children were born while Lucy and her husband were living in Madison, but in 1873, the family moved to Chicago, Illinois. However, before the family moved to Chicago, Lucy joined the Woman's Relief Corps, an organization that provided aid and employment to the wives and families of soldiers. This was Lucy Flower's first experience in public work (Farwell, 1924).

TURNING HER ATTENTION TO SAVING CHILDREN

While her husband was establishing himself in the legal community in Chicago, Lucy turned her attention to philanthropy and served on the Board of Trustees of both the Chicago Home for the Friendless and the Half-Orphan Asylum. The Chicago Home for the Friendless was founded in 1858, and as the population of Chicago was growing so dramatically, the organization tried to meet the needs for social services to women and children. As time went on, the organization served as an orphanage, a shelter for women and children, and also cared for older people in need. The Chicago Nursery and Half-Orphan Asylum was opened in 1860 as a place to provide day-care services for working mothers and also as a home for orphans and other dependent children. Its first constitution stated the objectives of the asylum as for the "care and maintenance of poor women's children, enabling the women to find employment; also the care and maintenance of such children as are deprived, by death or other cause, of either parent" (Chicago Historical Society, 2013, p. 1). The Chicago Nursery and Half-Orphan Asylum was incorporated in 1865, and in 1869, thanks to a bequest from a local philanthropist, a new building was planned. But that new home for the asylum was incomplete at the time of the Great Chicago Fire of 1871. Nonetheless, as building continued, the asylum began taking in children on a long-term basis, plus continuing to offer temporary care for more than fifty children who had become lost in the confusion of the fire (Chicago Historical Society, 2013).

Serving on these boards helped Lucy become more aware of the dismal conditions for poor children in Chicago, and as her involvement in the city's culture of Protestant charities increased, she began to forge some important friendships—including one with Julia Lathrop (Tanenhaus, 2002).

Lucy Flower became firmly ensconced as a bona fide child saver during the 1870s and 1880s. Like many other women in Chicago during this period, she was well educated (although Lucy had not gone that far in school), usually widely traveled, and typically had access to political and financial resources—often through their husbands (Platt, 2009). Kathleen McCarthy (1982) goes even further and refers to Flower and her friends as the "Gilded Age patrons" (p. 46). These were society women who generously supported the building of the city's charitable institutions like the Half-Orphan Asylum, on whose board Lucy served.

Lucy Flower took a leading role in organizing the Illinois Training School for Nurses, which was the first such nurses' training school in the Midwest, and she served as its president for several years (Farwell, 1924). However, due to her association with the Chicago Home for the Friendless and the Half-Orphan Asylum, she came to realize that many homeless boys needed a place to live, and by 1886, she had taken on a public role in advocating for the establishment of a State Industrial School in Illinois.

She wrote frequent columns for the Chicago newspapers and appeared before legislative committees pleading for a State Industrial School for homeless boys so they could keep their self-respect and have a chance at a successful life (Farwell, 1924). She was especially concerned about young boys being sent to Illinois jails and prisons, and she argued that it was a "disgrace" that young boys should be there. "They do not deserve to go out into the world with the stigma of a criminal institution upon them," she said (Farwell, 1924, p. 17).

Although a bill to institute a State Industrial School was defeated, her efforts sparked enough interest to bring about the establishment of a school for dependent children at Glenwood. Lucy helped raise funds for this semiprivate school which, in her own words, was dedicated to the "victims of careless and vicious parents and guardians" (Farwell, 1924, p. 18).

LUCY CALLS FOR A PARENTAL COURT

She assisted in organizing the Lake Geneva Fresh Air Association in 1888, and she served as chairman of the committee for the selection of children for this outdoor experience (Farwell, 1924). With her concern for poor, dependent, and delinquent children growing, Lucy Flower called for a "parental court," a court for children, as early as 1888 (Tanenhaus, 2002). In her mind, a parental court would hear the cases of dependent, neglected, and delinquent children under sixteen years of age (Tanenhaus, 2002). However, she was not alone in suggesting a separate court for juveniles. For instance, Adelaide Groves, a Chicago socialite, said that Chicago needed detention homes where boys could be placed both before trial and after trial so they didn't end up in jails and the Chicago House of Correction (Platt, 2009). While neither Chicago nor the state of Illinois was ready for a separate court for children yet, still, Groves, working with the Chicago Women's Club, started a regular day school for boys in the county jail. There was a developing movement to separate youth from adults in the House of Correction (Platt, 2009).

Given the flourishing friendship between Lucy Flower and Julia Lathrop, two important female reform traditions were converging. One was the child-saving tradition and the other was the child welfare movement. Their friendship brought these reform traditions together, but by so doing, Flower and Lathrop set the stage for a dynamic synthesis of Chicago philanthropists and welfare leaders who were calling for a juvenile court system (Tanenhaus, 2002).

Both Flower and Lathrop were keen lobbyists for dependent and delinquent children. Lucy Flower was an outspoken theorist proposing the reasons why children became delinquents. For instance, her belief was that delinquent young people developed as a result of poor homes and faulty child-rearing (Clapp, 1998). She believed it was the right of every child to be raised in a proper home, and she told the 1896 Illinois Conference of Charities that "Every child allowed to grow up in ignorance and criminality or in pauperism tends to lower the standards of the community in which he lives, as the evil of his life does not end with him but may be transmitted to his posterity, and the extent of his influence be incalculable" (Clapp, 1998, p. 33). The attitudes Flower expressed during the 1880s and 1890s were supported by other Chicago Women's Club members, most of whom believed, along with Flower, that juvenile delinquency was simply a symptom of a broader crisis among lower-class families (Clapp, 1998). As Elizabeth Clapp (1998) points out, Flower and her fellow club members reflected the bias of their social class when it came to their views about juvenile delinquency. Working-class and immigrant families, they fervently believed, should conform to middle-class ideas about how to raise children in a proper manner.

RELATIONSHIP WITH JULIA LATHROP

Julia Lathrop was younger than Lucy, and she was college educated. However, she made her home at Jane Addams's Hull House, a settlement house constructed to care for poor children from Chicago's slums. Not the wife of a well-to-do husband like Lucy, Julia Lathrop was a social worker who found living and working in Hull House to be tranquil for her (Platt, 2009). The partnership of Flower and Lathrop, one a Golden Age patron and the other a child welfare expert, made the crusade to bring about a children's court viable. They were both concerned with the twin problems of urban populations: crime and poverty. Neither believed that individual responsibility was an adequate explanation for crime and poverty in modern cities. And both challenged the idea that people made choices that shaped their lives. Instead, as Tanenhaus (2004) observes, they thought of crime and poverty as "environmental problems that required thorough investigation in order to discover and eradicate their root causes" (Tanenhaus, 2004, p. 5).

Although Lucy Flower and Adelaide Groves, among others, had publicly advocated for a children's court, by 1890 this appeared to be a remote possibility. As Anthony Platt (2009) points out, in that year, the Board of Public Charities found almost no public or political support for its efforts to reform conditions in county and city jails. Yet, there seemed to be a growing sentiment among child welfare experts and some child-saving organizations that children should not be handled in the criminal courts, nor should they be locked up with adult criminals (Platt, 2009). The records of the Chicago Women's Club show that in 1891, Mrs. Perry Smith, a member of the CWC, recommended the creation of a juvenile court so that children "might be saved from contamination of association with older criminals" (Platt, 2009, p. 128). Furthermore, other members of the CWC persuaded Judge Richard Tuthill to hold a separate court for children on Saturday mornings (Platt, 2009). The CWC assigned a representative to this special court who acted in the capacity of probation officer and adviser to the judge. Judge Tuthill was later quoted in the Annals of the Chicago Women's Club as saying about the CWC that:

> The work of this noble organization was initial, persistent and effective. Well do I remember how many years ago, when it became my turn to hold the Criminal court, I first visited the jail and found

the cells of the old jail filled with boys, some of them under what was then called the age of responsibility, ten years. I requested the State's Attorney to have a calendar of all the boys' cases made out for me, telling him that I wished to dispose of their cases before I began on the adults.... Mrs. Lucy Flower, Mrs. Perry Smith and others ... at once set to work to do what could be done to improve the situation ... The Club thereupon employed and paid for some two or three years a young lady who gave her service in behalf of the little children in the jail every day.... Then began the work of changing the law of Illinois with respect to the care and treatment of all boys and girls under 17 years of age, who were found in a condition of delinquency ... the Women's Club took a most important and effective part. (Platt, 2009, p. 129)

While momentum to establish a separate court for children was building, Chicago's Mayor Hempstead Washburne appointed Flower to be a member of the Chicago Board of Education, a position that gave her greater opportunities to show her concern for "neglected and mishandled youth" (Farwell, 1924, p. 20). She became the chairman of the committee on compulsory education and began lobbying for better handling of children who were constantly truant from school. Appearing before a legislative committee at the state capital in Springfield, Illinois, Flower said, "One of the inalienable rights of every American child should be the right to an elementary education; and there are in this city at least ten thousand children, helpless to protect themselves or to know what the deprivation means, who will be deprived of this right if you Illinois legislators fail to do your duty" (Farwell, 1924, p. 21). The legislature was moved by her words and passed the Parental School Law in Illinois. When in 1894, a new mayor was elected and he chose not to reappoint Flower to the School Board, there was such a hue and cry she was quickly nominated to be a candidate for a position of trustee of the University of Illinois. In the election that followed, she won by more than 184,000 votes—becoming the first woman in Illinois ever elected to this office (Farwell, 1924).

But back in 1891, a bill was introduced in the Illinois General Assembly proposing a children's court. The person most instrumental in introducing this bill was Timothy D. Hurley, president of the Catholic-controlled Chicago Visitation and Aid Society. The bill would give county courts the power to commit dependent children to any nonprofit child welfare organization incorporated under Illinois law (Tanenhaus, 2002). In addition, the bill proposed that county courts be empowered to commit to private child-saving organizations any child "being trained or allowed to be trained in vice and crime" (Platt, 2009, pp. 123–124). Lucy Flower supported this bill because it would give judges more discretion in handling dependent cases (Tanenhaus, 2002). She knew that under existing Illinois law, judges had few options in dealing with children. They could only commit youngsters to a limited number of training or industrial schools (Tanenhaus, 2002). But even with the support of Flower and other child savers, the bill did not pass. It may well have failed because its constitutionality was questioned, and it had almost no support from Protestant organizations (Platt, 2009). However, Flower learned something valuable from the defeat of this bill. A bill for a juvenile court would only get passed if she built a broad coalition of support.

BUILDING A POLITICAL BASE

By the early 1890s, the child-saving movement was gaining increased influence. With greater power, The Chicago Women's Club was working to establish a school in the city jail for young people, and they were lobbying for a central police station to be used exclusively by women and children (Platt, 2009). The annual congresses of both the National Conference of Charities and Corrections and the National Prison Association were held in June in Chicago. Both Frederick Wines and Lucy Flower attended these congresses.

Flower saw an opportunity for building the coalition and broad base she felt she needed to push through a bill for a parental court when John P. Altgeld, a reform-minded Democrat, was elected governor and began his term in office in 1893. One of the first official acts of the new governor was to appoint Julia Lathrop to the State Board of Charities (Tanenhaus, 2002). In this capacity, Lathrop visited every jail and poorhouse in Illinois's 102 counties. This task allowed her to make political connections across the state.

While Lathrop was building her political connections, Flower worked with various women's organizations to build support for sponsoring a new bill. In addition, she formed the Every Day Club, which brought together about forty civic-minded society and professional women. The club invited experts and specialists to come to their luncheons to discuss their work. Flower used the Every Day Club as a forum to keep the idea of a children's court in front of influential people.

At the same time, Governor John P. Altgeld was the kind of governor the child savers and philanthropists needed. He was a Progressive and a reformer who was concerned about the poor and the effect of the criminal law on the poor even before he became governor. During his one term as Illinois governor, he recommended the use of probationary parole and indeterminate sentences, and he established the state board of pardons and helped improve child labor laws (Platt, 2009). Unfortunately, he was defeated for a second term, and he left office in 1897.

But during the last decade of the nineteenth century, Lucy Flower was also conducting research of her own. For example, she went to Boston in 1895 to study how that city handled child welfare and how they used probation in juvenile cases (Tanenhaus, 2004). Far ahead of many other states, undoubtedly because of the pioneering work in probation by John Augustus, Massachusetts had passed legislation in 1891 requiring all criminal courts to appoint probation officers in all juvenile cases (Tanenhaus, 2004). When she returned to Chicago after visiting Boston, Flower drafted a plan to transfer all children's cases in Chicago's eleven police courts to a single, higher court. She showed the draft to her friend, S.S. Gregory, a lawyer and former president of the American Bar Association.

He disappointed her by telling her he thought the plan was unconstitutional under Illinois law (Tanenhaus, 2004). She and Lathrop decided to present the problem to a friend, Judge Harvey Hurd. Judge Hurd advised them to appeal to the Chicago Bar Association. Lathrop went directly to Ephraim Banning, who served with her on the State Board of Charities and was a member of the Chicago Bar Association. He was receptive, and in October, 1898, at the Chicago Bar Association's annual meeting, Banning introduced a resolution asking for a five-member committee to investigate the conditions related to dependent and delinquent children and to come up with legislation that would help to cure some of the existing evils surrounding how children were handled (Tanenhaus, 2004).

In the meantime, Lucy and Julia Lathrop worked behind the scenes to make sure that the proposed bill, which called for the establishment of a children's court, would be a legislative priority in 1899. Those efforts paid off when the theme was announced for the Third Illinois Conference on Charities for November 1898. The theme was to be "the Children of the State" (Tanenhaus, 2002).

The two-day Illinois Conference on Charities was held at the Eastern Hospital for the Insane in Kankakee. The conference helped to galvanize support for the creation of a juvenile court. Frederick H. Wines, the secretary of the State Board of Charities for almost thirty years, presented his vision of a children's court:

> In our system we make criminals out of children who are not criminals by treating them as if they were criminals. That ought to be stopped. What we should have, in our system of criminal jurisprudence, is an entirely separate system of courts for children, in large cities, who commit offences which would be criminal in adults. We ought to have a "children's court" in Chicago, and we ought to have a "children's Judge," who should attend to no other business. We want some place of detention for those children other than a prison. (Tanenhaus, 2002, p. 50)

Also at the Conference on Charities that year was Robert Smith, superintendent of the John Worthy School, a training school for delinquent boys. Flower and the Chicago Women's Club had earlier campaigned to establish the John Worthy School, which would be for boys who were locked up in Bridewell, the Chicago House of Corrections (Dohrn, 2002). Robert Smith told the attendees at the Conference on Charities that his institution could not possibly reform the diverse group of offenders who were sent to his school. "The John Worthy School," he said, "in its present condition is nothing more nor less than a school for crime, and until the city council of Chicago takes steps to isolate the boys from adult criminals, the evil will not be remedied" (Platt, 2009, pp. 128–129).

Chairing the Conference Business Committee, Julia Lathrop drafted a resolution to push for legislative change. Although the Legislative Committee and other committees of the conference would play only a minor role in the planning which led to the passing of the juvenile court law, the conference itself was significant in bringing the issues before a wider audience, focusing attention on the need for new legislation, and, in general, increasing the momentum toward reform.

A JUVENILE COURT IS CREATED

In 1899, the draft of a proposed bill prepared by a Chicago Bar Association committee was presented to the city's judges for their consideration and comments. Flower arranged for an Every Day Club luncheon and during the luncheon presented the bill to the city's circuit court judges, hoping to gain their approval (Tanenhaus, 2004). She held a similar luncheon for the city's clergymen with the idea that they might preach sermons about the need for a children's court.

The bill was brought to the legislature in early 1899 and was passed in April 1899. Lucy Flower's vision of a "parental court" for Chicago became a reality on July 1, 1899—when the new law took effect. Chicago now had the world's first juvenile court. The act that brought it about was called the Act to Regulate the Treatment and Control of

Dependent, Neglected and Delinquent Children, and it included these provisions, some of which sound like they could have been written by Lucy Flower:

> ... For the purposes of this act the words dependent child and neglected child shall mean any child who for any reason is destitute or homeless or abandoned; ... or who habitually begs or receives alms; or who is found living in any house of ill fame or with any vicious or disreputable person; or whose home ... is an unfit place for such a child; and any child under the age of 8 years who is found peddling or selling any articles or singing or playing any musical instrument upon the streets or giving any public entertainment. (Parry, 2005, p. 57)

But getting that legislation passed didn't mean the end of Lucy Flower's efforts on behalf of the juvenile court. She helped to raise funds necessary for the new court to begin its pioneering work, and she proposed that the Chicago Women's Club establish a separate organization to be known as the Juvenile Court Committee. Her idea was accepted, and this new committee was formed, with Flower as its first president. The committee ran a detention home and paid the salaries of fifteen probation officers (Tanenhaus, 2002).

RETIRING FROM CHILD SAVING

Lucy Flower remained involved with the juvenile court in Chicago until about 1902, when her husband became ill and the couple moved to California. In her biography of her mother, Harriett Farwell wrote: "There she cheerfully lived for the rest of her life far from the home she was used to, the friends that she loved, the life that stimulated her, and the interests that had so long been peculiarly her own" (Farwell, 1924, p. 39).

When Lucy Flower moved from Chicago to Coronado, California, her retirement from child saving symbolized the passing of a generation of Golden Age patrons from the political and social welfare scene. But staying behind in Chicago were her friend Julia Lathrop and other Progressives who continued to help shape the juvenile court into the entity it became until the landmark U.S. Supreme Court decisions of the 1960s changed the face of the children's court.

With the death of her husband in 1909, Lucy Flower soon became ill and incapacitated herself. However, in 1911, when she had been gone from Chicago for almost ten years, she was paid the tribute of having the first trade school for girls named in her honor: the Lucy L. Flower Technical High School. Lucy Louisa Flower died on April 27, 1920. Her daughter wrote after her death that "Her body might be in Coronado, but her mind was in every good cause, practical, philanthropic or educational, which was being waged anywhere in the world …" (Farwell, 1924, p. 42).

QUESTIONS FOR DISCUSSION

1. Would there have been a juvenile court in this country if it were not for the child savers? Why or why not?
2. What were the greatest concerns for Lucy Flower that motivated her to advocate for a separate court for children?
3. Why were neglected and dependent children included in the first juvenile court legislation?

IMPORTANT TERMS AND NAMES

Chicago Home for the Friendless: Founded in Chicago in 1858, the Chicago Home for the Friendless was an organization that provided a residence for orphaned children and provided social services for women and children.

Chicago Nursery and Half-Orphan Asylum: The Chicago Nursery and Half-Orphan Asylum, which opened in 1860, provided day-care services for the children of working mothers and also provided a home for orphaned and dependent children.

Chicago Women's Club: Founded in 1876, the Chicago Women's Club was a club for self-improvement and social reforms. It was instrumental in bringing about the first juvenile court.

Child savers: The child savers were wealthy and concerned women who worked to help poor and delinquent children in Chicago and other big cities in the nineteenth century.

Every Day Club: A club founded by Lucy Flower for a few dozen influential women in Chicago. They invited various experts and specialists to talk about their work at the club's luncheons.

Frederick H. Wines: The son of Enoch Wines, who founded the National Prison Association, Frederick Wines was the secretary of the Illinois State Board of Charities from 1969 to 1899.

Gilded Age patrons: A term used by Kathleen McCarthy, it referred to society women in Chicago who generously supported the establishment of the city's charitable organizations.

Jane Addams: Jane Addams was a Chicago social worker, author, and reformer, who opened Hull House, a settlement house and community center.

John P. Altgeld: John P. Altgeld was the Progressive governor of Illinois from 1893 to 1897. He appointed women to governmental positions, increased funds to education, and brought about improvement in child labor.

Judge Richard Tuthill: A circuit court judge in Chicago who was persuaded by the Chicago Women's Club to begin holding separate courts for children well before the legislation was passed creating a juvenile court.

Parental Court: When Lucy Flower first suggested a separate court for children, she referred to what she envisioned as "parental courts." In later years, she called them children's courts or juvenile courts.

State Board of Charities: A state board, composed of citizens, to regulate all organizations involved in charitable endeavors.

State Industrial School: Industrial schools were built in the nineteenth century as reform schools and boarding schools for juvenile delinquents.

FOR FURTHER READING

Dohrn, B. (2002). The school, the child, and the court. In M. K. Rosenheim, F. E. Zimring, D. S. Tanenhaus, & B. Dohrn, *A century of juvenile justice* (pp. 267–309). Chicago: University of Chicago Press.

Farwell, H. S. (1924). *Lucy Louisa Flower: 1837–1920: Her contribution to education and child welfare in Chicago.* Chicago, IL: Private printing.

McCarthy, K. (1982). *Noblesse oblige: Charity and cultural philanthropy in Chicago: 1849–1929.* Chicago, IL: University of Chicago Press.

Parry, D. L. (2005). *Essential readings in juvenile justice.* Upper Saddle River, NJ: Pearson Education, Inc.

Platt, A. M. (2009). *The child savers: The invention of delinquency.* New Brunswick, NJ: Rutgers University Press.

Tanenhaus, D. S. (2002). The evolution of juvenile courts in the early twentieth century: Beyond the myth of immaculate construction. In M. K. Rosenheim, F. E. Zimring, D. S. Tanenhaus, & B. Dohrn, *A century of juvenile justice* (pp. 42–73). Chicago, IL: University of Chicago Press.

Tanenhaus, D. S. (2004). *Juvenile justice in the making.* New York, NY: Oxford University Press.

REVIEW QUESTIONS

True or False

1. Lucy Flower has been called the Mother of the Juvenile Court.
2. Lucy Flower was a prison reformer who believed that children should be jailed with adults.
3. Lucy Flower may be the first woman in United States history who could be called a pioneer in the criminal justice field.
4. A "Gilded Age patron" was a society woman instrumental in supporting Chicago's charitable institutions.

Multiple Choice

5. The momentum for the creation of the first juvenile court likely occurred in Chicago because of
    a. The influence of the Half-Orphan Asylum.
    b. The collaboration between the child-saving movement, the Chicago Women's Club, and the Chicago Bar Association.
    c. The work of Governor Peter J. Altgeld.
    d. The behind-the-scenes efforts of Jane Addams.

6. Both Lucy Flower and Julia Lathrop believed that crime came about as a result of
    a. Alcoholism.
    b. Environmental problems.
    c. The choices people make.
    d. People having too much money.

7. By serving on various boards and committees, Lucy Flower had a growing concern about
    a. Neglected and mishandled youth.
    b. Children who were school truants.
    c. Boys who were imprisoned with adults.
    d. All of the above.

8. Years before there was a juvenile court, Lucy Flower traveled to Boston to
    a. Study probation in juvenile cases.
    b. Find a good juvenile court judge.
    c. Study secure detention facilities for young children.
    d. Discover how to prevent juvenile delinquency.

9. The world's first juvenile court went into operation in Chicago on
    a. September 1, 1905.
    b. September 1, 1901.
    c. July 1, 1899.
    d. July 1, 1895.

REFERENCES

Chicago Historical Society. (2013). Chicago nursery and half-orphan asylum. Retrieved from http://chsmedia.org/media/fa/fa/M-C/ChapinHall-inv.htm

Clapp, E. (1998). *Mothers of all children*. University Park, PA: Pennsylvania University Press.

Dohrn, B. (2002). The school, the child, and the court. In M. K. Rosenheim, F. E. Zimring, D. S. Tanenhaus, & B. Dohrn, *A century of juvenile justice* (pp. 267–309). Chicago, IL: University of Chicago Press.

Farwell, H. S. (1924). *Lucy Louisa Flower: 1837–1920: Her contribution to education and child welfare in Chicago*. Chicago, IL: Private printing.

Flower, Lucy Louisa Coues. (2011). *Britannica Online Encyclopedia*. Retrieved from www.britannica.com/print/articvle/211101

Hoeveler, J. R. (1971). Flower, Lucy Louisa Coues. In E. T. James, J. W. James, & P. S. Boyer, *Notable American Women: 1607–1950*. Cambridge, MA: Harvard University Press.

McCarthy, K. (1982). *Noblesse oblige: Charity and cultural philanthropy in Chicago: 1849–1929*. Chicago, IL: University of Chicago Press.

Parry, D. L. (2005). *Essential readings in juvenile justice*. Upper Saddle River, NJ: Pearson Education, Inc.

Platt, A. M. (2009). *The child savers: The invention of delinquency*. New Brunswick, NJ: Rutgers University Press.

Tanenhaus, D. S. (2002). The evolution of juvenile courts in the early twentieth century: Beyond the myth of immaculate construction. In M. K. Rosenheim, F. E. Zimring, D. S. Tanenhaus, & B. Dohrn, *A century of juvenile justice* (pp. 42–73). Chicago, IL: University of Chicago Press.

Tanenhaus, D. S. (2004). *Juvenile justice in the making*. New York, NY: Oxford University Press.

9

EARL WARREN
A Chief Justice Whose Supreme Court Changed the Criminal Justice System

He's been referred to as Super Chief, and he has been hailed as the greatest chief justice in the history of the United States Supreme Court. On the other hand, he has been vilified by some in law enforcement, and President Dwight D. Eisenhower thought nominating him to the Supreme Court was a mistake. One thing, though, is crystal clear about Earl Warren and his career on the Supreme Court. Under his leadership, the Supreme Court brought about a revolution in criminal procedure and law enforcement, literally changing how every police officer, every prosecutor, and every criminal court judge did their jobs.

All in all, though, he was a most unlikely Supreme Court justice, let alone Supreme Court chief justice. No one could ever have predicted that this man, who was born on March 19, 1881, in Los Angeles would ever rise to the level of a judge; certainly not to the highest court in the land. His early life was very normal and unpretentious.

His father and mother were both Scandinavian immigrants, and neither were well educated. His father, Mathias "Matt" Warren, born in Norway, worked as a car repairman and car inspector for the Southern Pacific Railroad (White, 1982). His mother, Christine "Crystal" Hernlund Warren, was born in Sweden and came to America as a baby, but grew up in Chicago and Minneapolis. Crystal and Matt met in Minneapolis, and after marrying moved to Los Angeles in 1889. His mother perhaps had less influence on his life than his father, because his father taught him some enduring lessons.

Of the lessons he learned from his father, one was to escape economic dependence through education (White, 1982). Matt Warren made it one of his life's missions to see to it that Earl and his older sister, Ethel, had good educations. To accomplish this, Matt Warren worked hard and handled his money very carefully. He taught his children to live simply and save their money (Warren, 1977). His father warned young Earl to never let himself be caught broke. "Saving is a habit, like any other, and once established will last you a lifetime," he told his son (Cray, 1997, p. 16). When Earl was a teenager, his father helped see to it that his son worked for Southern Pacific Railroad, and that, too, provided an important life lesson for Warren. As he writes in his memoirs, he saw that a giant corporation like Southern Pacific Railroad could wield significant power in the economic and political life of a community. He observed that railroad workers could be laid off without pay and without warning for weeks before the end of a fiscal year in order that the corporate stock might pay a higher dividend (Warren, 1977). He also was aware that the company would bring minority groups into the county to provide cheap labor, only to be fleeced out of much of what they earned at the company store where they were obliged to shop.

The young Warren helped carry men to the emergency room for amputation of an arm or leg that had been crushed because there were no safety measures taken in the shops and yards to prevent such injuries. And if an injured man even considered suing the railroad company, he could be fired. Furthermore, the Southern Pacific Railroad provided no compensation for injured workers. As a worker himself, Warren became familiar with the long workdays—usually ten- and even twelve-hour days—seven days a week. By careful observation, Earl Warren learned about monopolistic power, political dominance, corruption in government, and their effect on the people of a community. He considered what he learned valuable lessons that would tend to shape his career for the rest of his life (Warren, 1977).

Although his father taught him some valuable life lessons, Matt Warren left behind some bitter memories as well. As Matt Warren got older, he grew more and more irascible and crotchety. So much so that Warren's mother left his father a number of years before Matt Warren was murdered by an unknown assailant in 1938. That murder was never solved (White, 1982).

However, by the time of his father's death, Earl had graduated from the University of California at Berkeley. During his undergraduate years, although never a serious student or a scholar, he did, however, discover he had an interest in political matters (Cray, 1997). Earlier in his life, he made the decision to become a lawyer, and to that end he majored in political science. However, his real awakening to this burgeoning interest came about because he volunteered to work with a student organization called the Lincoln-Roosevelt League. When the vice president of the league, Hiram W. Johnson, decided to run for governor of California, and was elected, Warren had found a new interest.

Hiram Johnson was a Progressive, and from that point on, Progressive tenets became the reference point for Warren's future political life (White, 1982). Hiram Johnson represented to Warren the very model of progressivism and reform, and Ed Cray (1997) states that Johnson became a hero for the young Earl Warren, capturing the college student's imagination. In his autobiography, Warren says of Johnson that in his campaign he promised to "... and after his election did, put an end to Southern Pacific domination of the political life of our state" (Warren, 1977, p. 38). Warren continued to view Governor Johnson with high regard, saying that after his (Johnson's) election as governor of California, "There ensued an administration of reform measures never equaled in California or probably any other state before or since" (Warren, 1977, p. 39).

When Earl Warren graduated from UC–Berkeley's law school, he had no contacts and few, if any, prospects. Looking around for a job, he landed a job at the law office of Associated Oil Company in San Francisco. By all accounts, he spent a miserable year there and after resigning took a new position with the Oakland firm of Robinson and Robinson. He lasted there for a year and a half before deciding that maybe he should open up his own law office. However, before he could open his own law practice, the United States declared war on Germany. Instead of pursuing a law practice, Warren signed on with the U.S. Army, requesting an officer ranking. He wasn't accepted as an officer, but he was assigned to Camp Lewis in

Washington State with the assignment of training draftees. After a few months, he became an officer at Camp Lee in Petersburg, Virginia, with the task of training replacement troops (White, 1982).

In November 1918, he was reassigned to Camp MacArthur in Waco, Texas, where he became a bayonet instructor. However, two days into this assignment, the Armistice was signed—and the war was over (Warren, 1977). Leaving the Army the next month, he still had no prospects for a job or career, but a friend told him about an opportunity as a clerk to the judiciary committee of the 1919 California legislature. He immediately decided to take the clerkship, and this was his first step in what was to become a fifty-year career as a public servant (Warren, 1977).

When the legislative session ended, Warren worked as a deputy city attorney for the city of Oakland. A year later, at age twenty-eight, he was offered a position as deputy district attorney in Alameda County. If this wasn't exactly a stepping stone to becoming the governor or the chief justice of the Supreme Court, at least it gave him his first practical experience with the criminal justice system.

In this new job, Warren tried criminal cases, defended civil and criminal suits against county officials, advised county boards of education about civil liability issues, and wrote legal opinions on various issues—such as real estate matters—for the county board of supervisors. Along the way, though, he discovered that his real first love was law enforcement and public service. Within three years, Warren had become the Alameda County district attorney's chief deputy. The county district attorney was Ezra Decoto, but in 1925, Decoto resigned. Earl Warren was chosen by the county's board of supervisors to fill the unexpired term left by Decoto's resignation. The next year, at the end of the term, Warren ran for the position and became Alameda County's duly elected district attorney.

Although still a young man, Earl Warren brought a number of assets to his new job. He was efficient, loyal, industrious, and could manage an office skillfully (White, 1982). He also brought with him to the position a kind of civic morality and the air of one who was nonpartisan (White, 1982). That meant that he could vigorously pursue the prosecution of various illegal activities against public officials and others taking graft. As a result of his record as the district attorney, Warren was building a broad base of support that led him to easy victories in the elections of 1930 and 1934.

His record of sterling accomplishments was growing in Alameda County. For instance, he engineered a plan to coordinate the law enforcement agencies of the entire state of California; a plan that helped him and other district attorneys fight corruption and organized crime. Warren was especially looking to bring together various law enforcement agencies in order to better combat Prohibition-era racketeers (Warren, 1977). As he himself acknowledged in his memoirs, he was in a good position to take some initiative in this effort since he was chairman of the Board of Managers of the California Bureau of Criminal Identification. This bureau ran a crime lab and provided communication between sheriffs in rural communities. Since Earl Warren also had an interest in creating schools to train police officers, his leadership helped bring about a liaison with criminology classes at San Jose State College.

However, after more than two terms as the Alameda County district attorney, Warren set his sights on a new job—that of attorney general for the state of California. He was well aware that the way the attorney general in his state operated was as a lawyer with no particularly defined law enforcement powers. His idea was that if he got elected, he would expand the jurisdictional reach of the attorney general's office (White, 1982). In his own words, he saw becoming the attorney general as an opportunity for "developing it into an extremely important arm of the state government" (Warren, 1977, p. 109). To realize that goal, though, it would entail at least one amendment to California's constitution. Consequently, he waited for the right opportunity to come along to achieve this.

He didn't have to wait long. In 1934, there was a series of payroll robberies and a vigilante lynching of two confessed kidnappers in California. Seizing on these events, Warren called for the adoption of four new amendments to the state's constitution. The most important of these amendments called for the creation of a State Department of Justice, the expansion of the jurisdictional powers of the attorney general, and an increase in the attorney general's annual salary. All of these amendments were approved by California voters. Thus, these amendments paved the way for Warren to run for the attorney general position. There was only one stumbling block: California already had an attorney general in Ulysses S. Webb, a man who had been in that office since 1902. Warren viewed Webb as an honorable attorney general, and he went to Webb, telling him that as long as he wanted the office, Warren would never run against him (Warren, 1977). A few years later, with Earl Warren patiently waiting in the wings, Webb informed him that he would retire at the end of his term in 1938. Once that actually happened, Earl Warren officially announced he would be running for the office.

Rather than select one party for his candidacy, he chose to file as a candidate for the Democratic, the Republican, and the Progressive tickets. He got the nod from all three parties, but in addition, he had the support of all law enforcement officers in California. During the campaign, Warren constantly emphasized four main issues: California's rising crime rate; the need for more rehabilitation in state prisons; greater coordination among law enforcement agencies; and reshaping the office of attorney general into a true Department of Justice (Cray, 1997). Although running a modest campaign, he toured the state and managed to pick up endorsements from most newspapers and the support of a diverse number of organizations. As a result, he won the election with relative ease.

THE ATTORNEY GENERAL

As the new attorney general of California, Warren had every intention of using the new powers and responsibilities of the office. Swinging right into action on his first day in office, he immediately dealt with the selling of pardons for prisoners through the governor's office. Soon thereafter, he began shutting down illegal dog tracks, taking a close look at bookmaking at horse race tracks, closing down brothels, and padlocking speakeasies. All of these activities were avenues for public corruption, and that is something Earl Warren could not tolerate. Neither could he ignore organized crime. He would say in his autobiography many years later that the main

thrust of his activities as attorney general was attempting to keep organized crime out of California (Warren, 1977).

As it turned out, though, not everything Warren was doing sat well with
the governor, Culbert Olson. Remembering this period of time, Warren
would write about his difficulties with Olson by remarking in his memoirs
that Olson bypassed him as attorney general and, in addition, disregarded
the plans and programs of the law enforcement, health, and fire-fighting
officials of the state, whom Warren had helped to weld into an enthusiastic and cooperative organization for civilian defense. The governor also
refused to recognize Warren in the State Council for Defense, although
Warren had worked for two years in getting vital forces of the state to take
part. Finally, the governor had vetoed an appropriation bill of $214,000 for
Warren's office. These things widened the chasm between the two men
(Warren, 1977).

By April 1942, Warren was ready to take on Olson in a bid to become
governor. But America was in the midst of a world war, and early on there
was a movement to intern all Japanese Americans—an idea Warren
supported.

Speaking out in favor of placing Japanese Americans in camps for
the remainder of the war, at the time Earl Warren thought that was the
best thing to do. He had heard military intelligence state that Japanese
American fishermen, who often went out into the Pacific Ocean at night,
might be signaling enemy submarines. While he had qualms about abro-
gating the civil rights of Japanese Americans, he was also a patriot who
wanted to support the war effort.

However, after World War II had ended and Japanese Americans were
released from camps and centers where they were held, Earl Warren was
vocal in protecting the safety of those who would return to California.
Their rights, he declared, should be protected. And in his memoirs, he
notes that he was guilt-ridden by his error in supporting the internment of
Japanese Americans. In fact, he wrote that he subsequently deeply regret-
ted the removal order and his own testimony advocating it. He said in his
1977 book that placing Japanese Americans in internment camps was not
in keeping with our American concept of freedom and the rights of

citizens. He wrote that whenever he thought of the innocent little children who were torn from home, school friends, and congenial surroundings, he was conscience stricken. He concluded that it was wrong to act so impulsively, without positive evidence of disloyalty on the part of Japanese Americans (Warren, 1977).

Governor Earl Warren Conversing With a Young California Miner.

https://commons.wikimedia.org/wiki/
File:Earl_Warren_with_young_miner.jpg.
Copyright in the Public Domain.

Despite this wartime humanitarian crisis, he had already decided to run for governor. And a strong reason, besides the widening chasm between the governor and him, was the overall sense that as attorney general under Olson, he believed he could not be as effective as he wanted to be as long as Olson was governor. In the ensuing campaign, Earl Warren explained to the electorate that he had the ability to lead the state and not be influenced by politics. To prove this, he again filed for his candidacy as both a Republican and a Democrat. And again, as in previous elections, he won rather handily.

GOVERNOR EARL WARREN

Although becoming governor was a major transition in his life, still Warren desired to continue to operate much as he did as district attorney and as attorney general. That is, he wanted to function independently, stay clear of political affiliations, and expand the jurisdictional boundaries of the office while bringing professionalism to the staff that surrounded him (White, 1982). However, like it or not, he was now in a position that was undoubtedly political; furthermore, being governor of California meant he was part of national Republican politics.

Early in his term as governor, his policies were trending in a conservative direction. He pushed for frugal government spending, a reduction in taxes, and the establishment of a budget surplus. But later in his term, his progressive leanings were evident as he advocated for the elderly, the mentally ill, and the disabled. It was difficult to label him as either a conservative or a liberal, but perhaps the closest description was as a California Progressive. According to one of his biographers, Edward White (1982), being a California Progressive meant that Warren stood for honesty in government, opposition to special interests, and paying close attention to public opinion. But California progressivism also meant that he tended to view California as a paradise that should be preserved against encroachment by aliens and ideologies. In addition, whatever political label might be put on him by others, he saw himself as being interested in civil rights, representative government, and equality of opportunity (White, 1982). In his own mind, he did not identify himself as a liberal or conservative, a Republican or Democrat; he was a Progressive.

When Warren became governor, he was well aware that for almost a decade, the state legislature had ignored reports calling for progressive programs in California's prison system. He was also aware that California prisons were often run like country clubs. Guards and wardens were susceptible to receiving gratuities in exchange for lax treatment or even furloughs from incarceration. Warren had for a long time complained that prisons did nothing to break the cycle of crime and punishment (Cray, 1997). "Caging men like animals, penning them within walls, then expecting them to become better men, is fallacious," he had argued as early as 1931 (Cray, 1997, p. 145). Soon after becoming governor, when Warren got word that two of Folsom Prison's felons were getting passes to spend weekends in San Francisco, he ordered them arrested. He then appointed a staff member to study prisons and come up with a plan to reorganize the prisons in California. Following his usual pattern, once the report was done, Warren waited for the right opportunity to implement prison reform. When that opportunity presented itself, Warren garnered support from the public, the media, and law enforcement to back his plan. But within two months of the report being completed, Warren called a special session of the legislature to enact the committee's recommendations for reform. By the end of the week, the California legislature passed a package of bills to reorganize the entire state penal system (Cray, 1997). Following that, he found a new director of prisons. As a result, the California prison system would become a model emulated by other states (Cray, 1997).

During his three terms as governor, Warren worked hard to separate partisanship from activism. But according to Edward White (1982), this led to a misunderstanding of Earl Warren. Most people assumed he was a moderate Republican, but he was, in fact, not a moderate, but an activist. However, that was overlooked by the national Republican Party; he was a candidate for president of the United States twice by 1952 and was Thomas Dewey's vice presidential running mate in 1948. President Dwight Eisenhower nominated Warren for chief justice of the U.S. Supreme Court because Eisenhower thought that Warren was a middle-of-the-road Republican (White, 1982). Warren himself quoted President Eisenhower as calling Warren's appointment to the Supreme Court as the "biggest damn fool thing I ever did" (White, 1982, p. 129).

As a politician on the national stage, by all accounts, Earl Warren was miserable (White, 1982; Cray, 1997). Valuing his independence, when he was on the campaign trail, he always felt like he couldn't say what he really wanted to say in his speeches. And although a popular figure in California, he didn't excite the national media or, perhaps, the national electorate. Somehow, when he was away from California, he was not viewed the same as he was by the people who lived in his home state. For instance, the *New York Times* said of him: "An attractive vote-getter ... [but] a plodding, routine ... District Attorney ... and an equally unspectacular Attorney General" (White, 1982, p. 136). *Time* magazine said: "... his critics saw him as a bull-headed, plodding mediocrity who never says or does anything out of the ordinary," and that only his admirers characterize him as "bold, patient, dependable" (White, 1982, p. 136). And John Gunther, in his 1947 book *Inside U.S.A.*, described Earl Warren as "someone who will never set the world on fire or even make it smoke; he has all the limitations of all Americans of his type with little intellectual background, little genuine depth, or coherent political philosophy; a man who has probably never bothered with an abstract thought twice in his life; a man ... with little inner force" (Cray, 1997, p. 182).

After winning his third term as California's governor in 1950, since he won by the largest majority of any governor in the history of California—over a million votes—he himself thought about national politics and announced his candidacy for president in November 1951. But when Dwight D. Eisenhower also threw his hat into the ring a couple of months later, it was obvious to Warren that he probably didn't have a chance of defeating the general, who was a beloved military hero. As the campaign went along, Warren threw his support to Eisenhower. Eisenhower, in turn, began to consider Warren as a part of his cabinet—perhaps secretary of labor or of the interior. And after Eisenhower was elected, he and Warren held a discussion in which the new president told Warren that he would offer him the first Supreme Court vacancy that occurred (White, 1982). Following that conversation, though, Warren didn't hear anything from the president until a month later, when Eisenhower nominated him for chief justice of the U.S. Supreme Court.

Why was Earl Warren nominated for chief justice?

Edward White (1982) says one reason was that Eisenhower knew Warren would accept the nomination. But another reason was that Eisenhower and his staff were well aware of how much Warren contributed to support Eisenhower during the campaign. Also, while attorney general of California, Warren had argued cases before the Supreme Court. Finally, there was an unexpected vacancy on the Supreme Court when Chief Justice Fred Vinson died of a heart attack. Holding a conversation with Eisenhower's attorney general, Herbert Brownell, in September 1953, in which they talked about what positions in the government Warren might be willing to accept, they discussed whether Warren generally agreed with Eisenhower's policies and programs. Warren told Brownell that he was supportive of Eisenhower's programs and that he was ready to accept the nomination for chief justice. On September 30, 1953, Eisenhower officially nominated Earl Warren to be chief justice of the U.S. Supreme Court.

In a letter to his brother Milton, the president defended Warren's nomination by writing:

> I believe that we need statesmanship on the Supreme
> Court. Statesmanship is developed in the hard knocks
> of a general experience, private and public. Naturally,
> a man occupying the post must be competent in the
> law—and Warren has had seventeen years of prac-
> tice in public law, during which his record was one
> of remarkable accomplishment and success, to say
> nothing of dedication. He has been very definitely a
> liberal-conservative; he represents the kind of polit-
> ical, economic, and social thinking that I believe we
> need on Supreme Court. Finally, he has a national
> name for integrity, uprightness, and courage that,
> again, I believe we need on the Court. (Cray, 1997,
> p. 262)

It seems apparent that Eisenhower nominated Warren thinking he was an "Eisenhower Republican." He was not. What he was, in fact, was a man who, as a district attorney, an attorney general, and as a governor had a set of skills which he brought to every position he held. Those skills included using the powers of whatever office he was in to solve problems. Thus, he could be said to be an activist, something he had never tried to hide: something President Eisenhower and his staff should have been savvy enough to recognize.

EARL WARREN'S MARRIAGE AND FAMILY LIFE

While Warren was being the dedicated public servant that Eisenhower appreciated, he was also a man who valued his family life. In 1921, Earl Warren met and fell in love with Nina Palmquist Meyers, a widow with a young son, and like Warren himself, had parents who were Scandinavian immigrants. When they met, Nina Meyers managed a women's specialty shop in Oakland, California. In his autobiography, Warren wrote that meeting Nina was the greatest thing that ever happened to him. In fact, that is the dedication in his book: "To NINA, the best thing that ever happened to me" (Warren, 1977).Two years later they were engaged, and two years following that, in 1925, they were married.

Their marriage was one that revolved around closeness, mutual admiration, and the complementary roles they played. Nina was the quiet observer of her husband's public and political life, and she managed the home and the family. She was not interested in being a public figure; she left that up to him. But together they worked hard at maintaining a family life that was distinct from Earl Warren's public life.

By 1943, when Warren first became governor of California, they had six children, including Nina's son that she brought into the marriage. Their children, James, Virginia, Earl Jr., Dorothy, Nina, and Robert, ranged in age, in 1943, from seven to twenty-two. Up to the time Warren became governor, the family lived in Oakland. But when he took over the office of governor, it was necessary for the whole family to move to the governor's mansion in Sacramento.

Prior to that first campaign for governor, neither Nina nor the children were exposed to the limelight. Things changed when he ran for governor. It was then that everyone began to grasp the potential political capital that this family possessed for garnering votes. In fact, Nina and the children were frequently touted in the press as the family next door. Although Warren, too, could see the value of letting the public get a glimpse of his family, Warren always had a rule that the family came first and politics came a distant second. His dominant priority throughout his fifty-year career was preserving the closeness of the family and his family relationships. He always tended to view himself as an average family man who just happened to be a public figure (White, 1982). But he believed that the values he espoused and practiced at home—equality, fairness, and unpretentiousness—could be transferred to public life. Because of these values and principles, Earl Warren was a different kind of politician—and a different kind of Chief Justice.

CHIEF JUSTICE OF THE UNITED STATES SUPREME COURT

According to various observers, the Court Warren inherited had been badly administered and greatly divided since the days of Franklin Roosevelt (Cray, 1997). Fred Vinson, the previous chief justice, lacked the ability to unite the justices on the Supreme Court. One divisive aspect of the Supreme Court in its daily functions was that there was antagonism between Hugo Black and Robert Jackson. Within the resulting hostile atmosphere of the Court when Warren took over, there were frequent dissenting opinions and plenty of bad feelings between the associate justices. Although Robert Jackson was rumored to be a possible successor to Harlan Fiske Stone, the retiring chief justice, in 1946, it was reported that William O. Douglas and Hugo Black would resign if Jackson became the chief justice. In addition, Felix Frankfurter and Black were constantly at odds, further polarizing the High Court.

When Earl Warren came to Washington, D.C., to assume the role of chief justice, he brought with him an awe of the Supreme Court. That was one reason that in his first few months, he played a passive role on the Court as he held back hoping to get a better sense of how the Court operated and what his role would be (White, 1982). However, he would not be allowed to continue to take that inactive stance for very long. By December 1953, five cases came along that were lumped together and were thereafter known as *Brown v. Board of Education*. It was this case that established Earl Warren's role on the Supreme Court.

As Edward White points out, given Warren's history in California, his views on race relations could best be described as "undeveloped" (White, 1982, p. 162). That might also be said to be true of other issues that would come before the High Court, such as enforced equality in schools. Now, though, in his first year as chief justice and with the cases known as *Brown v. Board of Education* before him, he would be forced to develop his own views. He even assigned the writing of *Brown v. Board of Education* to himself. This, too, would demand a thorough understanding of all the issues involved.

Although the Supreme Court that Warren inherited from Vinson was divided in other ways, it was also split over the issue of equality in schools.

There was disunity in their opinions about whether to accept or overturn the 1896 ruling in *Plessy v. Ferguson*, which had previously established the doctrine of separate but equal.

Although the Supreme Court then ruled that the Fourteenth Amendment's injunction forbade any state to make or enforce a law that abridged the privileges or immunities of any U.S. citizen, still, the Court decided in 1873 that this only applied to the federal government. When Congress passed public accommodation acts in subsequent years, those were struck down by the Court, too. That paved the way for Louisiana in 1890 to adopt an act that required all railway companies carrying passengers to provide "equal but separate accommodations for the white, and colored, races" (Hall, 2005, p. 739). This law mandated that passengers must sit in the sections designated for their race and that there would be a penalty that included jail time for any violation of this act.

When Homer Adolph Plessy, who was one-eighth black, tested this law by taking a seat in the whites-only section of a Louisiana Railway train, he was arrested. Plessy contended that the segregation law violated his rights under the Fourteenth Amendment (Newton, 2006). The case was appealed up to the U.S. Supreme Court in 1896. The Court ruled 7–1 to uphold the Louisiana statute, with Associate Justice John Marshall Harlan, the lone dissenter, writing a dissenting opinion. In his dissent, he wrote that "Our Constitution is color-blind, and neither knows nor tolerates classes among citizens ... In respect of civil rights, all citizens are equal before the law" (Newton, 2006, p. 294). Nonetheless, the separate but equal doctrine of *Plessy v. Ferguson* stood firm from 1896 until new school cases came before the Court in the 1950s.

The Reverend Oliver Brown filed suit against the Topeka, Kansas, Board of Education. Brown wanted to send his eight-year-old daughter, Linda, to a school closer to home. However, that school was reserved for whites only. That case, along with similar suits from Virginia and Delaware, a South Carolina case, and another from the District of Columbia, were all taken up by the Supreme Court and grouped together as *Brown v. Board of Education*—beginning in 1951. There were oral arguments in June 1951 and more in December 1952. Chief Justice Vinson sought to delay any decisions and perhaps lacked the vision or ability to unite the justices (Cray, 1997). Then, Vinson died, and Warren came on the Court.

Warren approached this case with the attitude that there was a simple decision to be made, mainly because he thought that separate but equal just didn't work and to continue *Plessy v. Ferguson* was to allow an injustice to continue (White, 1982). But beyond this, he recognized that a very real problem was that if *Plessy* was overturned, and segregation was outlawed in public schools by the Court, how exactly could this be implemented across the country?

But first, bringing his unique managerial style to bear in the position of chief justice, Warren desired to forge a unanimous decision. After the justices all voted and it was found that only one justice (Stanley Reed) was against overturning *Plessy*, Warren went to work on convincing Reed that it would be in the best interests of the country if there were a unanimous decision. When he was able to pull this off in *Brown v. Board of Education*, his presence on the Court was suddenly established. If it was apparent to those outside of the Supreme Court, it was equally apparent within the Court itself. The other justices found out that Earl Warren was a force to be reckoned with. At least in retrospect, though, it can also be seen that the *Brown* decision was the beginning of an activist Court that would support "liberal" policies; policies and positions that would be revealed as a theme of the Warren Court. Warren wanted to achieve the morally right results; he wanted results and decisions that were just. When he sensed pressure from justices that interfered with his idea of what was right and just, he could become very stubborn and a formidable opponent. This was a pattern that was part and parcel of his long experience as a leader. He disliked dissension, and he tended to dominate any office he held. He was not about to change his administrative style just because he was chief justice of the Supreme Court.

It was crystal clear within that first year that Earl Warren's Court would be active; it would uphold equality of opportunity for all citizens; and it would promote the cause of justice (White, 1982). In so doing, he moved away from Associate Justice Felix Frankfurter and moved closer to the liberal bloc on the Court, spearheaded by William O. Douglas and Hugo Black.

THE WARREN COMMISSION

After that fateful day in November 1963, after Earl Warren learned of the assassination of President John F. Kennedy, he initially asked his law clerk, Frank Beytagh, to drive him to Andrews Air Force Base to be present when the president's plane arrived. Warren felt it was his duty to be on hand to show the world the government and the nation were still carrying on (Newton, 2006). The very next evening, Jacqueline Kennedy called the chief justice's apartment and asked him to deliver one of the eulogies at the memorial service the next day. Warren readily agreed and then struggled to write a meaningful address. The next day, he spoke at the Capitol Rotunda, saying: "What moved some misguided wretch to do this horrible deed may never be known to us, but we do know that such acts are commonly stimulated by forces of hatred and malevolence, such as today are eating their way into the bloodstream of American life. What a price we pay for this fanaticism" (Cray, 1997, p. 414).

A week later, he would be approached by Solicitor General Archibald Cox and Acting Attorney General Nicholas Katzenbach to chair a commission to investigate and report on the assassination. After thinking about it for a few days, Warren declined, as it seemed to be a duty that would be too political (Cray, 1997). However, President Lyndon Johnson was not so easily put off. He called Warren to the White House and applied all the pressure he could muster to convince Warren that the country needed him to do this. Ultimately, when Johnson appealed to him in terms of what was good for the country, Warren capitulated (Newton, 2006). The agreement with the president was that he would remain at the Supreme Court, handling his usual duties there, he would have full cooperation from other governmental agencies, and he would receive whatever funding he needed to produce a report.

After putting together a prestigious committee, Warren would devote much of the succeeding ten months to the investigation, but, in effect, he had two full-time jobs during that period. The commission delivered its report to President Johnson on September 24, 1964. Early reviews and reactions were mostly positive (Newton, 2006), but public regard for the eight-hundred-plus pages of the Warren Commission Report was short lived. The commission concluded that Lee Harvey Oswald acted alone and was not part of a conspiracy. In his memoirs, Warren points out that with one exception—the assassination of Abraham Lincoln—all presidential assassinations have been carried out by mentally deranged individuals (Warren, 1977). Warren was convinced that the commission came to the right finding. Although he didn't live very long after that, he was aware that conspiracy theories abounded in the aftermath of the report, but what he would not live to learn was that those conspiracy theories would continue to flourish (and likely will continue since the release in October 2017 of JFK Assassination Records by the National Archives). What he said in his auto-

An Official Photograph of U.S. Supreme Court Chief Justice Earl Warren.

Harris & Ewing, https://commons
.wikimedia.org/wiki/File:CJ_Warren.tif.
Copyright in the Public Domain.

biography was that "Many people in this country believe in the conspiracy theory because they are of the opinion that a crime of this magnitude could not be committed by one disoriented man" (Warren, 1977, p. 363). He and his committee conducted hundreds of hours of testimony, collected thousands of pages of reports (from the CIA and the FBI, among various governmental agencies), and reviewed the autopsy, after which Warren wrote that there are "no facts upon which to hypothesize a conspiracy" (Warren, 1977, p. 366). One biographer (Jim Newton, 2006) has written that the Warren Commission Report has grown more solid over time and that today the findings of the commission are "beyond reasonable doubt" (Newton, 2006, p. 449).

LAW ENFORCEMENT AND CRIMINAL JUSTICE CASES

In the years after *Brown v. Board of Education*, under Warren's lead, the Supreme Court ruled segregation invalid in all public buildings, housing, transportation, and recreational and eating facilities. The Court steadfastly struck down every segregation law brought before it (Schwartz, 1983). Beyond what his Court was doing, Earl Warren was dealing with discrimination within the Supreme Court building itself. When he arrived at the Court, there was a separate bathroom for Negroes. He changed that very soon after he arrived. Furthermore, no one who worked for the Supreme Court was black, but again, that soon changed. By mid-1954, the Supreme Court had its first black page. That was followed by the hiring of black secretaries and law clerks. With Thurgood Marshall's appointment to the High Court in 1967, the Court itself was integrated (Schwartz, 1983).

In other areas of the law, the new chief justice moved more slowly. In the early years of his tenure, he sided mostly with the conservatives on the Court, usually supporting the government and law enforcement in criminal cases (Schwartz, 1983). Back when he was a prosecutor and district attorney, Warren was a rather tough-minded politician (White, 1982). However, in the course of his Supreme Court career, he was often characterized as soft on crime and inclined to protect criminals. He himself disagreed with this and said he had done nothing really wrong. He only insisted that a man has a right to counsel, is entitled to fair treatment at all times, and to due process in the trial of his case (White, 1982).

But he also thought that things had changed since he was a district attorney. The professional criminal of the Prohibition and Depression eras knew what he was doing and took his chances. The average criminal of the 1950s and 1960s, though, might have turned to crime because of disadvantages or because of degradation (Warren, 1977).

The criminal procedure cases coming before the Warren Court involved, from Warren's point of view, principles of fairness and equality that were all part of the Constitution. It was cases like *Irvine v. California*, which came up before the Court early in Warren's first year, that began to shape his thinking and activism. In this case, police officers secretly entered Irvine's house and planted a hidden microphone in the bedroom. Evidence from the hidden listening device was used to convict Irvine of bookmaking. In the appeal that came up to the Supreme Court, the conviction was challenged on the basis of an illegal search and seizure. Warren voted with the majority to uphold the conviction. However, that case bothered Warren, and later in his career, he indicated that had he to do it over again, he would vote differently (Schwartz, 1983).

But in 1954, he joined the majority in the *Hernandez v. Texas* case, in which the Court ruled that discrimination against defendants of Mexican background by seating a jury excluding Mexican Americans was wrong (Schwartz, 1983). For the most part, during his first year on the Court, Warren was influenced by the judicial restraint philosophy of Felix Frankfurter (Schwartz, 1983). As time went on, however, Warren and the rest of the justices rejected Frankfurter's federalism, based on the view that the Constitution did not impose the same limits on state and local law enforcement as it did on federal law enforcement (Belknap, 2005). Michael Belknap points out in his book *The Supreme Court Under Earl Warren: 1953–1969* (2005) that "Once he saw the American justice system from the vantage point of the Supreme Court, he was struck by the gap between the enlightened law enforcement that he favored and the inequality and coercion so common in many places" (p. 220).

Despite the fact that both Warren and his fellow justices tended to lean in a pro-prosecution direction, the early Warren Court made rulings that suggested a shift in the opposite direction. For instance, in the 1956 case of *Griffin v. Illinois*, a lower court ruled that the defendants, Judson Griffin and James Crenshaw, convicted of armed robbery, were not entitled to a copy of the trial record for an appeal. The defendants, both poor men, could not afford a transcript, and the lower court denied their request because it was not a capital case. The Supreme Court reversed the lower courts, contending that poverty should not be a factor in whether one had constitutional rights (Belknap, 2005). Belknap (2005) suggests that this case was a broadside in the shifting view of the Supreme Court. The Court clearly said in this case that there should be economic equality in the criminal process.

Another case, this one involving evidence seized without a warrant, again pointed toward a shift in terms of how the Court viewed illegally obtained evidence. The *Elkins v. United States* case was decided by the Court in 1960. Elkins had been convicted in a federal court of wiretapping. The evidence against Elkins was taken from his home by state police officers acting without a warrant (Schwartz, 1983). Warren voted with the majority to overturn the conviction. Just a year later, the seminal case of *Mapp v. Ohio* (1961) would present itself to Warren's Court.

Previously, in a 1949 decision (*Wolf v. Colorado*), the Supreme Court expanded some of the protections of the Fourth Amendment; however, it did not go so far as to apply those protections to the states. Specifically, the exclusionary rule (the rule that states that illegally obtained evidence may not be used against a defendant) was not applied to the states. *Mapp v. Ohio* was an opportunity to do just that. The *Mapp v. Ohio* case originated in Cleveland and concerned a situation in which police officers broke into the home of Dollree Mapp, claiming they had a search warrant. They told Ms. Mapp an informant had told them that a suspect wanted in a bombing was hiding in her home and that they had a tip that gambling paraphernalia was hidden there (Hall, 2005). In fact, an extensive search of her home revealed neither a suspect nor gambling equipment. What they did find were several allegedly obscene books and pictures. Ms. Mapp was arrested and convicted of the possession of obscene literature, and she was imprisoned (Hall, 2005).

Both in the Ohio Supreme Court and initially in the U.S. Supreme Court, the main issue seemed to be whether the state's possession-of-obscenity statute violated the First Amendment (Belknap, 2005). A majority was in favor of overturning Ms. Mapp's conviction on First Amendment grounds. However, U.S. Supreme Court justice Tom Clark, who wrote for the majority, changed the emphasis from the First Amendment to the Fourth Amendment. By so doing, *Wolf v. Colorado* was overruled, and the protections of the Fourth Amendment were now afforded to defendants in state courts (Schwartz, 1983).

Further Fourth Amendment cases were forthcoming to the Supreme Court. In 1961, the High Court ruled in *Silverman v. United States* that when the police drove a "spike mike" through the common wall separating the house of a gambling suspect from the row house next door, they had, in effect, conducted a warrantless search, which violated the Fourth Amendment (Belknap, 2005). Then, the High Court held in *Berger v. New York* (1967) that a New York State law authorizing the ex parte order for eavesdropping was unconstitutional. Later that same year, in deciding *Katz v. United States* (1967), the Supreme Court held that the FBI had violated the Fourth Amendment rights of a suspect by attaching a listening and recording device to the outside of a public telephone booth without first obtaining a search warrant (Belknap, 2005).

The rights of citizens protected by the Sixth Amendment were also the subject of important decisions by Warren's Court. One of the most famous of these cases was *Gideon v. Wainwright* (1963). According to some observers, the Court was looking for an opportunity to overrule a 1942 Supreme Court decision in *Betts v. Brady*. That decision held that a state defendant had a constitutional right to appointed counsel only if his or her case involved special circumstances. In actuality, as some of the Court's justices were aware, almost no cases ever qualified under the *Betts* ruling (Belknap, 2005). The case of Clarence Earl Gideon was the right case at the right time. The circumstances of the case were simple. Clarence Earl Gideon, an uneducated Florida man, was charged with breaking into a poolroom with intent to commit a misdemeanor, which was a felony under Florida law (Hall, 2005). Since he had no funds for an attorney, Gideon requested that the court appoint a lawyer for him. Florida's trial court refused because it was not a capital case. Gideon thus was forced to defend himself. The jury convicted Gideon, and he was sent to prison.

Availing himself of the prison's library, Gideon learned how to file a habeas corpus petition, sending it to the Florida Supreme Court. That court denied him relief, and next Gideon wrote out an appeal in longhand to the U.S. Supreme Court (Hall, 2005). The Court voted to hear his case and assigned a prominent Washington, D.C., attorney, Abe Fortas (who would later become an associate justice of the Supreme Court) to represent Gideon in oral arguments before the High Court. The main question that was argued before the Court was whether *Betts v. Brady* should be overruled (Hall, 2005). Voting unanimously, Warren's Court ruled that *Betts* should be overturned, and that the Sixth Amendment, as applied to the states by the Fourteenth Amendment, should apply to defendants in state court trials when charged with a serious offense (Hall, 2005). Justice Hugo Black wrote for the Court and declared "that in our adversary system of criminal justice, any person hauled into court, who is too poor to hire a lawyer, cannot be assured a fair trial unless counsel is provided for him" (Belknap, 2005, p. 236).

A few years later, the Supreme Court held in *United States v. Wade* (1967) that the accused is entitled to counsel at a lineup, because that is a critical stage in a criminal prosecution.

Although the *Wade* case had more to do with the right to be represented by counsel, it was also related to confessions that were made during incarceration—often without any legal representation. It was one of the features of the criminal justice system that evoked the most emotion for Warren. In 1959, in the case *Spano v. New York*, Earl Warren wrote the majority opinion, reversing a conviction in a confession case. Mr. Spano was a suspect in a murder investigation. He had surrendered to a district attorney in New York, and before his lawyer left, he cautioned Mr. Spano to answer no questions (Belknap, 2005). Upon his lawyer leaving the building, Mr. Spano was subjected to eight hours of intensive police interrogation, after which a confession was obtained. Warren wrote the majority opinion overturning the conviction. The ethical principle for Warren in *Spano* was that the police must "obey the law while enforcing the law" (White, 1982, p. 266). Not only in this case but in others, Warren believed that police behavior in questioning suspects was often unjust and that such police behavior robbed citizens of their dignity and humanity. To the chief justice, many of the criminal justice decisions of the Court were mostly aimed at police and police procedures; they were not rulings that allowed guilty people to go free. As White (1982) suggests, Warren perceived law enforcement cases not as efforts to cripple the police, but to rid law enforcement of its coercive and unethical features. This can be seen in several other monumental cases that came from Warren's Court.

The first of two such cases relating to interrogation and the right to have an attorney present was *Escobedo v. Illinois* in 1964. In this case, the Court ruled that individuals have the constitutional right to counsel as soon as the police focus on a person as a suspect and begin questioning at police headquarters (Schwartz, 1983). In this case, the evidence used to convict Danny Escobedo of murder included an incriminating statement and eventually a confession after he had been subjected to lengthy and perhaps deceptive questioning by Chicago detectives (Belknap, 2005). Escobedo, who had little previous experience with law enforcement, was never advised of his constitutional rights, and although he repeatedly asked to talk to his attorney (who was present in the police department trying to see his client), he was not allowed to consult with his lawyer (Hall, 2005). Convicted in a subsequent trial, Escobedo was sentenced to prison. But the Supreme Court, after listening to oral arguments, voted to reverse his conviction. In the opinion written by Associate Justice Arthur Goldberg, the Court held that refusing to allow Escobedo to talk to his attorney was a denial of assistance of counsel, and this was a violation of his Sixth Amendment rights (Belknap, 2005).

Escobedo raised questions about what standards police needed to meet in order to conduct a constitutionally valid interrogation. Although as many pundits, including *Time* magazine, suggested, legislation should spell out the standards for the police rather than depending on future court cases to define those standards. However, politicians engaged in taking potshots at the Supreme Court rather than enacting laws to regulate police procedures (Belknap, 2005).

The second case, even more famous than the *Escobedo* case, was *Miranda v. Arizona* (1966). Another confession case, this one concerned Ernesto Miranda, an indigent, twenty-three-year-old man living in Phoenix, Arizona. Accused of kidnapping and rape, he was arrested and transported to a Phoenix police station (Hall, 2005). There, Miranda was placed in an interrogation room, where he was questioned for two hours, and after this interrogation, the police emerged from the room with a signed, written confession of guilt (Hall, 2005). In a split decision, with Chief Justice Earl Warren writing the majority opinion, the Court reversed Miranda's conviction. A suspect, Warren wrote, must be given an opportunity to have a lawyer present before interrogation begins, unless the person knowingly and intelligently waives that right. Furthermore, the burden of proof that there had been such a waiver is on the prosecution. Also, a suspect must be given the now-familiar four-part "Miranda" warning that begins, "You have the right to remain silent ..." (Hall, 2005). Warren wrote: "Prior to any questioning, the person must be warned that he has a right to remain silent, that any statement he does make may be used as evidence against him, and that he has a right to the presence of an attorney, either retained or appointed" (Belknap, 2005, pp. 245–246).

Although in one other case (*Terry v. Ohio*, 1968), the Warren Court gave latitude for police officers to do stop-and-frisks based on reasonable suspicion, the public and the law enforcement community tended to be outraged over both *Escobedo* and *Miranda*. Los Angeles police chief William Parker accused the Supreme Court of "handcuffing the police" (Belknap, 2005, p. 243). Former New York police chief Michael Murphy was vocal in stating his belief that the High Court was "unduly hampering the administration of criminal justice" (Belknap, 2005, p. 243). And the 1964 Republican presidential standard bearer, Barry Goldwater, used these decisions in his campaign, railing against those who were soft on crime and blaming the Supreme Court for a breakdown of law and order (Belknap, 2005). The emotional torrent unleashed by the *Miranda* decision was perhaps even greater than the storm following *Escobedo*. Police officers believed that the end of effective policing had arrived (Schwartz, 1983). North Carolina senator Sam Ervin criticized the ruling, saying that the Court's action emboldened criminals while at the same time curtailing the police, and all at the expense of victims (Schwartz, 1983).

Earl Warren, of course, did not see himself as playing a part in undermining law enforcement. Instead, he saw the decisions of his Court as ennobling law enforcement (White, 1982). In fact, he was of the opinion that the Supreme Court's decisions related to criminal justice and police procedures made law enforcement a stronger profession.

WARREN'S THEORY OF JUDGING

In his well-written biography of Earl Warren in 1982, Edward White argues that Warren thought of the U.S. Constitution as embodying the values Warren himself believed in. In addition, to Warren, the Constitution granted judges, like himself, the power to protect those values. From his point of view, the Constitution's imperatives for the Court were ethical imperatives (White, 1982). His own ethical imperatives reflected his personal morality, in that he held a set of values that he believed represented moral truths about decent and civilized life. The rights enumerated in the Constitution were simply the "natural rights of man." He believed that the protections afforded by the Bill of Rights could be applied to new situations and to do so was necessary in the pursuit of justice. The pursuit of justice, as Warren defined it, was thus a "continuing direction for our daily conduct" (White, 1982, p. 223).

Earl Warren assumed that the Bill of Rights necessarily changed with time, and thus it needed revisions with time. "We will pass on," Warren said, "a document that will not have exactly the same meaning it had when we received it from our fathers. But, it would be a better Bill of Rights that will be burnished by growing use and it would be a worse one if neglected" (White, 1982, p. 224).

From the beginning of his sixteen years on the Supreme Court when he was confronted with *Brown v. Board of Education*, Warren's ethical and moral beliefs came into play. For example, he believed that the practice of racial segregation in the public schools, based on assumptions of racial superiority, were immoral and therefore wrong. The Supreme Court's duty was to eradicate this wrong. In *Brown v. Board of Education*, as in so many other cases, his sense of the fairness or justice of a case was crucial to his ultimate decision. But so, too, was the concept of decency, one of Warren's cherished values. Decency, he thought, was basic to a civilized society, and he had a simple test for decency. Decency, Warren believed, was what people of average sensibility would recognize as wholesome and upright conduct (White, 1982). So, using this definition, a number of activities would be indecent because they appealed to mankind's baser instincts and dissuaded people from living wholesome and honorable lives. Gambling, prostitution, bootlegging, drug dealing, trafficking in pornographic materials—all, to Earl Warren, were indecent activities.

When it came to obscenity issues and cases, Warren took a rather paternalistic approach. To him, pornographers were common criminals, and their activities warranted vigorous prosecution. But he was also dubious about the value of governmental regulation of pornography. That, he thought, would lead to governmental censorship.

THE LAST YEARS OF EARL WARREN

After Felix Frankfurter retired in 1962, and after first Arthur Goldberg and then Abe Fortas succeeded the long-time justice, Warren found himself in the majority of a number of equal justice cases. These included *Loving v. Virginia*, *Harper v. Virginia Board of Elections*, *James v. Maryland*, *Escobedo v. Illinois*, and *Miranda v. Arizona*.

In spite of the criticism of his Court's rulings, in the 1960s and 1970s, a number of commentators regarded Earl Warren as one of the greatest justices ever to serve on the U.S. Supreme Court. Maybe, some contended, such as Associate Justice Thurgood Marshall, he was the best chief justice we ever had (Belknap, 2005). But in March 1966, Warren turned seventy-five. Two years later, in June 1968, he informed President Johnson, first in person and then by letter, that he intended to resign from the Supreme Court. He did, in fact, retire in June 1969.

In retirement, Warren's time was given over to speeches, ceremonies, visits to the Supreme Court chambers, lectures, conferences, and pleasure trips, including trips to visit his family members. But he also had begun writing his memoirs, which no retired chief justice had ever done before. When his autobiography was published (Warren, 1977), they revealed few facts about the inner workings of the Supreme Court. He apparently didn't want to hurt others or expose himself. Nor, as it turned out, was there much about his personal feelings or his relationships with his wife and children.

With *The Memoirs of Chief Justice Earl Warren* written, it was time to pay attention to his health, which had been slowly declining over the years. He had an operation for stomach cancer in 1951, although afterward his health remained generally sound, despite his constant battle with a weight problem. But in 1972, he began to experience angina pectoris and was found to have some blocked arteries. Two years later, Warren experienced chest pains and was hospitalized in California for a week, where angina and coronary artery disease were diagnosed. The doctors advised him to cut back on his activities, which he did. But in May 1974, he was again hospitalized after experiencing chest pains. On July 2 of that year, he was admitted to a hospital with congestive heart failure. Earl Warren died on July 9, 1974, of cardiac arrest.

His body lay in state in the foyer of the Supreme Court Building—the first time such a ceremony had taken place on the death of a Supreme Court justice. Ironically, his enemy, President Richard Nixon, attended his funeral and then resigned the presidency on August 9, 1974. Earl Warren was buried on July 12, 1974, with military honors at Arlington National Ceremony.

THE LEGACY OF EARL WARREN

One of Earl Warren's core beliefs was that public office should be treated as a public trust. That belief, which he modeled daily in his own life as a public servant, serves as a benchmark for others who serve the public. He was one—perhaps one of a very few major public servants—who believed that the future would be better than the past, that public morality and private morality were the same, and that under the American system of government, justice would eventually prevail.

Edward White (1982) writes that there are three words that might best describe Warren and his legacy: morality, patriotism, and progress. The restoration of morality in American life was an abiding theme in his career. He believed that the eradication of crime was possible by improving the conditions of our citizens and by getting rid of ghettos; and by ensuring that every youngster is afforded a decent education and given some skill by which he can compete in the marketplace. Crime, he believed, was a social condition that could be reduced by the elimination of the environmental factors that encouraged its growth.

As chief justice of the United States, he retained the Progressives' belief in affirmative government. He sought to shift the focus of affirmative government action to the federal judiciary. In addition, he tended to extend his commitment to civil rights and civil liberties well past the point that most Progressives were prepared to go. In his role on the Supreme Court, Warren cast controversies in ethical terms, identified instances of injustice, and sought to use the power of his office to provide a remedy. All in all, he functioned on the Court much as he had as governor. That is, he identified needed reforms and sought to undermine the positions of those opposing reforms by emphasizing that their opposition perpetuated injustices.

The principal criticism of Warren as a judge was directed at his interpretation of his office rather than on the substance of his results (White, 1982). Anthony Lewis (1969) said of him that he was "The closest thing the United States has had to a Platonic Guardian, dispensing law from a throne without any sense of the limits of power except what was seen as the good of society. Fortunately, he was a decent ... honorable, democratic Guardian" (pp. 2726–2727).

Without a doubt, Warren was one of the major figures in twentieth-century American history, and as such, as chief justice of the Supreme Court, he dramatically altered the legal relationship between blacks and whites in America. In so doing, he contributed a profound shift in the way Americans thought about race and skin color as a determinant of worth.

Edward White contends that Warren's greatest strengths and most memorable qualities were intangibles: presence, capacity for growth, persuasiveness, inner conviction, decency, persistence, and reasonableness (White, 1982). And, as Bernard Schwartz (1983) confirms, Earl Warren was capable of growth and change. It was said that he at one time was a racially biased attorney general of California who changed to become a world leader in the fight for universal brotherhood (Schwartz, 1983). That speaks well for him that he could grow. In fact, Alan Barth, a civil libertarian, concluded that Warren grew "prodigiously" (Schwartz, 1983, p. 489).

He presided over a historic Supreme Court that thoroughly transformed American constitutional law (Horwitz, 1998). The range of the Warren Court's influence, as Harvard law professor Morton J. Horwitz has written, was enormous, as it initiated a revolution in race relations; expanded the guarantee of equal protection under the law; increased the protections of freedom of speech and of the press; improved constitutional protections for defendants in criminal cases; and recognized a constitutional right to privacy (Horwitz, 1998).

But perhaps a more fitting tribute to the man who would engineer changes in our society could not be found than a quote from Associate Justice William O. Douglas: "I like to think that the spirit of Earl Warren is abroad in this land, quickening the conscience of our people" (Douglas, 1980, p. 241).

QUESTIONS FOR DISCUSSION

1. Did Earl Warren begin his Supreme Court career with a pro–law enforcement bias or an anti–law enforcement bias?
2. What were the personal qualities that made Earl Warren succeed as a leader in every administrative position he held?
3. What caused the shift in Warren's position from a Supreme Court justice who supported law enforcement to a justice who championed placing limits and restraints on law enforcement procedures?
4. What role did Warren's Progressive philosophies play in the criminal justice cases in which he voted?

IMPORTANT TERMS

Exclusionary rule: This rule has established that any evidence obtained by law enforcement officers in violation of a suspect's Fourth Amendment rights cannot be used against them in a criminal trial.

Progressivism: Progressivism began as a social movement near the end of the nineteenth century and became a political point of view. Not only did

Progressives look for practical solutions to the problems in society, but they believed that a good education, a safe environment, and an efficient workplace could help overcome many of society's ills. In addition, Progressives were concerned about corporate greed and public corruption.

Warren Commission: The Warren Commission was appointed by President Lyndon Johnson a week after the assassination of President John F. Kennedy. Headed by Chief Justice Earl Warren, the purpose of the commission was to determine the facts concerning the assassination. After nearly a year-long investigation, the Warren Commission submitted its report, concluding that Lee Harvey Oswald acted alone in killing President Kennedy.

FOR FURTHER READING

Compston, C. (2001). *Earl Warren: Justice for all*. New York, NY: Oxford University Press.

Newton, J. (2006). *Justice for all: Earl Warren and the nation he made*. New York, NY: Riverhead Books.

Powe, L. A. (2000). *The Warren Court and American politics*. Cambridge, MA: Belknap Press.

Scheiber, H. N. (Ed.). (2007). *Earl Warren and the Warren Court*. Lanham, MA: Lexington Books.

Schwartz, B. (1983). *Super chief: Earl Warren and his Supreme Court, a judicial biography*. New York, NY: New York University Press.

Warren, E. (1977). *The memoirs of Chief Justice Earl Warren*. New York, NY: Doubleday & Co., Inc.

REVIEW QUESTIONS

True or False

1. Early in his career, Earl Warren found his first love was law enforcement.
2. As governor of California, Warren was not interested in prison reform.
3. When Earl Warren became chief justice of the Supreme Court, the Court itself was deeply divided.
4. Early in his career as chief justice, Earl Warren sided with the government and leaned toward supporting law enforcement.

5. One reason that Earl Warren began voting for placing limits and restrictions on police behavior was because he saw the police acting in ways that were coercive and unjust.

Multiple Choice

6. *Mapp v. Ohio* (1961) was a case in which Earl Warren's Court decided to apply
   a. The protections of the First Amendment to individuals.
   b. The exclusionary rule to states.
   c. The Fourth Amendment protections to federal defendants.
   d. The First Amendment protections to police officers.

7. Under Warren's stewardship, the Supreme Court decided many cases in which there were issues concerning
   a. The Fourth Amendment.
   b. The Sixth Amendment.
   c. The Eighth Amendment.
   d. All of the above.

8. In overturning the conviction of Clarence Earl Gideon in 1963, the Supreme Court ruled that
   a. Anyone facing the death penalty was entitled to legal counsel.
   b. Anyone charged with a misdemeanor was entitled to a lawyer.
   c. Anyone who was rich was entitled to an attorney.
   d. Anyone facing serious charges was entitled to legal counsel.

9. A major factor influencing Earl Warren in confession cases was Warren's growing understanding that
   a. Police behavior during interrogations needed to be tough.
   b. Police behavior during interrogations should not be too physical.
   c. Police behavior during interrogations often robbed citizens of their dignity and respect.
   d. Police behavior during interrogations should use the good-cop-versus-bad-cop approach.

10. Both *Escobedo v. Illinois* (1964) and *Miranda v. Arizona* (1966) were concerned with
    a. The right of a suspect to have an attorney present during interrogation.
    b. The right to refuse to answer any and all police questions.
    c. The right to legal counsel only after going to trial.
    d. The right of a suspect to be treated with dignity and respect during an arrest.

11. While there was a firestorm of criticism leveled at Earl Warren and the Supreme Court following some of the criminal justice rulings of the 1960s, including both *Escobedo* and *Miranda*, Earl Warren held the belief that
    a. The rulings his Court made produced a stronger police profession.
    b. The rulings of his Court would lead to his impeachment.
    c. The rulings of his Court would reduce the status of police officers.
    d. The rulings of his Court would embolden criminals.

12. Earl Warren's Court literally transformed American constitutional law. His Court
    a. Initiated a revolution in race relations.
    b. Increased the protections of free speech and a free press.
    c. Improved the protections for criminal defendants.
    d. All of the above.

REFERENCES

Belknap, M. R. (2005). *The Supreme Court under Earl Warren: 1953–1969*. Columbia, SC: University of South Carolina Press.

Cray, E. (1997). *Chief justice: A biography of Earl Warren*. New York, NY: Simon & Schuster.

Douglas, W. O. (1980). *The court years: 1939–1975. The autobiography of William O. Douglas*. New York, NY: Random House.

Hall, K. (Ed.). (2005). *The Oxford guide to the Supreme Court*. New York, NY: Oxford University Press.

Horwitz, M. J. (1998). *The Warren court and the pursuit of justice*. New York, NY: Hill and Wang.

Lewis, A. (1969). Earl Warren. In L. Friedman & F. Israel (Eds.), *The justices of the United States Supreme Court: Their lives and major opinions* (pp. 2726–2727). New York, NY: Chelsea House.

Newton, J. (2006). *Justice for all: Earl Warren and the nation he made*. New York, NY: Riverhead Books.

Schwartz, B. (1983). *Super chief: Earl Warren and his Supreme Court, a judicial biography*. New York, NY: New York University Press.

Warren, E. (1977). *The memoirs of Chief Justice Earl Warren*. New York. NY: Doubleday & Co., Inc.

White, G. E. (1982). *Earl Warren: A public life*. New York, NY: Oxford New Press.

10

CLARENCE DARROW
The First Great Defense Attorney

He was born in Kinsman, Ohio, on April 18, 1857, the fifth child of Amirus Darrow and Emily Eddy Darrow. But the rustic town of Kinsman would not be able to hold on to Clarence Darrow for very long, for he was destined to become a nationally known attorney who would command the world's attention as he defended some of the most notorious criminal defendants during the first three decades of the twentieth century.

Unlike his father, Amirus, a poor, but bright, man who loved books but had no special abilities for making a living, Clarence would grow up to have a unique talent for making a living. Not that he rejected his father's values. Clarence once wrote that his father was the village infidel and over time accepted, and perhaps even took delight in, his reputation. Darrow commented that he had no doubt that his father always thought he was right (Tierney, 1979). In his autobiography, Darrow wrote that he was mainly the product of his mother "Who helped to shape the wanton instincts of the child" (Darrow, 1996, p. 17), but he acknowledges that he was also influenced by the "gentle, kindly, loving human man whose presence was with me for so many years" (p. 17). In some ways, he emulated his father, whether consciously or not. For instance, Clarence would grow up with a deep moral commitment and the courage of his convictions. And, in fact, as Clarence Darrow grew into adulthood, his suspicions of popular opinion, his attraction to heresy, and his dislike of established authority—all came from observing his father (Tierney, 1979). Perhaps the greatest quality he would inherit from his father was the capability of standing up to the crowd and not being swayed by the opinion of others.

Also, because of his father's love of books, Clarence grew up surrounded by books. And while Clarence never enjoyed formal education, he was captivated by what he read in books. He loved reading Voltaire, for instance, whose rationalism had a strong influence on his intellectual development. But his wide-ranging interests included the writings of the agnostic, Robert Green Ingersoll, whose pursuits—as a speaker, political leader, and a man who poked fun at conventional religious beliefs—was so very much like Darrow's own interests and later activities. Both Ingersoll and Voltaire provided a foundation in rational thinking, but in time Darrow also was influenced by the writings on Marxist economics and Darwinian determinism (Tierney, 1979).

Although he attended the preparatory school of Allegheny College, by the age of sixteen, Clarence Darrow's formal education ended, except for a year of law school. But before law school, he took a job as a school teacher in Vernon, Ohio, which was about seven miles away from Kinsman. He taught for three years before his father and his older sister Mary encouraged (or more likely insisted) him to attend the University of Michigan Law School. Both Amirus and Mary had attended what was not yet a law school but a law department at the University of Michigan, and in 1877, Clarence was off to Ann Arbor to study law.

As was often the custom in those days, Darrow didn't stay long at law school, but departed after a year to get a practical education in law in a practicing attorney's office. However, his short stay at the University of Michigan emphasized personal characteristics. First, he was no scholar; second, he was not well disciplined and could not apply himself to study (Darrow, 1996). Those traits showed up at various times in his life, and were responsible for him spending just a few months in a law office in Youngstown, Ohio. He was anxious to get out in the world and apply his skills as a lawyer, but first he had to take the bar exam. At age twenty-one he passed the exam and now felt he was ready to practice law.

GETTING STARTED AND GETTING MARRIED

On April 15, 1880, Darrow and Jessie Ohl, a girl he had grown up with in Kinsman, were married. They immediately moved to Andover, Ohio, where they expected he could set up a law practice and make a living.

He quickly realized that was not an easy thing to do and that he needed to make contacts and get his name known. One way to do this was to offer his services as a public speaker and another way was to become involved in politics. By 1883, he was a speaker in the Andover area, and he joined the Democratic Party. When later that year Jessie gave birth to a son, Paul Edward Darrow, that provided more reason to find a way to supplement his meager earnings from his fledgling law practice. Because of his developing political connections, he decided to run for the city solicitor position in Ashtabula, Ohio. He was successful, becoming city solicitor in April 1885. This job would provide him with a regular income.

Darrow quickly learned some things that would help determine his destiny. First, he learned that he enjoyed going to court and pleading for his clients. Second, he discovered that this kind of work increased his self-confidence. Third, he found that he got immense satisfaction from fighting hard and winning for clients. And finally, he learned that he was at his best when he put his heart and soul into his client's cause (Tierney, 1979).

Around this time, because of his interest in politics, he began reading the writings of John Peter Altgeld, a judge and later a governor of Illinois. One of the first things he read by Altgeld was a short book titled *Our Penal Machinery and Its Victims*. Published in 1886, the book was an attempt to change prevailing attitudes toward crime, and although Altgeld rejected the current explanations that viewed crime as caused by the innate sinfulness of criminals, he also called for a closer examination of the causes of criminal behavior (Joshi, 2005). The book impressed Darrow, and he would remember its influence on him for a long time. He was quoted as saying that until reading that book, he had a conventional view of crime and criminals. He thought that criminals were somewhat different from other men; that they were evil and malignant, choosing very consciously a way of life. Darrow had never considered that a person's environment might play a role in a criminal's behavior (Tierney, 1979).

As Darrow gained more self-confidence and looked at his prospects in Ashtabula, he began to see that there were limits on what he could achieve by staying where he was. Somewhat impulsively, he decided that he and his family should move to Chicago, which they did in 1887. He believed that although the competition among lawyers would be fiercer in Chicago, so, too, were the opportunities. And so, too, he would quickly discover was the corruption in politics. What he saw was far different from what he experienced in small cities in northern Ohio. But he also recognized that this was a way of life in Chicago, and he came to accept that graft and corruption were an aspect of doing political business. However, to Darrow, corruption in business and politics was morally indistinguishable from the kind of ordinary criminality that got poor people sent to prison (Tierney, 1979). In his biography of Darrow, Tierney makes the point that Clarence Darrow liked politicians and had difficulty with the concept of punishing them for their dishonesty. Therefore, he came to the somewhat surprising conclusion that nobody should be punished (Tierney, 1979).

In the course of working in the Democratic Party, Darrow soon became acquainted with John Peter Altgeld, and, finding him a congenial mentor, he became a faithful supporter of him. This did not go unnoticed by Altgeld, who made sure that Darrow was able to obtain a patronage job in the Chicago City Hall. But Darrow was also attending meetings and lectures and always took advantage of opportunities to speak or debate topics. By 1888, it dawned on Darrow that he had the ability to cast a spell over an audience, and he possessed the capability of impressing people who listened to him give speeches or heard him voice his opinions. One of those people was Chicago's mayor, DeWitt Cregier. So impressed was Mayor Cregier that he offered Darrow the job of special assessment attorney for the city of Chicago. Darrow immediately accepted.

The job of special assessment attorney involved looking after the legal aspects of the city, building new roads and improving existing streets. Generally, Darrow's job was to work with citizens and property owners who were distressed by the city taking their property and charging them fees. He was so successful at this that he was quickly assigned the position of assistant corporation counsel for the city. This job soon led to him being named acting corporation counsel. While busy in the work of helping to manage the city's business, Darrow was also active in Altgeld's campaign for state governor. But when Cregier was defeated as Chicago's mayor in the next election, Darrow knew he would soon be out of a job. However,

Altgeld came through, helping him secure a position as an attorney in the law department for the Chicago and Northwestern Railway (Farrell, 2011).

Being a lawyer for the Chicago and Northwestern Railway was a busy job and demanded that Darrow juggle many different assignments at the same time. He loved this kind of frenetic life style; however, this way of living caused serious problems for his marriage to Jessie. She liked his financial success and the house they lived in, but she wanted a husband who did more than drop in occasionally to sleep (Tierney, 1979).

THE EUGENE PRENDERGAST CASE

On October 28, 1893, Chicago mayor Carter Harrison was shot to death by a man named Patrick Eugene Prendergast. Somehow, Prendergast was operating under the delusion that he was due the job of city corporation counsel. The outrage of the citizens over this assassination made Clarence Darrow fearful about the angry mob mentality of the people, and that this poor, demented Patrick Prendergast would not only be found guilty but also be condemned to death (Farrell, 2011).

By this point in his life, Clarence Darrow was a strong opponent of capital punishment and was moving toward a point of view that legal accountability for a crime was based on a false assumption. That fallacious assumption was that there was moral blameworthiness (Tierney, 1979). People like Prendergast, he believed, could not be held accountable for their actions because they were sick, not immoral.

Consulting two of Chicago's best-known attorneys, Darrow came to the conclusion that the only hope for Prendergast was for him to be declared insane. The insane could not be executed. Along with one of the two attorneys he met with, James S. Harlan, it was announced that the two of them—Harlan and Darrow—would challenge Prendergast's sanity at a special inquest (Farrell, 2011). Nonetheless, despite the best efforts of Darrow and Harlan, Prendergast was found by a judge to be sane, and his hanging was set for July 13, 1894. Darrow appealed to his friend, Governor Altgeld, to pardon Prendergast, but Altgeld refused. Patrick Prendergast was hanged on July 13, 1894.

THE PULLMAN STRIKE

Happening at almost the same time as the Prendergast case was the strike against the railway companies brought on by the Pullman Company reducing workers' wages but resisting lowering the rent Pullman charged the company's employees for living in the city Pullman created for its employees. Then, the Pullman Company began to fire employees. The railway union refused to allow their members to work on trains if a Pullman car was attached. In response to this strike, President Grover Cleveland sent federal troops to Chicago, which was the hub of most railway lines, to keep order (although there was apparently no disorder) (Tierney, 1979).

Clarence Darrow was well aware of the situation, and he was sympathetic to the strikers' cause. This despite the fact that he worked for a railway company. Feeling he needed to get involved, Darrow went to the president of the Chicago and Northwestern Railway and offered his resignation. However, the president supported his desire to get involved, and although he accepted his resignation, he kept him on half pay (which actually continued for several years). He also offered to continue to send him business.

When labor leader Eugene V. Debs was arrested in connection with the Pullman strike, Darrow had a significant reason to get involved; he took on the defense of Debs. In so doing, he realized his voice and his true calling. He showed to himself and others that he was a passionate, radical advocate for Eugene Debs, as well as for the working-class laborer. This case revealed, to himself and others, that he could be a fiery advocate who could spew venomous remarks toward the prosecution and directly at prosecution witnesses. By taking on the case of *United States v. Debs*, Clarence Darrow took advantage of another opportunity, this time to practice his courtroom technique—a technique that he would use many times in the future to defend labor leaders and others. His strong style was described as an acrimonious duel to the death that brooked no compromise (Tierney, 1979).

Despite his style, Darrow could not successfully defend Debs, but even in defeat, Darrow became the romantic hero of the labor movement.

Recognizing that he had developed a broad political base, Darrow ran for a seat in the House of Representatives in 1896. However, with William Jennings Bryan heading up the Democratic ticket for president against the Republican William McKinley, Bryan and other Democrats like Clarence Darrow were soundly trounced by Republicans. That seemed to end Darrow's political career, at least for the time being.

But that also meant returning to a private law practice, which he found, for the most part, mundane and uninteresting, especially when he was not in court.

DARROW'S LIFESTYLE AND DIVORCE

Working on the Prendergast case and defending Eugene Debs was exciting work, though it was work that kept him away from home. Jessie was interested in their home and family, not in Clarence's work. While she wanted her husband at home, he usually preferred to be elsewhere. He knew this and finally approached her about a divorce. However, ever the supportive wife, she told him that if she filed against him on the basis of desertion, it would do irreparable damage to his career. Better that he file accusing her of desertion. He agreed and filed for a divorce, which she did not contest. They were divorced in 1897. Jessie got the house, $25,000, and Clarence agreed to pay her $150 a month for the rest of her life (Farrell, 2011).

Free of the constraints of marriage, Clarence Darrow was now forty-nine years old, and he could pursue his life in his own way. As told in some detail in John A. Farrell's biography, *Clarence Darrow: Attorney for the Damned* (2011), for the next six years, Darrow embarked on the life of a bachelor in which he had relationships with other women while advocating the virtues of free love. Also, it was during this period in his life when he wanted to become an author and to become accepted as a writer. However, Darrow didn't have either the discipline or the talent to be a writer of books, but he was resourceful enough to come up with a plan to overcome these deficits. He decided he would have his closing arguments to juries published, since it was clear that his major talent was speaking. By publishing his long closing arguments, it would be like writing a book.

To that end, in 1898, Darrow accepted the defense of Thomas I. Kidd of the Amalgamated Woodworkers' International Union (AWIU). Kidd was charged with criminal activities related to his strike-organizing efforts at the Paine Lumber Company in Oak Brook, Illinois. Specifically, Kidd was charged with criminal conspiracy to interfere with the business of the lumber company by organizing a strike. In exchange for the AWIU agreeing to publish his closing argument after the trial, Darrow accepted the case for a lower fee (Farrell, 2011).

The Kidd case gave Darrow a chance to refine some of the techniques he had used in past cases. He continued to make venomous attacks on one or more persons on the side of the prosecution, but he honed his overall approach in terms of how he addressed the jury and how he presented the case. His approach was developing into one in which he ranged well beyond the facts of the case, sensing that facts often got in the way of presenting the point of view of the defense. An effective defense, he concluded, meant not getting bogged down with too much detail about the evidence. Instead, he could argue from theory and principle while describing the social context of the case (Tierney, 1979). In defense of Kidd, he told the jury point blank that his main concern was not Thomas I. Kidd. Rather, he was asking the jury to acquit Kidd as a vindication of a general principle; in this case, that general principle centered around whether unions were good for society. In the Kidd case, as in subsequent cases, he invited the jury to ignore all of the evidence brought forth in the trial and to simply consider whether workers had a right to strike (Tierney, 1979).

The jury, after listening to Darrow's persuasive arguments, deliberated for less than an hour before acquitting Kidd and his codefendants. As a result, Darrow's reputation continued to grow among labor unions, and, perhaps more importantly to Darrow, his final address to the jury was published as a pamphlet and received wide circulation. What wasn't so widely publicized was that Darrow was only a co-counsel for the defense and that addresses to the jury were also made by his co-counsel and, of course, by the prosecution. Clarence Darrow got the publicity, thus making it appear that he stood alone defending the rights of the working man. What also was never brought to the public's attention was that his published jury addresses were often edited by Darrow and were sometimes significantly altered from the original closing remarks (Tierney, 1979). That never seemed to bother him.

HIS SON PAUL AND A PROFOUND LOSS

When Darrow and Jessie were divorced, his son Paul told his father he never wanted to see him again. However, when Paul became an adolescent, Darrow discovered a new-found interest in his son. One of Darrow's hopes was that Paul would follow in his footsteps and go into law or politics. In addition, he hoped his son would adopt the same point of view on social and political issues. However, Paul was of a different temperament. Not only did he lean toward a more conservative philosophy, but he was also more interested in business—not law or politics. In later years, father and son would reconcile, and Paul would help his father with investments.

Recognizing that his son was walking down a different path was not the greatest loss Clarence Darrow would endure. Perhaps the most profound loss he would experience came after March 1902, when his mentor and friend, John Peter Altgeld, died. Up to his death, for nearly fifteen years prior to that, Darrow had almost daily conversations with Altgeld, discussing various aspects of law and politics.

Paying tribute to him at his funeral, Darrow said: "My dear, dead friend, long and well have we known you, devotedly have we followed you, implicitly have we trusted you, fondly have we loved you … But, though we lay you in the grave and hide you from the sight of man, your brave words will speak for the poor, the oppressed, the captive and the weak; and your devoted life inspire countless souls to do and dare in the holy cause for which you lived and died" (Darrow, 1996, p. 487).

POLITICAL CAREER REVIVED

Although his loss in the House of Representative elections several years before had seemingly ended his political ambitions, in November 1902, Darrow gave in to requests and became a candidate for the Illinois House of Representatives. This time, however, he was elected. He served out his term, saw both the good and bad sides of politicians, and in the process decided that this kind of politics was not for him. He noted in his autobiography that while he served in Springfield, Illinois, he conscientiously tried to serve all the people of his state, "And from my standpoint I succeeded" (Darrow, 1996, p. 126).

Even if he ruled out politics, he hadn't ruled out a second marriage. In the spring of 1899, he met Ruby Hamerstrom, a journalist nineteen years his junior. They were married in 1903 and together embarked on a lengthy European honeymoon. During this honeymoon and in just two months, he wrote *Farmington*, a fictionalized account of his youth. The book was subsequently published, although it met with only marginal success.

Darrow was not adept at compromising in his relationships, but fortunately Ruby was, and somehow she had the resources to put up with her husband. It turned out to be a close and stable marriage that lasted until his death thirty-five years later. The reason for the success of this marriage was perhaps best summed up by Darrow himself when the journalist and author Lincoln Steffens asked about their relationship. "Fine, because Ruby and me, we both love Darrow," he replied (Tierney, 1979, p. 182). She was a loyal, protective, and possessive wife whose interests always revolved around her husband.

After his honeymoon and his return to the United States, Darrow was asked to represent the United Mine Workers in their negotiations with the Pennsylvania Coal Company following a prolonged strike by the miners. President Theodore Roosevelt had ordered arbitration, and Darrow agreed to become involved. Along with other negotiators, Darrow was able to win hour and wage concessions from the mine owners. This victory, too, helped increase Clarence Darrow's reputation, although it may not have resulted in much change for the miners (Farrell, 2011).

In the first several years of the twentieth century, Darrow was in a law practice in which he frequently had conflicts with his law partners, as his work habits were a source of irritation. He preferred speaking and handling occasional trials as defense counsel, but he didn't like the mundane work that brought in money, and his partners complained that he took more money out of the business than he brought in. His work as a defense counsel in high-profile cases served as both an attractive trait for law partners and as a constant irritant. His fame brought new clients to his law firms, but he could be out of town for long periods of time and he often lowered his fees. His next big case illustrates this.

In 1906, he was asked to aid in the defense of the secretary-treasurer of the Western Federation of Miners (WFM), William D. Haywood, who was accused of murdering Frank Steunenberg, the ex-governor of Idaho. As governor, Steunenberg was involved in a labor dispute in the Idaho mines, and at one point, he brought in federal troops to quell riots. On December 30, 1905, Steunenberg was killed when a dynamite trap exploded at the front gate of his home. It was suspected that it was the radical officers of the Western Federation of Miners who were responsible. Finally, it was "Big Bill" Haywood who was charged. Darrow took on the case without consulting his law partners. What made it worse from the point of view of Darrow's partners was that there were actually five WFM officers charged with the murder, and each were to have a separate trial. Haywood's trial would be the second trial, but perhaps the most important one.

The trial of Big Bill Haywood attracted national attention because it seemed to be a classic case of labor and the working class pitted against management and the business leaders. But because the trial was held in Boise, Idaho, it would be the first trial in American history to be covered by the wire services. In fact, it was the first great reporting success by the Associated Press (Tierney, 1979). This feat was made possible because of the advances in the telephone and telegraph systems.

Tierney (1979) makes the point in describing Darrow's handling of the Haywood case (Clarence Darrow was lead co-counsel, but there were fourteen other attorneys for the defense) that it was a matter of controversy at the time whether the way Darrow handled the Haywood case helped or hurt his client. Darrow had a tendency to justify violence, to disparage religion, to preach political doctrines not always shared by the jury, and to deliver personal attacks on the other side's lawyers and witnesses. Many people at the time thought these tactics were potentially hazardous for his clients and an abuse of his role as a lawyer (Tierney, 1979). However, despite these usual Darrow tactics, Haywood was acquitted.

Shortly thereafter, when Darrow announced that he was going to Los Angeles to defend another client in a murder case, it spelled the end of the law partnership he had maintained in Chicago. Nonetheless, Darrow headed to Los Angeles.

The case was related to an explosion at the downtown plant of the Los Angeles Times in the early morning hours of October 1, 1910. The headlines in the Los Angeles Times the next day read: "Unionist Bombers Wreck the Times." Fifty people were killed or injured in the bombing.

At the moment that the explosion occurred, Earl Rogers, a well-known defense attorney, was entering his office nearby. He knew some of the people who were victims of the bombing, and he felt compelled to offer his services as a special prosecutor. It was Rogers's subsequent investigation that led to the arrest in April 1911 of the alleged perpetrators: James B. McNamara and Ortie McManigal in Detroit, and two weeks later the arrest of James's brother, J.J. McNamara, a union official. Clarence Darrow arrived in Los Angeles in April to head up the defense team.

The American Federation of Labor (AFL), led by Samuel Gompers, pledged the funds for the defense, but the money was slow coming in, and Darrow worried about that. Also of concern was the news by the time Darrow showed up in Los Angeles that Ortie McManigal had turned state's evidence, signing a detailed confession implicating the McNamara brothers. McManigal's story seemed to reflect the facts, but he stated that the orders for the bombing were in written form and that document was in the vaults of the Iron Workers' Union in Indianapolis. By appealing to President William Howard Taft, the prosecution got federal approval to seize the records of the Iron Workers' Union.

Reviewing the evidence against his clients, Darrow understood that they were likely guilty. There could be no explanation for the bombing that would result in their acquittal. The best he could do was to try to keep them from being hanged (Farrell, 2011). Going against the wishes of the American Federation of Labor, Darrow arranged to have the McNamara brothers plead guilty, and once that was done, Darrow would try to negotiate a sentence less than the death penalty. On December 1, 1911, the brothers pled guilty (Farrell, 2011).

However, on November 28, 1911, Bert Franklin, Darrow's chief investigator, was arrested for the attempted bribery of a prospective juror. Neither Franklin nor other investigators he had hired denied the charges. Darrow knew he might be indicted on the same charges, so rather than return to Chicago, he and Ruby rented an apartment in Los Angeles and awaited further developments.

Darrow and Ruby didn't have to wait very long. In January 1912, he was indicted on bribery charges. He immediately gave himself up to the police and then posted bail. He knew he needed a good attorney to defend him, and he turned to Earl Rogers. Rogers, as it turned out, admired Darrow and agreed to defend him.

The trial began on May 15, 1912. Helping out with his defense, Darrow himself conducted the voir dire. When the jury was seated, the prosecution began its case, and in his opening statement, the prosecutor described Clarence Darrow as corrupt and crooked (Tierney, 1979). Both sides called witnesses, and when it was time to give closing arguments, Rogers gave a very effective closing. Darrow then had an opportunity to give his own closing speech. At the beginning, he said:

> I am not on trial for having sought to bribe a man named Lockwood. I am on trial because I have been a lover of the poor, a friend of the oppressed, because I have stood by labor for all these years, and I have brought down upon my head the wrath of the criminal elements of this country.... Suppose I am guilty of bribery—is that why I am prosecuted in this court? Is that why, by their most infamous methods known to the law and outside the law, these men, the

> real enemies of society, are trying to get me inside the penitentiary? No that isn't it, and you twelve men know it. I have committed one crime, one crime which is like that against the Holy Ghost, which cannot be forgiven. I have stood for the weak and the poor. I have stood for the men who toil. And therefore I have stood against them, and now is their chance. All right gentlemen, I am in your hands. (Farrell, 2011, pp. 259–261).

That's the way he began his address, but several hours later, he ended it on this note:

> No man is judged rightly by his fellow men. We go here and there, and we think we control our destinies and our lives, but above us and beyond us are unseen hands and unseen forces that move us at their will.... After all, *Life is a game of Whist. From unknown sources/The cards are shuffled and the hands are dealt....* I have taken the cards as they came; I have played the best I could. I know my life, I know what I have done. My life has not been perfect; it has been human, too human.... But I have felt the heartbeats of every man who lived. I have tried to help in this world. I have not had malice in my heart. I have had love. (Farrell, 2011, p. 263)

According to many witnesses, it was his greatest closing argument up to that point in his career (Tierney, 1979). When he finished, some of the jurors were crying. The judge was struggling to control his emotions (Farrell, 2011). Then, the prosecutor had to follow this emotional closing with his own closing remarks. After the prosecutor was finished addressing the jury, the jurors filed out to deliberate.

Thirty minutes later, the twelve men returned, with the jury foreman announcing a verdict of "not guilty."

However, three months later, the prosecutor came back with another charge of bribery and proceeded to trial. While Darrow took this charge more lightly, it actually was more serious. Unfortunately, Rogers was no longer available to defend him, and his new attorney for this trial was Jerry Geisler, who was the junior counselor for the first trial. Darrow was even more involved in this trial, and it ended with a hung jury. Darrow and Ruby returned to Chicago after the trial, but Darrow felt like there was a dark cloud hanging over his head because he was not acquitted. But, by the end of 1913, the district attorney in Los Angeles decided not to pursue another trial.

Clarence Darrow in 1913

Underwood & Underwood, https://commons.wikimedia.org/ wiki/File:Clarence_Darrow_ cph.3b31130.jpg. Copyright in the Public Domain.

But, was Clarence Darrow guilty of attempting to bribe a juror?

That's a question that Kevin Tierney asks in his biography of Darrow. Piecing together the evidence, Tierney (1979) writes that a good many people—including reporters and other attorneys, such as Earl Rogers—thought he was guilty. Perhaps, Tierney says, paraphrasing what Darrow said in cases he was defending, sometimes the end justifies the means, and maybe this was a philosophy that was more than just courtroom rhetoric. Alan Dershowitz has also weighed in on the charges against Darrow: "There is now persuasive evidence that he may, in fact, have been guilty" (Dershowitz, 1996, p. v.). However, Geoffrey Cowan, author of the book *The People v. Clarence Darrow* (1993), puts the issue in a contemporary context:

> With considerable justification, and a bit of paranoia, Darrow felt that the judicial system was rigged against his clients. The prosecutors controlled the police and the grand jury, and they were backed by Burns' detectives, by the Erector's Association's money and by a generally hostile press led by a *Times* that was bent

on revenge. His clients had been illegally kidnapped, dragged across state lines and forced to face criminal charges. Their friends were harassed, their witnesses intimidated. The judge was a member of the most elite club in the city, and no one would be allowed on the jury who did not own property and who was not acceptable to the prosecution. The jurors all knew they would be rewarded for voting to convict the McNamaras and punished if they voted for an acquittal.... The forces of capital bribed jurors too but the approach was a bit more subtle. (Geoffrey Cowan as cited in Dershowitz, 1996, p. vi)

Returning to Chicago and after months as a defendant, with newspapers nationwide reporting the details of his legal battles, Clarence Darrow was sinking into a deep depression because he thought his career was in ruins (Tierney, 1979). He lost friends, especially those acquaintances who thought he was guilty of bribery. However, within a few months, he was sufficiently recovered to begin public speaking again. But he was not at all sure that he wanted to continue practicing law. On the other hand, he had to do something to earn a living. Public speaking was likely to be the most lucrative. He signed up for a series of Chautauqua (a 19th- and early-20th-century traveling institution that featured speakers and performers throughout the United States) appearances, and Darrow not only enjoyed these appearances that were, for the most part, more entertainment than serious lectures, but he relied on them for a significant part of his income for the rest of his life.

However, he needed to go back to the law, and when he had an opportunity to form a law practice with a young, Jewish Socialist by the name of Peter Sissman, he took it. Recognizing that his best bet for money was in defense work, he took on more criminal cases. Fortuitously, the war in Europe came along—hastening his return to respectability. His speeches were supportive of the war and the views of President Woodrow Wilson. He even acknowledged in his public addresses that some people needed to be detained for the good of the war effort. This took up even more of his time once the United States entered the war in 1917. By the time the war ended on November 11, 1918, it can be said that Clarence Darrow had made a public demonstration that he supported the war. That made him a respectable man once again.

Chicago, though, wasn't any less corrupt following the Great War, and public officials who got indicted frequently turned to Darrow for their defense. One of those officials was Oscar DePriest, the first African American alderman in Chicago, who was charged with conspiracy to allow gambling dens and houses of prostitution to operate in the Windy City. Playing the race card and claiming that money that came to DePriest was campaign donations—not bribery—DePriest was acquitted. Another was the chief of police, Charles C. Healy, facing the same charges as DePriest. And, like DePriest, Darrow won his acquittal.

Although earning a good living again, Darrow didn't enjoy the stigma that went along with being a defense attorney (Tierney, 1979). But he could also pick and choose among the clients seeking his services. No longer did he have to depend on violent union officials or corrupt politicians. He began to represent a new type of client: those charged with illegal wartime activities, including those accused of advocating the overthrow of the government. In one particular case, he successfully defended Fred Lundin, the campaign manager of Mayor William Hale ("Big Bill") Thompson. Lundin was charged with misappropriating more than a million dollars in school funds.

CRIME AND ITS CAUSES

In 1922, Darrow's book *Crime: Its Causes and Treatment* was published. According to Tierney's biography, readers did not find it a gratifying book because it failed to suggest any particular ways of curing crime (Tierney, 1979). Darrow criticized then current methods of treatment but offered no alternatives. The *Saturday Evening Post* magazine turned down an article by Darrow in which he proposed to talk about his book because it was "thoroughly one-sided" and took the position that all criminals were strongly influenced by their early environment and poverty (Tierney, 1979,

p. 318). The book was also criticized for being carelessly written and for suggesting that criminals became law violators through no fault of their own; they were victims of their environment and their heredity. In the 1920s, and for a good time after that, criminal law was predicated on the theory that criminals became offenders because of a lack of moral responsibility. Darrow ascribed criminality to anything but personal immorality.

In the book, he writes that:

> The criminal is not hard to understand. He is one who, from inherited defects or from great misfortune or especially hard circumstances, is not able to make the necessary adjustments to fit him to his environment.... Almost always he is a person of practically no education and no property. One who has given attention to the subject of crime knows exactly where the criminal comes from and how he will develop. The crimes of violence and murder, and the lesser crimes against property, practically all come from those who have been reared in the poor and congested districts of cities and large villages. (Darrow, 2009, p. 26)

It may be instructive to review what Darrow said about crime and its causes in another context. While he frequently talked about crime in his speeches and addresses, one of the most interesting and straightforward lectures about crime and criminals took place in 1902, when he was invited by the warden of the Cook County Jail in Chicago to speak to the inmates. Following are excerpts from this speech:

> If I looked at jails and crimes and prisoners in the way the ordinary person does, I should not speak on this subject to you. The reason I talk to you on the question of crime, its cause and cure, is that I really do not in the least believe in crime. There is no such

thing as a crime as the word is generally understood. I do not believe there is any sort of distinction between the real moral conditions of the people in and out of jail. One is just as good as the other. The people here can no more help being here than the people outside can avoid being outside. I do not believe that people are in jail because they deserve to be. They are in jail simply because they cannot avoid it on account of circumstances which are entirely beyond their control and for which they are in no way responsible....

If every man and woman and child in the world had a chance to make a decent, fair, honest living, there would be no jails and no lawyers and no courts. There might be some persons here or there with some peculiar formation of their brain, like Rockefeller, who would do these things simply to be doing them; but they would be very, very few, and those should be sent to a hospital and treated, and not sent to jail....

Hanging men in our county jails does not prevent murder. It makes murderers. And this has been the history of the world. It's easy to see how to do away with what we call crime. It is not so easy to do it. I will tell you how to do it. It can be done by giving the people a chance to live—by destroying special privileges. So long as big criminals can get the coal fields, so long as the big criminals have control of the city council and get the public streets for streetcars and gas rights—this is bound to send thousands of poor people to jail. So long as men are allowed to monopolize all the earth, and compel others to live on such terms as these men see fit to make, then you are bound to get into jail. The only way in the world to abolish crime and criminals is to abolish the big ones and the little ones together. Make fair conditions of life. Give men a chance to live. Abolish the right of private ownership of land, abolish monopoly, make the world partners in production, partners in the good things of life. Nobody would steal if he could get something of his own some easier way. Nobody will commit burglary when he has a house full. No girl will go out on the streets when she has a comfortable place at home. The man who owns a sweatshop or a department store may not be to blame himself for the condition of his girls, but when he pays them five dollars, three dollars, and two dollars a week, I wonder where he thinks they will get the rest of their money to live. The only way to cure these conditions is by equality. There should be no jails. They do not accomplish what they pretend to accomplish. If you would wipe them out there would be no more criminals than now. They terrorize nobody. They are a blot upon any civilization, and a jail is an evidence of the lack of charity of the people on the outside who make the jails and fill them with the victims of their greed. (Weinberg, 2012, pp. 3–4, 9, 14–15)

Clearly of the opinion that it was the environment and poverty that caused crime, the next big criminal case he would take on did not at all fit his theories of criminology.

LEOPOLD AND LOEB

Richard Loeb, 18, and Nathan Leopold, 19, were not poor kids with inadequate genetics. Instead, they both belonged to rich, Jewish Chicago families and both were academically successful. Nevertheless, they hatched a plan to commit the "perfect crime" by kidnapping and killing a fourteen-year-old boy (Robert Franks), who was a neighbor of theirs and who was selected at random. The murder was carried out on May 2, 1924, and by May 30, the police had solved the crime and arrested Leopold and Loeb. Darrow met with the two young men on June 3, 1924, and by that time both had confessed. It was clear to him that it would be a hopeless case to defend.

The case immediately garnered national attention and was universally described as a thrill killing; Leopold and Loeb were seen as examples of a golden generation gone wrong. Judge Ben Lindsey of Denver, Colorado, called the murder the "modern misdirection of youth" (Tierney, 1979, p. 328). The murder of the hapless Bobby Franks became the most publicized crime up to that time. Every day, there were front-page stories about the case. Darrow had only one aim: to save the boys from death.

The prosecutor in the case was Robert Emmet Crowe, who had a warm relationship with Darrow. But Crowe was an ardent proponent of capital punishment. He publicly demanded it in all murder cases in Cook County, Illinois, because he believed it to be a deterrent to future potential murderers (Tierney, 1979).

The date for the trial to begin was set for July 21, 1924, and up to that day, Darrow kept his defense strategy a secret. At the start of the trial, he announced that his clients were changing their pleas from not guilty to guilty of both charges—kidnapping and murder. Crowe was ready to prosecute, and he insisted on presenting his case. Darrow countered by insisting he be allowed to present his psychiatric witnesses; the judge allowed this. After Crowe presented his case and the defense's psychiatrists testified, all that was left were the closing arguments.

On August 22, 1924, Clarence Darrow rose to deliver his closing. The crowd that gathered trying to get in the courthouse to hear Darrow was huge. As a result of the unrelenting publicity about the case, Darrow had truly acquired national fame and recognition. That fame would remain for the remainder of his life. Those who got close enough to hear Darrow's closing argument would be treated to a great attorney at the top of his form as he sought to save the lives of Leopold and Loeb:

Your Honor, it has been almost three months since the great responsibility of this case was assumed by my associates and myself. I am willing to confess that it has been three months of great anxiety—a burden which I gladly would have been spared excepting for my feelings of affection toward some of the members of one of these unfortunate families. This responsibility is almost too great for anyone to assume, but we lawyers can no more choose than the court can choose.

Our anxiety over this case has not been due to the facts that are connected with this most unfortunate affair, but to the almost unheard-of publicity it has received; to the fact that newspapers all over this country have been giving it space such as they have almost never before given to any case. The fact that day after day the people of Chicago have been regaled with stories of all sorts about it, until almost every person has formed an opinion. And when the public is interested and demands a punishment, no matter what the offense, great or small, it thinks of only one punishment, and that is death. (Weinberg, 2012, pp. 19–20)

That's how Clarence Darrow's closing address to Judge John Caverly began. But he was just getting warmed up to his topic. He continued with an attack on the idea of sentencing these two young men to death:

We are here with the lives of two boys imperiled, with the public aroused. For what? Because, unfortunately, the parents have money. Nothing else.

I told Your Honor in the beginning that never had there been a case in Chicago, where on a plea of guilty a boy under twenty-one had been sentenced to death. I will raise that age and say, never has there been a case where a human being under the age of twenty-three has been sentenced to death. And, I think I am safe in saying, although I have not examined all the records and could not—But I think I am safe in saying—that never has there been such a case in the state of Illinois.

And yet this court is urged, aye, threatened, that he must hang two boys contrary to precedents, contrary to the acts of every judge who ever held court in this state. Why? Tell me what the public necessity there is for this. Why need the state's attorney ask for something that never before has been demanded? Why need a judge be urged by every argument, moderate and immoderate, to hang two boys in the face of every precedent in Illinois, and the face of the progress of the last fifty years?

I have heard in the last six weeks nothing but the city cry for blood. I have heard from the office of the state's attorney only ugly hate. I have heard precedents quoted which would be a disgrace to a savage race. I have seen a court urged almost to the point of threats to hang two boys, in the face of science, in the face of philosophy, in the face of humanity, in the face of experience, in the face of all the better and more humane thought of the age.... But here are the officers of justice, so-called, with all the power of the state, with all the influence of the press, to fan this community into a frenzy of hate; with all of that, who for months have been planning and scheming, and contriving and working to take these two boys' lives.

You may stand them up on the trap door of the scaffold, and choke them to death, but that act will be infinitely more cold-blooded, whether justified or not, than any act that these boys have committed or can commit. (Weinberg, 2012, pp. 21, 22, 26)

After several more hours arguing against the utility, the purpose, and the effectiveness of the death penalty, Darrow reaches the end of his closing argument:

Your Honor stands between the past and the future. You may hang these boys; you may hang them by the neck until they are dead. But in doing it you will turn your face toward the past. In doing it you are making it harder for every other boy who, in ignorance and darkness, must grope his way through the mazes which only childhood knows. In doing it you will make it harder for unborn children. You may save them and make it easier for every child that sometime may stand where these boys stands. You will make it easier for every human being with an aspiration and a vision and a hope and a fate.

I am pleading for the future; I am pleading for a time when hatred and cruelty will not control the hearts of men, when we can learn by reason and judgment and understanding and faith that all life is worth saving, and that mercy is the highest attribute of man.

I feel that I should apologize for the length of time I have taken. This case may not be as important as I think it is, and I am sure I do not need to tell this court, or to tell my friends that I would fight just as hard for the poor as for the rich. If I should succeed in saving these boys' lives and do nothing for the progress of the law, I should feel sad, indeed. If I can succeed, my greatest reward and my greatest hope will be that I have done something for the tens of thousands of other boys, for the countless unfortunates who must tread the same road in blind childhood that these poor boys have trod; that I have done something to help human understanding, to temper justice with mercy, to overcome hate with love.

I was reading last night of the aspiration of the old Persian poet, Omar Khayyam. It appealed to me as the highest that I can vision. I wish it was in my heart, and I wish it was in the hearts of all.

So I be written in the Book of Love,

I do not care about that Book above;

Erase my name or write it as you will,

So I be written in the Book of Love. (Weinberg, 2012, pp. 86–87

As Darrow finished his address, he was looking every bit as wrinkled and weathered as at any time in his long life. Tears were streaming down the judge's face, and there were tears filling the eyes of many spectators (Weinberg, 1989). According to Kevin Tierney (1979), at this moment, Clarence Darrow was in a class of his own, and there was no lawyer in America who could be compared to him. Tierney goes on to write that no lawyer (at least up to the writing of Tierney's biography of Darrow in 1979;

some might argue that because of television, perhaps Johnnie Cochran, who led the O.J. Simpson defense team, might have surpassed Darrow in the 1990s) has ever achieved the fame that came to Darrow. And it came to him at age sixty-seven.

Darrow's closing argument lasted two days. During those two days, he talked about the prosecution, the death penalty, how different the two defendants were from "normal people," and the role of the philosopher Nietzsche in Leopold and Loeb's own philosophies. Many concluded that Darrow was at his best in delivering his closing argument, which was addressed to the judge and the public, since there was no jury because of the guilty verdicts.

On the day of sentencing, Judge John Caverly returned to court with his findings. The judge sentenced both defendants to life in prison for the murder and another ninety-nine years for the kidnapping. Darrow had achieved his goal.

Alan M. Dershowitz has written that the Leopold and Loeb case might be the case that Darrow himself might have liked to be remembered for. He points out that not only did Darrow save the lives of two young thrill killers, but he proved that there was redemption and rehabilitation. Furthermore, Dershowitz states that "Most death penalty lawyers I know have read his masterful closing argument and many use parts of it in their pleas for life" (Darrow, 1996, p. xi).

Worn out after this case, Clarence Darrow went on the lecture circuit, and he said he would not take on another case unless it promised less anguish and more amusement than the Leopold and Loeb case. It wasn't until after the beginning of 1925 that an opportunity came along that he couldn't resist.

THE SCOPES MONKEY TRIAL

In 1925, a young Tennessee schoolteacher named John T. Scopes defied the state's law prohibiting the teaching of evolution. Scopes was arrested, and the case immediately got national headlines, causing William Jennings Bryan to announce his intention to join the prosecution. Then, the American Civil Liberties Union (ACLU) got involved and offered to defend Scopes. When Darrow heard about the case, he said he would defend the schoolteacher free of charge. To Darrow's thinking, Bryan was the embodiment of all those aspects of rural America that Darrow had escaped so many years before.

The reality of the situation was that it was not a trial in the strict sense of the term. Instead, as Tierney (1979) points out, it was a set piece; a contrivance. The anti-evolution law was out of date in Tennessee and elsewhere, and perhaps no one really expected it to be enforced. For their part, both Bryan and Darrow were essentially also out of date. So were their arguments and their styles of making speeches during the trial. It was all staged by Scopes, by the ACLU, and by the town of Dayton, Ohio, as well as by Bryan, too (Tierney, 1979).

Darrow saw it as an opportunity to defend science, revile Bryan, and to poke fun at fundamentalism, the Bible Belt, and Southern justice. The trial was dubbed the "Monkey trial" to show that it was about debating the theory of Darwin that both humans and monkeys had a common ancestry. As the trial began, William Jennings Bryan scored points and had the sympathy of the people who packed the courtroom. But as the trial wore on, Bryan, who had not prepared ahead of time, found himself "ravaged, out-classed, out-maneuvered and out-argued" by Darrow and the defense team (Tierney, 1979, p. 366). After the judge ruled that expert testimony from the many scientific minds the defense had assembled would not be allowed, Darrow and the defense saw no further benefits in letting the trial proceed. Consequently, Darrow pled Scopes guilty. This prevented any closing arguments by either Darrow or Bryan, although Bryan had prepared one and desperately wanted to deliver it.

For a brief period after the end of the Scopes trial, Darrow was proclaimed the hero, despite Scopes being convicted. Bryan had, essentially, been humiliated, and he died five days after the trial was finished. Scopes's conviction was reversed by the Tennessee Supreme Court in 1927. And, in 1968, in the case of *Epperson v. Arkansas* (393 U.S. 97), the U.S. Supreme Court ruled that an anti-evolution law was unconstitutional, because for the state to pass such a law, it would be establishing a state religion.

Following the Leopold and Loeb trial and the Monkey Trial, Darrow was a national icon. He could have taken any case back in Chicago for any amount of money he demanded. Instead, he would go to Detroit to take on a case for meager wages.

THE OSSIAN SWEET TRIAL

On September 9, 1925, several shots were fired from inside Dr. Ossian Sweet's house on the east side of Detroit. One man was killed and another was wounded. Everyone inside the house—his wife, other relatives, and friends—were arrested. For several nights leading up to September 9, crowds gathered outside of the home of Dr. Sweet, an African American who bought a house in a previously all-white neighborhood. On that night, many people ringing the house were throwing rocks at the house.

After Dr. Sweet and the others were arrested, the National Association for the Advancement of Colored People (NAACP) got involved, raising $75,000 for their defense. The NAACP hired Darrow and Arthur Garfield Hays as counsel and cocounsel. The objective of the NAACP was to pursue the cause that a man had a right to self-defense to protect his castle. Darrow hoped for a jury trial in order to send a clear message to white people (Farrell, 21011). In a first trial, Darrow's three main lines of defense were: 1) objection to the conspiracy charge; 2) strong objection to the police conduct throughout the events leading up to the shooting; and 3) that what Dr. Sweet had done was acceptable self-defense.

But in giving his closing arguments, Darrow wanted to make sure the twelve white men on the jury understood that this was a case about race:

> My friend Mr. Moll [a prosecutor] says, gentlemen,
> that this isn't a race question. This is a murder case.
> We don't want any prejudice; we don't want the other
> side to have any. Race and color have nothing to do
> with this case. This is a case of murder.

I insist there is nothing but prejudice in this case; that if it was reversed and eleven white men had shot and killed a black while protecting their home and their lives against a mob of blacks, nobody would have dreamed of having them indicted. I know what I am talking about, and so do you. They would have been given medals instead. Ten colored men and one woman are in this indictment, tried by twelve jurors, gentlemen. Every one of you are white, aren't you? At least you all think so. We haven't one colored man on this jury. We couldn't get one. One was called and he was disqualified. You twelve white men are trying a colored on race prejudice.

Now, let me ask you whether you are not prejudiced. I want to put this square to you, gentlemen. I haven't any doubt but that every one of you is prejudiced against colored people. I want you to guard against it. I want you to do all you can to be fair in this case, and I believe you will. A number of you have answered the question that you are acquainted with colored people.... Some of the rest of you said that you had employed colored people to work for you, are even employing them now. All right. You have seen some colored people in this case. They have been so far above the white people that live at the corner of Garland and Charlevoix that they can't be compared, intellectually, morally and physically, and you know it. How many of you jurors, gentlemen, have ever had a colored person visit you in your home? How many of you have invited them to dinner at your house? Probably not one of you. Now, why gentlemen? There isn't one of you men but what knows just from the witnesses you have seen in this case that there are colored people who are intellectually the equal of all of you. Am I right? Colored people living right here in the city of Detroit are intellectually the equals and some of them superior to most of us. Is that true? Some of them are people of more character and learning than most of us. (Weinberg, 2012, pp. 233–234)

Darrow then went on to discuss the mob outside the home and, finally, the right of a homeowner to defend himself: "Now let me tell you when a man has the right to shoot in self-defense, and in defense of his home; not when these vital things in life are in danger, but when he thinks they are" (Weinberg, 2012, p. 250).

After the jury deliberated for 48 hours without a verdict, Judge Frank Murphy (who would go on to become an associate justice of the U.S. Supreme Court) had no choice but to declare a mistrial. However, the prosecutor decided to try the case a second time, but this time he only charged Dr. Sweet. Darrow followed a similar strategy in this trial, which took place in April and May 1926, but the results were different. Ossian Sweet was acquitted.

Following the second trial, and for the next few years, Clarence Darrow would spend a considerable portion of his time furthering the cause of Negro rights. However, he did this from a lecture platform as he traveled around the country.

WINDING DOWN A CAREER

Approaching seventy years of age after the Sweet trial, Darrow began to experience serious health problems. He was advised to cut back on his hectic schedule, and, complying with his doctor's advice, he did, in fact, begin to wind down. However, he couldn't quite bring himself to retire from his law practice until 1928. But in 1927, he only took on two cases. One was the case related to Theodore Dreiser's book *An American Tragedy*, in which a man was accused of selling Dreiser's novel, which was considered obscene and banned in some cities. This case, like the Scopes trial, was more show than substance. However, the other case had to do with the murder of two well-known anti-Fascists. Darrow won an acquittal for the two New York Fascists he represented at the trial.

After that victory, he and Ruby set sail for Europe, viewing the voyage as a second honeymoon. But, like the first honeymoon, Darrow was working on a book during their travels. This time it was his autobiography, titled *The Story of My Life*. After it was published, though, the author Irving Stone commented that the title of the book should have been *The Story of My Philosophy*, since the book left out many details of his life and career (Tierney, 1979). Despite its flaws—lack of details of his personal life, misspellings of names, careless use of dates, and inaccurate facts—the book became a best-seller, but even Darrow conceded to a friend that it was as much propaganda as biography (Farrell, 2011).

Clarence Darrow During the Scopes Trial in 1925.

Underwood & Underwood, https://commons.wikimedia.org/wiki/File:Clarence_Darrow_during_Scopes_Trial_cph.3a44036.jpg. Copyright in the Public Domain.

When the financial crash came in 1929, Darrow and his son Paul were hit hard. Instead of being comfortably well off, Darrow found that he had to go back on the lecture and debate circuits. For the most part, he was content being more of an entertainer than what he had been earlier in his life—a pleader of causes. In fact, *Variety*, the Hollywood showbiz paper, described him as "America's greatest one-man stage draw" (Tierney, 1979, p. 399).

Finally, in 1932, he joined another law partnership with a group of younger attorneys. The law firm was called Darrow, Cronson, Smith & Smith, and it would be the last law partnership for him. That same year, the NAACP asked him to join in the Scottsboro Boys case. But the International Labor Defense, a Communist organization, was already involved, and the conditions they placed on Darrow's participation forced him to walk away from the famous case. However, that year, he was invited to go to Hawaii to take on the Massie case. He was subject to a great deal of criticism for agreeing to handle the defense in this case—since he would be on the wrong side of a racially tinged case—but he couldn't turn down the money (Farrell, 2011).

To his friends, he said he was going to Hawaii because he had never been there and he wanted to promote racial harmony. Although he lost the case, he did get to Hawaii, and maybe he achieved the goal of promoting better race relations. The case involved the alleged rape of Thalia Massie, the wife of Navy lieutenant Thomas Massie, who was stationed in Hawaii. Thalia's mother, Grace Fortescue, a wealthy socialite, came to Hawaii to help Massie and his friends get revenge for the rape. In the course of events, Massie, Fortescue and others kidnapped some Hawaiian natives, killing one of them. They were charged with murder, and after a trial they were all convicted, although they received very light sentences. But this would finally be Darrow's last big case.

As Darrow and Ruby returned to the United States, they quickly learned about the kidnapping and murder of Charles Lindbergh Jr. This would have been the case—it was one of those crimes dubbed "the crime of the century"—that a few years before would have surely been offered to Clarence Darrow. But it wasn't; his time had passed.

As the 1930s rolled on, Darrow was in steadily declining health, and his activities were limited by his reduced financial resources. In 1934, he was invited to become the chairman of the National Recovery Review Board (NRRB) in Washington, D.C. This was a godsend because he needed the money, and he was appointed by President Franklin Roosevelt in March 1934. Consequently, he and Ruby moved to Washington, D.C., and took a suite at the Willard Hotel.

This was an unusual position for Darrow, who was no supporter of the president, because the NRRB was created to deflect criticism away from the National Recovery Administration. Darrow, born in a small Ohio town in the middle of the nineteenth century, was totally out of touch with Roosevelt's New Deal politics. Philosophically, he was mistrustful of the government—any government—and had taken on this job with a partisan perspective. As a result, the reports the NRRB produced did not please the president or his administration, so they were suppressed, although Darrow himself tended to leak those reports. All in all, it was clear to many that indeed time had passed Darrow by. Throughout his career, he had ranted about monopolies and big business, but that's exactly what the New Deal was about. Darrow was a radical individualist and, as should have been expected by the administration, the report that came from the Review Board was critical, charging the NRA with fostering monopolistic practices that favored influential interests. This did not sit well with Roosevelt or his staff (Farrell, 2011).

Clarence Darrow's last public statement of any consequence came in January 1936 after his former client, Richard Loeb, was stabbed to death in Joliet Prison. Loeb was better off than Leopold, Darrow told the press: "He's better off dead" (Tierney, 1979, p. 437).

From then on, suffering from arterial blockages and damage from earlier heart trouble, Darrow began displaying significant signs of senility; Ruby was essentially caring for an invalid. He died on March 13, 1938, at age eighty. A memorial service was held at Bond Chapel at the University of Chicago, where thousands paid their last respects to him. Among the throng were even some people he had wronged. Yet, they were there to offer a tribute to a unique spirit.

Clarence Darrow was a giant of a man who was a voice for the inarticulate and the poor; a defender of the oppressed. Although he expected others to take his place and carry on his work as an icon in American society, ultimately, there was no one who could do that. Alan M. Dershowitz, the famed Harvard Law School professor, writes that "… Even if Clarence Darrow no longer qualifies as a role model [because of his probable bribery of a potential juror], his remarkable career still deserves study by all citizens who care about liberties and our legal system. Darrow's long career spanned the history of the first third of this [twentieth] century and his advocacy was instrumental in defending many of the most crucial cases of the day. His cases have become the stuff of legend, drama and film" (Dershowitz, 1996, pp. vi–vii).

As Kevin Tierney writes about Clarence Darrow, there have not been many men who left behind a void that posterity could not fill. Tierney also concludes that Darrow not only did this, but at the same time, his vigorous independence left an example for later generations to respect (Tierney, 1979).

QUESTIONS FOR DISCUSSION

1. What were the factors in Clarence Darrow's life that helped shape his views on the causes of criminal behavior?
2. In the 1890s, with the Prendergast case, Darrow discovered his first real cause. What was this cause, and what strategies did he use in this cause? Was he successful?
3. Why was Darrow initially drawn to politics?
4. What was Darrow's theory of the causation of crime, as expounded in his book *Crime: Its Causes and Treatment*?

IMPORTANT TERMS AND NAMES

Chautauqua: Chautauqua was an adult education movement that started in the late nineteenth century in the small town of Chautauqua, New York. In the twentieth century, it featured speakers and entertainers who traveled the country giving lectures and speeches. Two very popular speakers on the Chautauqua circuit were Clarence Darrow and William Jennings Bryan.

John Peter Altgeld: John Peter Altgeld was a Chicago politician who was elected a judge; later, he was elected as the governor of Illinois, from 1893 to 1897. A reform-minded Democratic politician, he espoused many of the same causes that were backed by Clarence Darrow. Darrow and Altgeld were friends for more than fifteen years.

National Recovery Administration: The National Recovery Administration was a government agency established by President Franklin D. Roosevelt in 1933 during the Depression to help stimulate economic recovery through the establishment of fair practices codes and minimum wages. It was ultimately declared unconstitutional by the U.S. Supreme Court.

Patrick Eugene Prendergast: Patrick Eugene Prendergast went to the home of Carter Harrison, the mayor of Chicago in 1893, and shot him three times. He was under the mistaken impression that he should have been appointed corporation counsel for Chicago by the mayor. Darrow got involved in the case because he saw Prendergast as a mentally ill individual who should be spared the death penalty. Darrow's attempts to save Prendergast from execution were unsuccessful, and Prendergast was hanged in July 1894.

Pullman strike: The Pullman strike occurred in 1894 when George Pullman, who founded the Pullman Palace Car Company, reduced the wages of his employees but refused to reduce the rent he charged those employees. The Pullman cars were sleeping cars used by almost all railroads at the time. Pullman built Pullman City and forced his employees to live in the city and pay rent to him. When the strike was called by the American Railroad Union, a union founded by Eugene V. Debs, the Illinois attorney general got a federal injunction to block the strike. This led to violence, and federal troops were called in to quell that violence. Debs was arrested and charged with interfering with the U.S. mail, because trains transported the mail.

Eugene Debs: Eugene V. Debs founded the American Railroad Union (ARU) to protect workers who were employed by the railroad companies. He was arrested and charged with interfering with the U.S. mail, because trains transported the mail, during the Pullman strike of 1894. He was defended by Clarence Darrow, but was convicted. After serving several months in jail, Debs was released to find the ARU no longer existed. He later would found the Industrial Workers of the World, would help establish the Socialist Party of America, and would run for president of the United States several times on the Socialist Party ticket.

William Jennings Bryan: A Democratic and populist party leader, he would run unsuccessfully for president of the United States three different times. He was Darrow's opponent in the Scopes Monkey trial in 1926. Bryan would die a few days after that trial ended in Dayton, Ohio.

Big Bill Haywood: Secretary-treasurer of the Western Federation of Miners, William D. "Big Bill" Haywood was defended by Clarence Darrow in 1906 when he was accused of the bombing murder of Frank Steunenberg, the former governor of Idaho. Darrow won an acquittal of Haywood, who would go on to be a leader in the Industrial Workers of the World.

Thomas I. Kidd: Thomas I. Kidd was an official of the Amalgamated Woodworkers' International Union and helped organize a strike at the Paine Lumber Company in Oak Brook, Illinois, in 1898. He was charged with criminal conspiracy, but defended by Clarence Darrow and was acquitted.

McNamara brothers: James B. McNamara and John J. McNamara were brothers who were charged, along with Ortie McManigal, in the bombing of the *Los Angeles Times* in 1910. Fifty people were killed or wounded. They worked for the Iron Workers' Union. McManigal turned state's evidence, but Clarence Darrow took on the defense of the McNamara brothers. However, the evidence against the brothers was overwhelming, and Darrow convinced them to plead guilty.

Nathan Leopold and Richard Loeb: Leopold and Loeb were two wealthy Chicago students who kidnapped and murdered fourteen-year-old Robert Franks in 1924. Their families hired Clarence Darrow to defend them, but since the young men were not denying their guilt, the only goal for Darrow was to work to avoid their execution. He had them plead guilty and then argued that their lives should be spared. They were given life sentences in prison.

Massie case: This was the last big trial in which Clarence Darrow would act as defense counsel. The case started in Hawaii in 1932, when Thalia Massie, the wife of a Navy lieutenant stationed in Hawaii, claimed she was raped by several men. Her mother, Grace Fortescue, came to Hawaii to help out, and Mrs. Fortesecue, Lt. Massie, and others went looking for the men, seeking revenge. They kidnapped several Hawaiian natives and ended up killing one of them. Darrow was invited to defend Mrs. Fortescue and the others who were charged. They were all convicted, and it was clear that Darrow had only taken on this case for the money.

Scopes Monkey Trial: Formally known as the *State of Tennessee v. John Thomas Scopes*, this was a case in which John Scopes, a science teacher, was charged with the misdemeanor crime of teaching the theory of evolution. William Jennings Bryan volunteered to lead the prosecution, and Clarence Darrow agreed to lead the defense. For both Darrow and Bryan, it was an opportunity to defend their religious and scientific beliefs. Ultimately, Darrow convinced Scopes to plead guilty. However, it was an opportunity for Darrow to gain even more fame as an attorney.

Ossian Sweet trial: In September 1925, Dr. Ossian Sweet and his wife moved into a house on Detroit's east side in a previously all-white neighborhood. After several days of mobs gathering outside the home every night, shots were fired from inside the house on September 9, and one man among the throng outside the house was killed. Dr. Sweet and others were arrested and charged with murder. Clarence Darrow led the defense and argued that a man had a right to protect his home when he was threatened. The first trial ended with a hung jury, but in the second trial, Darrow won an acquittal for Dr. Sweet.

FOR FURTHER READING

Boyle, K. (2004). *Arc of justice: A saga of race, civil rights, and murder in the jazz age.* New York, NY: Henry Holt and Co.

Darrow, C. (2009). *Crime: Its cause and treatment.* New York, NY: First Rate Publishers.

Darrow, C. (1996). *The story of my life.* New York, NY: Da Capo Press.

Farrell, J. A. (2011). *Clarence Darrow: Attorney for the damned.* New York, NY: Vintage Books.

Joshi, T. (2005). *Closing arguments: Clarence Darrow on religion, law, and society.* Athens, OH: Ohio University Press.

Lief, M. S., Caldwell, H. M., & Bycel, B. (1998). *Ladies and gentlemen of the jury: Greatest closing arguments in modern law.* New York, NY: Scribner.

McRae, D. (2009). *The last trials of Clarence Darrow.* New York, NY: William Morrow.

Standard, D. E. (2005). *Honor killing: How the infamous "Massie Affair" transformed Hawai'i.* New York, NY: Viking.

Vine, P. (2004). *One man's castle: Clarence Darrow in defense of the American dream.* New York, NY: Amistad.

Weinberg, A. (Ed.). (1989). *Attorney for the damned: Clarence Darrow in the courtroom.* Chicago, IL: University of Chicago Press.

REVIEW QUESTIONS

True or False

1. Clarence Darrow never graduated from law school.
2. In 1893, Darrow believed that Patrick Eugene Prendergast should be executed for the assassination of the mayor of Chicago.
3. In his defense of labor leaders, Darrow tended to justify violence.
4. Darrow was once indicted and prosecuted for bribing a juror.

Multiple Choice

5. Clarence Darrow's theory of criminology was that criminals became offenders because
   a. They were immoral.
   b. They chose to commit crimes.
   c. They were poor and raised in crowded neighborhoods.
   d. They came from the privileged classes.

6. In speaking to inmates of Cook County Jail in 1902, Clarence Darrow was succinct in his views of crime and criminals. He stated that
   a. People end up in jail because of their circumstances.
   b. People go to jail because they made poor choices.
   c. People are in jail because they are just irresponsible.
   d. People end up as inmates because they could have controlled their behavior.

7. The murder case of Richard Loeb and Nathan Leopold did not fit Darrow's theories of criminology because
   a. They were rich and privileged.
   b. They were poor, downtrodden students.
   c. They believed that they were inferior to other people.
   d. They had low IQs.

8. In his defense of Leopold and Loeb, Clarence Darrow argued that
   a. The death penalty was against modern science.
   b. The death penalty was about hatred and cruelty.
   c. The death penalty should not be applied to young men.
   d. All of the above.

9. A major issue in the Dr. Ossian Sweet trial was that
   a. A man has a right to live in Detroit.
   b. A man has a right to self-defense to protect his castle.
   c. A man has a right to shoot at a mob threatening him.
   d. A man has a right to bear arms.

10. The last big case of Darrow's career was the

   a. Scopes Monkey trial.

   b. Leopold and Loeb trial.

   c. Charles Lindbergh Jr. trial.

   d. Massie trial.

REFERENCES

Darrow, C. (1996). *The story of my life*. New York, NY: Da Capo Press.

Darrow, C. (2009). *Crime: Its cause and treatment*. New York. NY: First Rate Publishers.

Dershowitz, A. M. (1996). Introduction. In *C. Darrow: The story of my life* (pp. v–xi). New York, NY: Da Capo Press.

Farrell, J. A. (2011). *Clarence Darrow: Attorney for the damned*. New York, NY: Vintage Books.

Joshi, T. (2005). *Closing arguments: Clarence Darrow on religion, law, and society*. Athens, OH: Ohio University Press.

Tierney, K. (1979). *Darrow: A biography*. New York, NY: Thomas Y. Crowell.

Weinberg, A. (Ed.). (1989). *Attorney for the damned: Clarence Darrow in the courtroom*. Chicago, IL: University of Chicago Press.

Weinberg, A. (Ed.). (2012). *Attorney for the damned: Clarence Darrow in the courtroom*. Chicago, IL: University of Chicago Press [reprint ed.].

CREDITS

Clarence Darrow, Excerpts from Address to the Prisoners in the Cook County Jail. Copyright in the Public Domain.

Clarence Darrow, Excerpts from Closing Statement, *State of Illinois v. Nathan Leopold Jr. and Richard Loeb*. Copyright in the Public Domain.

Clarence Darrow, Excerpts from Final Arguments, Ossian Sweet Trial. Copyright in the Public Domain.

11

JOHN AUGUSTUS
Father of Modern American Probation

Frank Schmalleger and John Ortiz Smykla call him the first unofficial probation officer (2009). Dean Champion calls him "the Father of Probation in the United States" (Champion, 1996, p. 34). Authors Siegel and Worrall and Bohm and Haley acknowledge that he is considered the "father of modern probation" (Siegel & Worrall, 2012, p. 480; Bohm & Haley, 2012, p. 438). But, as Champion (1996) writes, it was this man—John Augustus, a shoemaker in Boston—who developed the concept of probation in America.

Most criminologists agree that the volunteer work of John Augustus led to the widespread use of probation services today. In fact, more than 4 million adults are on federal, state, or local probation in any given year in this country, and one out of every fifty-four persons age eighteen or older is on probation (Schmalleger & Smykla, 2009). But this all started in 1841, when a man showed up in a Boston police court and offered to help a man straighten out his life.

JOHN AUGUSTUS'S EARLY LIFE

John Augustus was born in 1784 in Woburn, Massachusetts. Unfortunately, little is known about his family background or his childhood. What little is known about him comes not from a small book he wrote near the end of his career, but from brief reports and descriptions of him by people who knew him in the nineteenth century. His book, *A Report on the Labors of John Augustus, for the Last Ten Years, In Aid of the Unfortunate: Containing A Description of His Methods of Operations; Striking Incidents, and*

Observations Upon the Improvement of Some of Our City Institutions, with a View to the Benefit of the Prisoners and of Society, was published in 1852 and provides only a couple of sparse references to his life or his family. Virtually the entirety of the 104-page book is devoted to his efforts to help other people (Augustus, 1972).

What is gleaned from other documents and research, such as the foreword to the 1939 edition of *John Augustus: First Probation Officer* (Augustus, 1972), reveals that although born in Woburn, he moved to Lexington and started a shoemaking business. That business flourished, and at one time he had several assistants working for him. In 1827, he moved the business to Boston. Prior to that, though, in 1813, he married a woman with the first name of Sally and they had a daughter they named Harriet. Harriet died around the age of one, and Sally died soon afterward. Years later, Augustus would marry Harriet Stearns. Together, they had a daughter, who died at age ten, and two sons.

John Augustus is described in a book written by Ball Fenner, a newspaper reporter at the time Augustus was actively helping people in the Boston courts. In his book, *Raising the Veil, Or Scenes in the Courts* (Fenner, 2015), published in 1856, Fenner writes:

> Among the notables who have been in and about the Boston court house for the past twelve years, few are better known than the man John Augustus. That this man has done much good since he entered upon his career as a philanthropist, no one who knows anything of the subject can for a moment doubt. Many persons are of the opinion that for the few years past Mr. Augustus has done more harm than good, by bailing those who are arraigned before the courts for the commission of crimes that deserve and should receive severe punishment, and it is said that rogues have been allowed to escape through the interposition of this man.

There may be a few cases where this gentleman's philanthropy (or whatever else you please to term it) has so far outrun good judgment and discretion that it may have led him to interfere where strict justice would demand that the law should take its course. If the facts respecting such matters were fully known, methinks the public would find that where one truly guilty individual has escaped, by and with the aid of John Augustus, ten have been suffered to go at large by the connivance and direct assistance of police officers.

… There is one thing certainly that is praiseworthy in the character of John Augustus, and that is, he will never quarrel with any person on account of his political opinions or religious belief; neither will he express his own, even when urged to do so. By pursuing his course he is, like the Apostle Paul, enabled to make himself "all things to all men," believing that by so doing he can "save some."

There are but few men to be found who would, if they had been placed in precisely his situation, have stood the ordeal of public opinion of those who stand high in the community as the most charitable and beneficent citizens. I believe that whenever and wherever he has made mistakes, in his impetuous zeal in laboring for the good of others, it has been the fault of head and not the heart. (Fenner, 2015, pp. 282–284)

When Augustus started going to court and helping people, he was already fifty-seven years old, which was somewhat older than the average life span at that time. In one newspaper account of him, which was recorded by Augustus in his own book, he is described as a "thin, elderly man of medium height, his face somewhat wrinkled, and his features of a benevolent expression" (Augustus, 1972, p. 75). He has also been described as a very determined, quite independent man, who was a fast talker and a bundle of kinetic energy (Panzarella, 2002).

HIS CALLING BEGINS

His work was that of a shoemaker, but he evidently was drawn to the police courts while his assistants were operating his business, because he writes early on in his book that in August 1841, he was in court one morning when "the door communicating with the lock-room was opened and an officer entered, followed by a ragged and wretched looking man" (Augustus, 1972, p. 4). The man was charged with being a common drunkard. Before the man was sentenced, Augustus spent a few minutes talking to the man and found that he was "not yet past all hope of reformation" (Augustus, 1972, p. 5). The man told Augustus that if he could be "Saved from the House of Correction, he never again would taste intoxicating liquors; there was such an earnestness in that tone, and a look expressive of firm resolve, that I determined to aid him; I bailed him, by permission of the Court" (Augustus, 1972, p. 5). Leaving the courthouse, the man agreed to return to the court in three weeks and he signed a pledge to become a sober man.

Three weeks later, John Augustus accompanied the man back to court. No one in the courtroom could believe he was the same man because his appearance was much improved. The judge was very pleased with the man's reformation and instead of the usual penalty, which was imprisonment in the House of Corrections, he was fined one cent and assessed court fees of $3.76, both of which he immediately paid. The follow-up, as Augustus wrote, was that "The man continued industrious and sober, and without doubt has been by this treatment, saved from a drunkard's grave" (Augustus, 1972, p. 5).

Augustus himself was so pleased by the change in this one individual that between August and the end of 1841 he had paid the bail of seventeen other men who were facing similar charges; all seventeen were saved from the House of Corrections and only had to pay fines. When they couldn't afford to pay their own fines, Augustus paid it for them (Augustus, 1972).

A SEASON OF PROBATION

Robert Panzarella (2002) suggests that even in John Augustus's first case, there is implicit in his description of this case a family-focused social theory and a psychological theory. Although he talks about his first case, the man who seemed to be a common drunkard, in the first five pages of his book, later on he recommends that temperance societies, such as the Sons of Temperance, should emulate his practice of visiting the families of people who have alcohol problems (Augustus, 1972). The greatest support for the alcoholic in bringing about rehabilitation is the family. Augustus, therefore, had an approach to helping those who ran afoul of the law because of their drinking, and that approach was to make sure that his or her family supported them. It was important for Augustus for a man to be "a man again" (Augustus, 1972, p. 5). His theory of psychological rehabilitation had to do with a man becoming a man by supporting his family adequately. You become a man when you are the man of the house and you are doing your duty to your wife and children.

Augustus did not use the term probation as most people would use it today. In his book, he referred to "bailing on probation" (Augustus, 1972, p. 99). He called the activity that he was engaged in as "bailing." For instance, he writes, "This year [1848] I accomplished a greater amount of labor in bailing persons, than during any other single year since beginning my labors in the courts" (Augustus, 1972, p. 37).

When he did use the word probation, it was usually in the sense of "testing" or "trial." This would be similar to someone saying they were just hired at a job and would be on probation for ninety days. So, he referred to probation as that period of time prior to sentencing when the person had a chance to show that they were capable of reformation. If they could show they were capable of turning over a new leaf, they would be fined when they returned to court. If they could not satisfy the judge that it was possible to turn their life around, they would be subject to imprisonment (Panzarella, 2002).

Following up on his initial success, as indicated above, he helped out many unfortunate men in the next few months and in the next ten years. But not everyone he talked to or, as it often happened, who appealed to him for assistance, did he find amenable for his help. He carefully screened possible candidates by interviewing them, sometimes checking out their backgrounds, and learning more about their histories. He was most eager to offer his assistance to those who seemed to present a low risk, who had some form of family support, and who had not been involved in violent offenses. Those he chose to help, he sought to first bail them out, and then, to improve their behavior and keep them living a life as a respectable citizen (Lindner, 2007).

Bringing about change in a person's behavior, for John Augustus, meant trying to meet some of their social needs. For instance, he assisted those he bailed out by trying to help them find employment, find suitable housing, get an education, or deal with personal problems. Sometimes, he actually employed those he was helping in his shoemaking shop so they could learn a skill which might well lead to regular employment elsewhere (Lindner, 2007).

He tells in his book about his concern with the evils of alcohol and mentions that he belonged to several temperance societies. There was an active temperance movement in the nineteenth and early twentieth centuries that focused on discouraging people from drinking alcohol. There were many spokespersons for this movement, such as Susan B. Anthony and Carry Nation, but the work of the movement was generally carried out by societies. Two of the most notable societies were the Women's Christian Temperance Union and the Anti-Saloon League. Augustus belonged to a few of these temperance societies, including the Washington Total Abstinence Society. But Augustus was also interested in other social movements of the time, such as the antislavery movement and moral reform groups (Sieh, 1993). He identified himself as nonsectarian but belonged to various denominations, such as the Methodists, Universalists, Baptists, and Unitarians (Sieh, 1993).

Given his interest in social reform, especially as it related to the unhealthy effects of drinking alcohol, it is little wonder that his first endeavors to help people at the police court were limited to reforming drunkards. Panzarella (2002) notes that it was his active involvement in and support of the temperance movement—rather than religion, enlightenment philosophy, or civic duty—that motivated Augustus's work to help people who came before the courts.

A tool he began using early in his bailing-out work was his employment of the pledge. If the person he elected to help was a drunkard, Augustus usually insisted that they take the pledge; that is, that they promise to no longer drink liquor (Augustus, 1972). He writes that having people sign the pledge had a magical effect upon chronic alcoholics (Augustus, 1972).

Another approach he used was to allow homeless people to reside temporarily in his house. He does not ever write about what his wife thought about this, but there were times that he had as many fifteen of the individuals he was helping living with them. In his 1939 foreword to Augustus's book, Harvard professor Sheldon Glueck pointed out that some of the contemporary probation officers in Glueck's day only provided "Perfunctory, sporadic office check-ups" (Augustus, 1972, p. xxii). The monitoring and supervision that Augustus provided was anything but perfunctory or sporadic. With this level of support, it is less of a wonderment that he was so successful in effecting change in his clients.

Lindner (2007) also points out that a key component of the services Augustus offered was his meticulous record keeping. Although obviously time consuming, he kept a written record of every person he supervised. It's also why we can accept from his book that he supervised for a season of probation 1,152 men and 794 women and girls (Augustus, 1972). Furthermore, that leads to another important aspect of his work. After establishing his bailing out with men, he then began to help women and finally children.

At first, he refused to help out female drunkards. But when he was accosted by a woman in a jail cell in 1842, who begged for his help, he was persuaded to give in and help her, too. It is very likely he was strongly influenced in this first female case because he learned that she had a husband and children. But, thereafter, and for the rest of his bailing-out career, he would also help women.

Then, a year later, he happened to be in court when two children, sisters who were eight and ten years old, were arraigned for larceny (Augustus, 1972). The circumstances of the case, which he learned by listening to what was said in court, were such that Augustus thought that a great injustice was being done to the girls. This was confirmed by finding out that the girls' father was a drunkard, and the father thought that at least one of his girls ought to go to jail. This convinced Augustus to get involved, and he bailed the girls out, taking the younger girl home with him. The next day, he went to the girls' home, only to learn that their mother was an alcoholic, too. He couldn't allow the girls to return to that home, so he found a home for the older girl and decided that he and his wife would raise the younger girl.

This case set the tone for his approach with other children in the future. He would bail out many children, ages seven and older, who were being charged with petty crimes—often larceny. Not only would he look for a supportive family environment for the children to return to, but he would take in and board girls and women at his home, often for lengthy periods of time. Furthermore, his modus operandi became established for all of his work. He writes about that in his book:

> It became pretty generally known that my labors were upon the ground of reform, that I confined my efforts mainly to those who were indicted for their first offense, and whose hearts were not wholly depraved, but gave promise of better things; it was also known that I received no compensation for so doing, and it early appeared that the judges were favorably disposed toward my plan of operation. (Augustus, 1972, p. 19)

Not only did he work with women and children, but also with prostitutes and women who ran houses of prostitution. That was initiated in 1845, when Augustus was approached by a woman who ran a "house of ill fame." The woman said that if he bailed her out, she would leave the city and give up her career as a madam. He agreed, and it is likely that his motivation was to shut down houses of prostitution. However, that also caused opposition to his activities.

In his book, John Augustus suggests that the police and very possibly other court or city officials made money from houses of prostitution. As he comments in his report, "I then became aware that it was useless to attempt to break up a den of vice of this kind, as the strong arm of the law was averse to such an act"—shutting down such houses (Augustus, 1972, p. 22).

But that didn't stop him from working with young girls, usually between the ages of ten to thirteen, who were prostituting themselves in Boston. Augustus took a very strict stance when it came to working with prostitutes. He looked, as usual, for a girl who was being arrested for prostitution for the first time. A second arrest placed her beyond his hope for reform (Panzarella, 2002). But following the first arrest and his bailing her out, his program of reform consisted of placing a girl as a domestic servant. Since domestic service was the most common employment for girls and women at that time in the nineteenth century, it would provide the most likely type of job for a female (Lindner, 2007).

Augustus also continued to take girls and women into his own home; sometimes there were so many living in his home that Ball Fenner, in his book, referred to Augustus's house as like a harem. Fenner writes: "The house literally swarmed with females; and if some of them had been fairer looking, and all of them better clad, a stranger might have been led to suppose that he was in Sultan's Harem" (Fenner, 2015, p. 40).

In 1848, John Augustus met with a group of about twenty-five philanthropists in the Boston area. Augustus got them to agree to provide funds for a home where women could stay for as long as needed. He had come to the conclusion that such a shelter was necessary because of the overwhelming number of females who needed help (Panzarella, 2002).

SUPPORT AND OPPOSITION
TO JOHN AUGUSTUS'S WORK

As Charles Lindner points out in his article "Thacher, Augustus, and Hill: The Path to Statutory Probation in the United States and England" (Lindner, 2007), John Augustus's work is all the more noteworthy because of the opposition and obstacles, not to mention vicious attacks, that he encountered over the course of his ten-year career.

Augustus himself referred to the abuse and rudeness he encountered in his report. For instance, he writes:

> Often when I attempted to enter the courtroom, I was rudely repulsed by the officers and told that I could not go in, as their orders were imperative to admit no one except members of the bar.... [When allowed in] I was crowded back and not allowed a seat where the members of the bar sat, even though there were at the time a number of unoccupied chairs.... I subsequently took a seat, but was soon rudely expelled without the least cause. (Augustus, 1972, pp. 15–16)

Many court officials and judges often saw him as an outsider who had no business getting involved in the court's work. Furthermore, court officers, jailers, and police officers frequently viewed him as someone robbing them of their fees, since it was standard practice at the time that officials were paid when an individual was incarcerated (Lindner, 2007). The same people accused him of mollycoddling wrong-doers by offering them treatment and help, rather than subjecting them to punishment (Lindner, 2007).

Furthermore, near the end of his book, Augustus did address the opposition to his "bailing on probation." He wrote that some were opposed to his methods because they believed it was an incentive to crime and thus detrimental to society. He surmised that the opposition to his methods were often from people who thought he was robbing the law of exacting punishment. He cited statistics showing that during the previous several years, 16,000 people were placed in the House of Corrections in Massachusetts, and that half of them were not only incarcerated for drunkenness, but about the same number had been previously locked up (Augustus, 1972). He then wrote that it was time for an investigation into this situation so that the public may be better informed about the usual practice of constantly locking up "this unfortunate class of criminals" (Augustus, 1972, p. 101). He could, though, demonstrate by his careful records of the people he had helped, that of the nearly 2,000 he bailed out, only ten absconded and failed to return to court an improved person (Augustus, 1972).

Then there were the accusations that he took advantage of the people he helped by taking money from them and also profiting by accepting donations from individual philanthropists and charitable organizations (Lindner, 2007). In refuting the allegations that he personally benefited from helping people, Augustus noted that those he helped seldom offered him any remuneration. Despite the efforts of researchers to find that he was involved in any wrongdoing, nothing of that nature has ever been revealed (Lindner, 2007).

On the other hand, he had many supporters. There are many articles, letters, and quotes from supporters in his report, but among his supporters were Sheldon Glueck, who wrote the foreword to the book in 1939, and Horace Mann, the educational reformer and U.S. congressman. Mann wrote about John Augustus, stating:

> Your labors favor all classes; they tend to reform the prisoner; they render property more inviolable; they give additional security to every man's person, and every man's life; they make it less mournful to think of our common nature; and they help to remove one of the foulest stains from an age that aspires to be called Christian. You seem to be entitled to the aid and encouragement of all. (Augustus, 1972, p. 61)

William B. English, a newspaper reporter at the time, wrote the following about Augustus:

> The great philanthropist to whom we have briefly alluded, is one of the most active disciples in the course of modern reformation; he is a Philanthropist, not in theory alone, but in practice. Toward the unfortunate his heart was full of pity, and all its kindliest feelings were exercised in alleviating their distresses. To the poor inebriate and that class of unfortunate females who had fallen victims to misplaced affection, and who were driven still deeper into despair by the harsh breath of slander, his sympathies were ever excited. He sought them in the lone hovel, and in those dark abodes where few had moral courage to approach, and then it was his pleasure to administer the sweets of consolation, to bind up the bruised heart when hope had fled. (Augustus, 1972, p. 53)

Did he profit in any way financially from his work?

John Augustus addresses that question at the very end of his book, as there were "persons who believe, or affect to believe that I make money by such acts" (Augustus, 1972, p. 103). He writes that while his work has saved the county and the state of Massachusetts hundreds or thousands of dollars, "it drains my pockets, instead of enriching me" (Augustus, 1972, p. 103). He worked hard at his boot-making business during the first years of his probation endeavors, sometimes working all night to make up for the time he spent in court. As a consequence of his volunteer work, though, he indicates that he spent all that he earned at his trade. By the fourth and fifth years, he was gaining more notoriety, and money was contributed to his cause. During the years 1844 through 1846, he received about $1,200 each year. After that, he gave up his shoemaking business to devote more time to his volunteer labors. For the last five years, he took in contributions of an average of $1,776 annually, "All of which I expended, and have not a dollar of this sum" (p. 104).

The anonymous letter writer of 1858 describes his last years: "The unceasing calls made upon his time destroyed his business ...; but, absorbed in the good he was daily doing, he nevertheless continued it steadily and undeviating, undeterred by any discouragement of a pecuniary nature" (Lindner, 2006, p. 78). And Augustus concludes his book with these words:

> ... [M]y time has not been spent in getting out *books*, but in getting *persons* out of jail. If there are any who wish to render me assistance by pecuniary aid or otherwise, or any who desire information or assistance which I can render, in my field of labor, I should be happy to see them at my residence, No. 65 Chamber Street.
>
> It will, I trust, afford peculiar satisfaction to those who have aided me to know, that the funds which they have contributed have not been misapplied. I respectfully submit this sketch of my labors, to my friends and the public. (Augustus, 1972, p. 104)

Financially impoverished and suffering from a prolonged illness, John Augustus died on June 21, 1859, at the age of seventy-four. Charles Lindner (2006) states that Augustus sacrificed himself for the good of others, while contending that his contributions to the creation of probation were "so enormous and significant" that it is readily understandable why he is considered the father of probation (Lindner, 2007, p. 37).

During his lifetime, there were no paid probation officers in the United States. It was not until 1878 that Massachusetts passed a statute providing for probation officers. That law required the mayor of Boston to appoint a probation officer "to attend the sessions of the courts of criminal jurisdiction, to investigate the cases of persons charged with or convicted of crimes and misdemeanors, and to recommend to such courts the placing on probation of such persons as might reasonably be expected to be reformed without punishment" (Lindner, 2007, p. 38). Two years later, another law was passed in Massachusetts, the state where John Augustus performed his labors on behalf of others, extending to all cities and towns in the state the right to hire probation officers (Siegel & Worrall, 2012).

Once Massachusetts took these first steps, the concept spread to other states. Gaining momentum since Augustus's time, today, there are probation services and probation officers in both state and federal courts, and probation is the most frequently used sentence in criminal justice (Bohm & Haley, 2012). Altogether, there are about 2,000 adult probation agencies in the United States (Siegel & Worrall, 2012). As of the end of 2009, approximately 5 million adults in America were on probation or parole (Bohm & Haley, 2012).

QUESTIONS FOR DISCUSSION

1. In what ways do probation officers today still carry out practices of probation developed by John Augustus?
2. Which personal characteristics were important in Augustus's developing probation work in the courts?
3. What was John Augustus's theory of why people violated the law?

IMPORTANT TERMS AND NAMES

Bailing on probation: John Augustus did not view what he did as probation. Instead, he saw it as "bailing on probation." That is, he bailed people out of the court system or jail and that allowed them a few weeks to show that they should not be sentenced to a jail or prison term.

Ball Fenner: Ball Fenner was a newspaper reporter in Boston during the time that John Augustus was bailing people from the courts. Fenner wrote articles about Augustus, and when he wrote a book based on his experiences as a reporter, he included profiles of Augustus. He published his book in 1856, *Raising the Veil, Or Scenes in the Courts.*

Probation: The contemporary definition of probation is the conditional release of a criminal offender from other sentences of the court during which time he or she is under the supervision of a probation officer.

Temperance societies: Temperance societies were organizations that were dedicated to bringing about social reform in regard to the use of alcoholic beverages. Such societies either advocated for moderation or total abstinence from drinking intoxicating liquor.

Sheldon Glueck: Sheldon Glueck was a criminologist and researcher at Harvard University, who, often along with his wife, also a professor at Harvard, studied criminal behavior.

FOR FURTHER READING

Augustus, J. (1972). *John Augustus: First probation officer.* Montclair, NJ: Paterson Smith Publishing Corp.

Fenner, B. (2015). *Raising the veil, or scenes in the courts.* London, England: Forgotten Books.

Lindner, C. (2006). John Augustus, father of probation, and the anonymous letter. *Federal Probation, 70*(1), 77–78.

Lindner, C. (2007). Thacher, Augustus, and Hill: The path to statutory probation in the United States and England. *Federal Probation, 71*(3), 36–41.

Panzarella, R. (2002). Theory and practice of probation on bail in the report of John Augustus. *Federal Probation, 66*(3), 38–42.

Sieh, E. W. (1993). From Augustus to the Progressives: A study of probation's formative years. *Federal Probation, 57*(3), 67–73.

REVIEW QUESTIONS

True or False

1. John Augustus is known as the Father of American probation.
2. Most of what we know about John Augustus comes from several well-written biographies of him.
3. The very first case John Augustus took on was the case of a male drunkard.
4. Augustus seemed to have a family-focused approach to helping people who were charged with a crime.

Multiple Choice

5. In John Augustus's work, he seemed to use the term *probation* to mean
   a. An indeterminate sentence.
   b. Trial or testing.
   c. Community-oriented policing.
   d. A fine by a court.

6. Drunkenness and alcoholism were considered by John Augustus to be
   a. One of the great evils of his time.
   b. A minor problem.
   c. One of the comic aspects of society.
   d. A major cause of crime.

7. The voluntary probation work that John Augustus did in Boston was so popular that
   a. He collected great wealth.
   b. He never faced any opposition.
   c. He received a moderate number of donations.
   d. He received wide public acclaim and was regarded during his lifetime as a true American hero.

8. John Augustus's contributions to the field of probation were highlighted by
   a. The fact that Massachusetts was the first state to allow the hiring of probation officers.
   b. His being paid to be the first probation officer.
   c. Other states hiring paid probation officers during Augustus's lifetime.
   d. Augustus being appointed Massachusetts' attorney general.

9. What John Augustus meant by "bailing on probation" was
   a. That he was supervising people who were out on bail before returning to court for possible sentencing.
   b. People failing to return to court.
   c. Individuals who committed a crime having to see a probation officer regularly for six months.
   d. People having to pay exorbitant bail.

REFERENCES

Augustus, J. (1972). *John Augustus: First probation officer*. Montclair, NJ: Paterson Smith Publishing Corp.

Bohm, R. M., & Haley, K. N. (2012). *Introduction to criminal justice* (7th ed.). New York, NY: McGraw-Hill.

Champion, D. J. (1996). *Probation, parole, and community correction* (2nd ed.). Upper Saddle River, NJ: Prentice Hall.

Fenner, B. (2015). *Raising the veil, or scenes in the courts*. London, England: Forgotten Books.

Lindner, C. (2007). Thacher, Augustus, and Hill: The path to statutory probation in the United States and England. *Federal Probation, 71*(3), 36–41.

Lindner, C. (2006). John Augustus, father of probation, and the anonymous letter. *Federal Probation, 70*(1), 77–78.

Panzarella, R. (2002). Theory and practice of probation on bail in the report of John Augustus. *Federal Probation, 66*(3), 38–42.

Schmalleger, F., & Smykla, J. O. (2009). *Corrections in the 21st century* (4th ed.). New York, NY: McGraw-Hill.

Siegel, L. J., & Worrall, J. L. (2012). *Introduction to criminal justice* (13th ed.). Belmont, CA: Wadsworth.

Sieh, E. W. (1993). From Augustus to the progressives: A study of probation's formative years. *Federal Probation, 57*(3), 67–73.

CREDIT

Ball Fenner, Excerpts from *Raising the Veil, Or Scenes in the Courts*, pp. 282–284. Copyright in the Public Domain.

12

SAMUEL GRIDLEY HOWE
Setting the Stage for Prison Reform and Parole

Samuel Gridley Howe has been sometimes referred to as the Father of Parole in America, but it could be argued that he might better be called the Grandfather of Parole. He could also be labeled as one of the earliest and most articulate of the apologists of the Auburn Prison System. But, no matter where he might fit into the pantheon of criminal justice pioneers, one thing seems certain. Samuel Gridley Howe was a Renaissance man who is recognized as an inventor and pioneer in several fields: education of the disabled and blind, physician, philanthropist, soldier, advocate for the humane treatment of the mentally challenged, militant abolitionist, and prison reformer. And on top of those things, he was married to an accomplished poet—the woman who wrote the words to "The Battle Hymn of the Republic."

His life and a description of his work is fairly well documented, thanks to three biographies, including one written after his death by his wife, Julia Ward Howe. Although much of his life has little to do with criminal justice, still, it is such a remarkable life it demands that his story should be retold—and remembered.

The Howe family was one of the first of the settlers to make their way from England to the New World, arriving in 1630 in Massachusetts. Joseph Howe, Samuel Gridley Howe's father, was a maker of rope and cordage—mostly used by shipbuilders and cod fishers—in Boston, where the family lived, and along the New England seacoast.

Born on November 10, 1801, as young Samuel was growing up, he was an outspoken and headstrong boy who engaged in many fights because he wasn't shy about voicing his political views. He was born just after Thomas Jefferson had become the third president of the United States. Jefferson was a Republican who had battled the federalists, and both Joseph and Samuel identified themselves also as Jeffersonian Republicans and clearly on the side of democracy, republicanism, and "the people" (Meltzer, 1964). But America was still a very young country and still embroiled in conflict. One of the most embittered conflicts was over whether America would have a strong central government or whether people and the separate states would retain the power. Those who feared a strong central government thought that a central government invited tyranny. On the other side were federalists, who welcomed a strong government. Thomas Jefferson, like Joseph and Samuel Howe, were firmly in the camp of those who, following the watchwords of the French revolution, believed that liberty, equality, and fraternity were concepts to fight for.

And fight, young Samuel did—often getting pummeled by bigger boys at his school, the Boston Latin School. Sometimes tiring of the fights, he complained to his father, asking why he had to stay in school. His father wanted him to finish school and go to college (Schwartz, 1956).

During the early years of the nineteenth century, America was still battling Britain, but by 1815, the conflict was ended and the British army and navy had stopped trying to retake America. But during the more than ten years of battles, the Howe family business had suffered (mainly because the government needed the ropes that the Howe Company made and had taken over the business), and it would be years before they would be solvent and wealthy again. Samuel's mother had just died, and Joseph Howe was left to raise six children. As a result of the family's financial difficulties, Joseph could only send one of his boys to college. He selected Samuel because, he reasoned, he was the best reader and the most likely to be a success in college (Schwartz, 1956).

Neither Joseph nor Samuel liked the idea of attending Harvard University because they agreed it was a hotbed of federalism—and he was likely to be in more fights. His father suggested Brown College in Rhode Island, and Samuel Gridley Howe entered Brown in 1817 (Howe, 2015).

The adolescent Howe didn't much like college. Students were expected to memorize their studies and repeat them back to the instructors, without ever injecting any of their own thoughts or ideas. To deal with the routines and boredom of the regimented college life he was forced to endure, Howe turned to pranks and jokes. Despite everyone else—students and faculty alike—recognizing he had a first-rate mind, he continued to engage in pranks. His father and his teachers wondered what would become of this prankster who didn't seem to be much of a scholar. But they needn't have worried, as it didn't take Howe long to decide and then announce to his father that he wanted to become a doctor. Also, he was determined to go to Harvard Medical School. His father agreed that he could do that, as long as he settled down and took his studies seriously (Meltzer, 1964). After graduating from Brown, he enrolled in Harvard Medical School in 1821, where he would be taught by some of the best physicians and surgeons in America.

He did settle down to become a more serious student, and he graduated with distinction in 1824. At about the same time as he was leaving Harvard Medical School, the Greek revolt against Turkish rule was taking place. Many young American men left to help Greece emancipate their country. Howe thought that he could offer free medical skills in the war. However, when he told his father his plans, Joseph Howe was not supportive of his son going off to a war in Greece. Young Samuel Howe offered his reasoning: "Battlefield surgery will teach me more about practice than in this quiet place," he said (Meltzer, 1964, p. 27). The elder Howe accepted his son's rationale, but requested that he wait until he actually received his diploma as a Doctor of Medicine. Acceding to his father's wishes, Howe waited until November, 1824; and then, packing up his surgical instruments, he sailed for Greece.

Once he arrived in Greece and began working on injured soldiers, however, he found that it was necessary for him to take an active part in the war by becoming a guerrilla and a fighter himself (Meltzer, 1964). A year later, he became the head physician-surgeon at the hospital at

Nauplia. During this time in Greece, he was becoming fluent in French and Greek while also learning to converse in German. In the fall of 1826, he left the post at the hospital and was commissioned director of the medical department of the fleet. Stationed on the ship *Karteria*, the ship sailed the waters around the Greek islands, sometimes engaging Turkish ships in battles. After a tour of duty, Howe went to work in another hospital, this time in Paros. Finally, with the help of allied troops, the war ended and it was time for reconstruction. Howe wondered how he could best help the Greeks to rebuild after the war.

The Greek government asked Howe to return to America to raise funds. He accepted this request and left for America, arriving in New York in February 1828. One of his objectives was to raise funds for a two-hundred-bed hospital in Greece, which he agreed to direct for a year. When he made his way to his home in Boston on his fund-raising tour, he found that he had won both local as well as national acclaim because of his regular letters home about the Greek war for independence. Drawing on his wartime experiences, Howe began writing a historical sketch of the Greek revolution, while he continued to actively raise funds to take back to Greece (Schwartz, 1956).

Howe was able to complete his book in a few months, and when it was published, it was a success. With that success, he was able to raise even more money. And before the end of 1828, he was ready to return to Greece with funds, along with food and clothing. He debarked on Greek soil in Aegina, but the port there had been virtually destroyed in the war, and he thought that it would be helpful in reconstruction if the port were repaired so it could accommodate shipping. He directed the efforts of hundreds of people in proceeding with this public project. But with the rebuilding of the port under way, his thoughts turned to how he could best help feed Greek citizens who were struggling to survive after the war. Organizing an effort to distribute seeds to people, he began giving out seeds in exchange for a promise that part of the harvest of every farmer would be given to help build a school. The president of Greece heard about his idea, supported it, and Howe chose people to farm in surrounding communities.

But a setback came to his ambitious projects when he contracted malaria and almost died. Although he planned to return to America in 1830, to aid his recovery he traveled from Greece into other parts of Europe. When he arrived in Paris, he decided he would stay there a while to take more medical training. After a few months, he sailed for home, arriving in Boston in April 1831. He was now twenty-nine years of age—with no clear direction for his life.

His father advised that he could become wealthy by opening up his own medical practice. But Samuel Gridley Howe replied that he wanted to do more than just make money. "I want to do something no one else has done," he said (Meltzer, 1964, p. 60).

DOING WHAT NO ONE ELSE HAD DONE

While seeking out a direction in life, Dr. Howe applied for government positions, considered being a newspaper editor, and wrote magazine articles. Nothing seemed quite right. One day, in talking with a friend, Dr. John D. Fisher, he learned that Fisher planned to build the New England Asylum for the Blind. His friend asked Howe to be the director. Howe immediately said he'd do it.

In preparation for this, Dr. Howe returned to Europe to study how the blind were taught in Europe. He also expected to recruit some experts who could return to America to work for him. As he traveled throughout Europe, he visited many schools for the blind, wound up getting arrested in Prussia (where he would spend weeks in jail), and eventually got back to Paris before returning to Boston in mid-1832.

On his return home, he became aware of a tide of reform that was sweeping Boston and New England. Many of the wealthy residents of Boston were concerned about the plight of people they viewed as the unfortunates of society. But Howe's immediate concern was to inaugurate the New England Asylum for the Blind, which was a name and a concept, but it lacked a building. That didn't stand in the way of Howe, who persuaded his father to allow him to start his asylum for the blind in the family home. Soon, the first two blind students arrived—Abby and Sophia Carter, ages six and eight.

The work of teaching the blind was a new educational endeavor, and there were no tools for the job. Undaunted, Dr. Samuel Howe created his own. Within a few months, there were seven students in the asylum, but Howe had run out of money. Again, as with every obstacle he ever encountered, Howe found a way around the problem. He took his students to the Massachusetts legislature and requested an annual sum of $6,000 for the education and maintenance of twenty blind students. He got what he asked for, and then sought more. Based on his acquisition of donations and grants, he was able in 1833 to find a new home for the asylum, which was renamed the Perkins Institution.

As he innovated techniques of instruction, Howe became aware that there were only three books in America printed for the blind. That was unacceptable. Therefore, he began writing his own textbooks for grammar, spelling, geography and history. He also wanted his students to have classroom books, such as the Bible and books of literature and history. He bought printing presses to print books for the blind. Within a short period of time, his press had printed more books for the blind than had ever been printed in the English-speaking world (Meltzer, 1964).

And the number of students who found their way to the Perkins Institution continued to grow. By their second year, they had forty-two students, and the building they used for a school had to be enlarged, but was still inadequate. By 1839, the Perkins Institution moved to South Boston and took over a large hotel. The school would remain there for the next seventy-five years.

Continuing to reach out to blind students outside of New England, Howe traveled to Ohio, Kentucky, New Orleans, and even to the halls of Congress in Washington, D.C. During his conversations with people as he toured the country, he was asked his opinion of asylums. His response reflected the evolving Dr. Samuel Howe, as he frequently remarked that he objected to asylums. He often added that we had no right to send the old, the poor, and the blind to asylums because they belong in families and should not be deprived from loving relationships (Meltzer, 1964).

A new challenge appeared one day for Dr. Samuel Howe when he heard about a girl who lived in Hanover, New Hampshire, who was not only blind but also a deaf-mute. He went to see the girl, whose name was Laura Bridgman. After talking to her parents, it was agreed that Laura would come to live at the Perkins Institution. She arrived in South Boston in 1837; by 1839, Howe had taught her to read and write, and together they invented a form of sign language (Schwartz, 1956).

When Charles Dickens toured America in 1842, one of his stops was at the Perkins Institution. He had heard of Laura Bridgman and wanted to meet her himself. When he got a chance to spend time with her, he was amazed at what she could do. Dickens's enthusiastic account of Laura Bridgman brought worldwide acclaim for both Laura and Dr. Howe.

Near the end of the 1830s, Dr. Howe became reacquainted with Horace Mann, whom he had met when Mann was a tutor at Brown University. Now, Horace Mann was a state legislator in Massachusetts and president of the Massachusetts State Senate. When they met again, Mann had just put through a bill in the Senate creating a State Board of Education. He then resigned his Senate seat to take the job of secretary of the State Board of Education. Howe and Mann both recognized that they had many interests in common.

Around the same time, Howe would meet Dorothea Dix. She asked Howe to help her improve the treatment of the insane, as the mentally ill were called at that time. She also told him of the deplorable conditions in jails, which is where she taught the Bible on Sundays to women inmates. She said her plan was to investigate the jails, prisons, and poorhouses throughout Massachusetts. Howe pledged his help.

He took matters into his own hands by making an examination of the East Cambridge Jail, after which he wrote an article about "the horrors of the demoniac den" where people were treated worse than "animals in a zoo" (Meltzer, 1964, p. 114). And when Dix completed her investigation of jails, workhouses, and almshouses in the fall of 1842, Howe was appalled by what he read in her notebooks. Shocked by the conditions of these institutions, Howe wrote several articles for newspapers and magazines exposing the conditions of these facilities to the public.

That same year he ran on the Whig ticket for a seat in the Massachusetts state legislature. After winning, he took Dix's report and read it to the legislators. One of the purposes of her investigation was to show that the mentally ill were not only housed with a variety of criminals and other inmates of the institutions, they were treated abominably. A bill was proposed to build a hospital for the mentally ill where they could receive more scientific treatment. With Howe's support, this bill passed.

SAMUEL GRIDLEY HOWE TAKES A WIFE

Dr. Howe had reached the age of forty. He had confided to friends that once he passed thirty and wasn't married, he expected to live out the rest of his life as a bachelor (Schwartz, 1956). But then he met Julia Ward.

It was actually because of Laura Bridgman that they met. Julia Ward, who was twenty-two and lived in a wealthy family in New York, had heard about Laura and wanted to meet her at the Perkins Institution. She was beautiful and an accomplished singer, could speak several languages, and wrote poetry. They fell in love. Within a few months, they were engaged. It was agreed that after they married she would use the name Julia Ward Howe and that she would move to Boston and her husband would support her—although not quite in the style she had grown used to. They were married on April 23, 1843, after which, traveling with Horace Mann and his new bride, Mary Peabody, they honeymooned in Europe. Julia became pregnant during the honeymoon and gave birth to a daughter in March 1844.

An interesting aspect of their honeymoon in Europe was that the couple met a woman by the name of Florence Nightingale. She asked them if they thought it suitable for an English woman like herself to devote herself to works of charity in a hospital. Samuel Howe replied: "Choose your path, go on with it, wherever it may lead you, and God be with you!" (Meltzer, 1964, p. 125). Of course, Florence Nightingale would go on to be the social reformer who founded modern nursing.

Once they returned home, Howe and Horace Mann, who in 1839 had opened up the first American school to train teachers, teamed up to introduce articulation into the teaching of deaf-mutes. The same year as their return to Boston from Europe, Howe was elected to the Boston School Board. Throughout his term in this position, he and Mann worked together to improve schools by advocating for a change in the way students were taught and eliminating the flogging of students.

PRISON REFORMER

It was during the 1840s that Samuel Gridley Howe was most active as a prison reformer and an advocate for prison inmates. Although in general he was always a passionate voice for the helpless and the voiceless, it may have been the work of Dorothea Dix that moved Howe to get involved in writing about prisons and speaking out for prisoners. Then again, there was an ongoing public debate in the 1840s over the Massachusetts prison system.

Two rival systems contended for public favor. One was the solitary system, as practiced at the Eastern State Penitentiary in Philadelphia. The solitary system called for complete silence and discouraged prisoners from working or sleeping together. Each prisoner had a separate cell. The other was the silent, or congregant, system, which was the system used at the Auburn State Prison in New York. In this system, inmates worked together during the day and took meals together, but then returned to individual cells at night. When Dr. Howe became a member of the Prison Discipline Society of Boston, the society was leaning toward the silent system. Joining him on the Prison Discipline Society were his closest friends, Charles Sumner, who served in the Massachusetts legislature, and Horace Mann. The three of them were appointed to a committee to examine the rival prison systems. After Howe wrote their report, he read it to the Boston Prison Discipline Society at their 1846 annual meeting. The society refused to permit it to be published, so Howe got it published privately as a minority report (Schwartz, 1956).

In their report "An Essay on Separate and Congregate Systems of Prison Discipline; Being a Report Made to the Boston Prison Discipline Society,"

Howe, reflecting the combined opinions of Sumner, Mann, and himself, compared the two systems and came out in favor of the Pennsylvania model (Howe, 1846). Howe argues in this report that a penitentiary filled with convicts cannot be administered using the congregate system without frequent use of corporal punishment. But he states that the use of physical punishment is unwise. Corporal punishment, he contends, crushes the manhood of prisoners and destroys "the very feelings on which we must rest our hope of reform" (Howe, 1846, p. 55).

Howe goes on to write that the discipline in a prison should have one aim: reformation. Therefore, by cutting off contacts and communication with other prisoners, by introducing habits of sober industry, and by only permitting contacts with "good men whom he can learn to love and imitate" and good books and good thoughts, then reform is possible (p. 26). The congregate system defeats the idea of reform by allowing criminals to interact, and this can only lead to reinforced criminality and revolt.

By June of 1847, the dispute was ended, and the Prison Discipline Society voted for the Auburn system; thus, Howe and his friends suffered a defeat (Schwartz, 1956). Funds were then appropriated to add a cell block to the old Charlestown prison so that the Auburn system might be implemented.

However, it is significant that the term *parole* was perhaps first used in America by Samuel Gridley Howe when he wrote a letter to the Prison Association of New York on December 21, 1846. Howe wrote: "I believe there are many who might be so trained as to be left upon their parole during the last periods of their imprisonment with safety and with great advantage to themselves" (Klein, 1920, p. 417). In this letter, Howe emphasizes the difficulty inmates would have in governing themselves when released from jails or prisons if they gained their freedom without training (Klein, 1920).

Having spent some time in the argument on the two prison systems and writing about parole, Dr. Howe next turned his attention to those people who were mentally challenged or intellectually retarded. In Howe's day, they were called idiots, and often they were placed in jails or houses of correction (Meltzer, 1964). When Howe began speaking out on the topic, a commission was appointed by the Massachusetts legislature to study the question of developmentally delayed individuals; Dr. Howe was chosen to head this commission. For the next two years, the commission studied the problem throughout Massachusetts. He personally examined hundreds of people who were intellectually defective. In October 1848, the commission issued its report. The report received both national and international attention and was viewed as the definitive word on the causes and prevention of "idiocy" (Meltzer, 1964). In his report, Howe decries the practice of placing these people in jails and almshouses (Howe, 1993).

For a while, Dr. Howe experimented with teaching the intellectually challenged, and then the state created the Massachusetts School for Idiotic and Feeble-Minded Youth. Howe was appointed its general super-intendent, a post he held for twenty-five years (Meltzer, 1964). The school was the first of its kind in America.

At the same time he was exploring the plight of the mentally challenged, Samuel Gridley Howe got involved in abolition, and by 1846 had begun speaking out about slavery. A vigilance committee was formed in Boston to help runaway slaves, and Howe was elected as the chairman. That not only put him squarely in the midst of the debate over how Northern cities like Boston should handle runaway slaves, but he was quickly also involved in the Underground Railroad. In 1853, he became editor of *Commonwealth*, a newspaper that advocated for free speech and for abolition (Schwartz, 1956). His wife Julia began contributing articles, poems, and even plays to the *Commonwealth*.

JULIA WARD HOWE AND HER WRITING

Despite her husband's disapproval of her pursuing a writing career, Julia Ward Howe published her first book of poetry in 1853. Although it was initially published anonymously, it was successful, and she began earning royalties. Dr. Howe voiced his displeasure with her for publishing her work and letting her name be known, but that did not stop her. Her second book of poems was published in 1856, and the next year her play,

The World's Own, was produced in New York and Boston (Meltzer, 1964). Dr. Howe was coming around in terms of accepting Julia's secondary career as a writer, but he thought that her place was in the home, showing devotion to her children and husband. Although this was not mentioned in Julia Ward Howe's biography of her husband, apparently their quarrels over her writing led to heated conversations about them separating (Ruane, 2011). But neither could likely accept being separated from the children, and within a few years, they had come to reconcile themselves to the realities of their marriage and each other's pursuits (Meltzer, 1964). Howe was undoubtedly less than thrilled about her writing "The Battle Hymn of the Republic," which she penned in November 1861 after watching a review of Union troops in Washington (Ruane, 2011).

SAMUEL GRIDLEY HOWE AS AN ARDENT ABOLITIONIST

When the Fugitive Slave Law was passed by Congress in 1850, Dr. Howe and his Vigilance Committee became more irate and more inclined to take action to prevent runaway slaves from being captured in Massachusetts and returned to the South. When at one point Howe met John Brown, the two men recognized that they had something in common: a hatred of slavery. Not only was Howe supportive of John Brown, but Howe became a member of the "Secret Six," a group of men who supported Brown with money and arms (Schwartz, 1956). John Brown was convinced that slavery could only be abolished through bloodshed, and Howe accepted that Brown might be right.

There is some evidence that Howe and other members of the Secret Six knew about Brown's plan to raid the federal arsenal at Harpers Ferry in Virginia (Schwartz, 1956). When the raid took place, some of Brown's fellow raiders were killed, and Brown himself was wounded and captured. The failure of the raid led to public disclosure of the Secret Six and the support of Brown by Samuel Gridley Howe. Brown was tried, convicted, and hanged on December 2, 1859. Some people called for charges to be brought against the members of the Secret Six, and perhaps fearing this himself, Howe fled to Canada for a period of time. Talk of Howe's involvement in the raid at Harpers Ferry had pretty much blown over by April 12, 1861, when the first shots of the Civil War were fired at Fort Sumter, near Charleston, South Carolina.

The federal government created the U.S. Sanitary Commission in June 1861 to look after the health and comfort of all soldiers. Howe was appointed a director of this commission, and this allowed him to work again with Dorothea Dix, who was superintendent of the commission. While serving on the Sanitation Commission, he continued to meet with other antislavery leaders to discuss the end of slavery. Anticipating various problems when slavery was ended, they believed the country needed to be prepared to deal with the cessation of slavery. To this end, and aware that President Lincoln would issue an Emancipation Proclamation at any time, Howe sent a petition to the United States Senate urging Congress to take steps to study the difficulties newly freed slaves would encounter. Lincoln saw the value of this proposal and set up a Freedmen's Inquiry Commission, placing Howe on this three-man board (Schwartz, 1956).

A preliminary report from the freedman's commission to War Secretary Edwin Stanton pointed out that Negroes were very valuable to the war effort, and if properly treated, they could be even more important, especially if they were armed. Men who deserve freedom, the report stated, will be willing to fight for it (Meltzer, 1964). Adding his own thoughts to the official report, Howe advised that the color line be ignored. "I want to sink the difference of race and treat the blacks exactly as I would treat whites in their condition. I do not believe in black colonies, or black regiments" (Meltzer, 1964, p. 214).

Furthermore, Howe advocated for equal rights with no strings attached for Negroes. Slavery, he argued, had created handicaps for blacks by denying them the opportunity to grow and learn, and only freedom—full freedom, at that—would restore the humanity to former slaves (Meltzer, 1964). Unfortunately, no one seemed to listen to what Samuel Gridley Howe was saying.

After a trip to Europe in the late 1860s, Howe returned home to an invitation from the Massachusetts governor to chair the Massachusetts Board of State Charities. This committee was charged with reorganizing and reforming charitable institutions in a single system. In an early report from this committee, Dr. Howe set out a group of principles for public welfare. Looking back on these principles today, it can be seen that Howe's ideas were many decades ahead of his time. He believed that no person should be cut off from society, and he said that no single life should be wasted (Meltzer, 1964).

However, the recommendations that he espoused in his role as a member of the Board of State Charities echoed some of his ideas that he had voiced at least a decade earlier. For instance, in the mid-1850s, when a reform school for girls was proposed in Massachusetts, Howe made his position very clear. He said that the worst thing possible for wayward young women was to place them in an institution together (Schwartz, 1956). "Most persons, born without any strong tendency to either virtue or vice, are creatures of circumstance, and grow up to be virtuous or vicious according to the outward influences exerted upon them," he wrote (Schwartz, 1956, p. 273). Instead of placing them in an institution, he said, wayward young people should be dispersed. They should be sent to live with good families, "which has not, to my knowledge, ever had definite consideration in schemes of reform" he wrote to a friend in 1854 (Schwartz, 1956, p. 273).

An Etching of Samuel Gridley Howe.

Thomas Addis Emmet, https://commons.wikimedia.org/wiki/File:S.G._Howe_(NYPL_Hades-255526-431432).tiff. Copyright in the Public Domain.

In a Board of State Charities annual report, he would write that children who grew up in socially blighted communities could not help but absorb criminal behaviors (Schwartz, 1956). However, Howe maintained the progressive point of view that all social evils could be remedied. But he was of the opinion that what children needed were good homes, temperance, limitations of hours and work, and street cleanliness (Schwartz, 1956). He also believed that almshouses and prisons should be used only as a last resort for habitual paupers and hardened criminals.

One of his last contributions to public service was his tenure on a commission, appointed by President Ulysses S. Grant in 1871, to investigate conditions in Santo Domingo, which became the Dominican Republic.

However, by 1874, he was seriously ill and had to give up some of the positions he held on boards and commissions, although he retained his post as head of the Perkins Institution. On January 9, 1876, Howe died at his home in Boston.

THE LEGACY OF SAMUEL GRIDLEY HOWE

As his wife Julia Ward Howe writes in her memoir of her husband, "Thus ended one of the noblest lives of our day and generation. All that is most sterling in American character may be said to have found its embodiment in Dr. Howe. To the gift of a special and peculiar genius he added great industry and untiring perseverance, animated by a deep and comprehensive benevolence" (Howe, 2015, p. 61).

In a eulogy from the governor of Massachusetts shortly after his death, Howe was lauded for his long and noble career as a philanthropist that included his efforts to educate the blind and the deaf, to reform the discipline of prisons, to instruct the feeble minded, and to ameliorate the conditions of the insane (Howe, 2015). He displayed a great deal of empathy in caring for all people he considered unfortunates. That included his endeavors to improve the administration of prisons and to give a fair chance to released prisoners by training them to be better prepared to go back into society and deal with their freedom. He cared for and tried to help neglected children and youthful offenders, and he was well ahead of his time by advocating that young people should be kept out of prisons and institutions.

His friend, Edward Everett Hale, an author and Unitarian minister, offered a fitting epitaph for Samuel Gridley Howe. He said that Howe was a man who left the unfortunates of society cheerful and happy, and he left the blind "glad in the sunshine of the love of God" (Meltzer, 1964, p. 224).

QUESTIONS FOR DISCUSSION

1. What would be an argument for Samuel Gridley Howe being called the Father of Parole?
2. In your opinion, what was Samuel Gridley Howe's most significant contribution to criminal justice?
3. What was Samuel Gridley Howe's greatest concern as a prison reformer?
4. Looking back at Samuel Gridley Howe's concerns about prisons in the mid-1800s, what do you think he would say about prisons today?

IMPORTANT TERMS AND NAMES

Asylums: The name used in the eighteenth and nineteenth centuries for institutions for the disabled, the insane, and the criminal.

Auburn Prison System: The Auburn Prison System was put into place with the opening of Auburn Prison. The system was also known as the congregate system and employed corporal punishment, solitary confinement, and the practice of inmates working and eating together. This was in contrast to the Pennsylvania system, in which inmates were kept separate in solitary confinement and never allowed to meet together in groups.

Dorothea Dix: Dorothea Dix was a nineteenth-century author of several books and a social reformer. Her work led to better facilities for the mentally ill and criminals.

Freedmen's Inquiry Commission: Established by President Lincoln after the Emancipation Proclamation, the Freedmen's Inquiry Commission was formed to determine the conditions of freed slaves. Samuel Gridley Howe was one of three men serving on this commission.

Fugitive Slave Act: Passed by Congress in 1850, the Fugitive Slave Act was a law passed to return runaway slaves to their owners.

Horace Mann: Horace Mann, who lived from 1796 to 1859, spent his career promoting public education and teacher training while also serving as a legislator in Massachusetts.

John Brown: John Brown was a militant abolitionist who believed that the only way to stop slavery was by armed insurrection. After his ill-fated raid on the federal arsenal at Harpers Ferry, he was arrested. Following a trial, Brown was hanged in December 1859.

Julia Ward Howe: The wife of Samuel Gridley Howe, she was a successful poet and writer, who is best known today as the writer of the lyrics for "The Battle Hymn of the Republic." Following the death of her husband, she took on a more public role as a social reformer.

Massachusetts Board of State Charities: A board set up by the state of Massachusetts in the 1860s to reorganize and reform the various institutions in the state into a single system. Samuel Gridley Howe served as its first chairman.

Parole: A term that means that a prisoner gets a temporary release prior to the end of his or her maximum sentence. Samuel Gridley Howe is said to have been the first American to use the word.

Prison Discipline Society of Boston: Founded in 1825, the Prison Discipline Society investigated jails and prisons. Samuel Gridley Howe served in the society in the 1840s.

Secret Six: The Secret Six were a group of men, including Samuel Gridley Howe, who were opposed to slavery. They supported John Brown with money and arms.

Solitary Prison System: The solitary prison system was a name given to the Pennsylvania model of prison administration. This system required that prisoners be kept apart from each other and not allowed to communicate with each other.

U.S. Sanitary Commission: The U.S. Sanitary Commission was started by private citizens before it was officially brought into existence by President Lincoln in 1861. Its purpose was to ensure that Union soldiers had clean and healthy conditions in army camps. Samuel Gridley Howe served on this commission in 1861.

Vigilance Committee: The Vigilance Committee came into existence in Boston to resist the Fugitive Slave Act of 1850. Samuel Gridley Howe served on this committee.

FOR FURTHER READING

Howe, J. W. (2015). *Memoir of Dr. Samuel Gridley Howe*. London, England: Forgotten Books.

Howe, S. G. (1846). *An essay on separate and congregate systems of prison discipline; being a report made to the Boston Prison Discipline Society*. Boston, MA: William D. Ticknor and Co.

Klein, P. (1920). *Prison methods in New York State: A contribution to the study of theory and practice of correctional institutions in New York State*. New York, NY: Columbia University Press.

Meltzer, M. (1964). *A light in the dark: The life of Samuel Gridley Howe*. New York, NY: Thomas Y. Crowell Co.

Schwartz, H. (1956). *Samuel Gridley Howe: Social reformer, 1801–1876*. Cambridge, MA: Harvard University Press.

REVIEW QUESTIONS

True or False

1. Samuel Gridley Howe wrote about the similarities and differences of the two prison systems as a member of the Boston Prison Discipline Society.

2. Howe believed that prisoners should live in dormitory-style cells in prisons.

3. Samuel Gridley Howe initially gained fame by writing about the Greek Revolution.

4. Howe was trained as an attorney and used his training to defend criminals in court.

Multiple Choice

5. Samuel Gridley Howe's first investigations of conditions in jails led to the conclusion that

   a. Prisoners were treated well.
   b. Prisoners were treated worse than animals in zoos.
   c. Prisoners were usually pampered.
   d. Prisoners should be expected to support themselves by making crafts.

6. Samuel Gridley Hoe supported the Pennsylvania system of prison discipline because
   a. Criminals should never be allowed to communicate with each other.
   b. Dangerous criminals need companionship.
   c. Prisoners are easy to manage if allowed to talk to each other.
   d. Criminals just need loving care and a better education.

7. Due to a report that Samuel Gridley Howe wrote for the Boston Prison Discipline Society, the state of Massachusetts decided to
   a. Adopt the doctrine of separate but equal.
   b. Adopt the Pennsylvania system for its prisons.
   c. Adopt the Auburn model for its prisons.
   d. Adopt the principle that all prisons should be designed to allow prisoners to work and play together.

8. As an abolitionist, Samuel Gridley Howe believed that Negroes
   a. Had been treated admirably by slave owners.
   b. Had been afforded great schools in the South.
   c. Had been allowed opportunities to learn to read.
   d. Had been denied opportunities to learn and grow during slavery.

9. Instead of placing young people in reform schools and other institutions, it was Samuel Gridley Howe's opinion that they should be
   a. Sent to adult prisons.
   b. Placed with good families.
   c. Allowed to work out their problems in special schools.
   d. Sent to colonies in Santo Domingo.

10. Samuel Gridley Howe was of the opinion that children would grow up healthy and would avoid criminal behavior if
    a. They had religious training.
    b. They were exposed to alcohol at an early age.
    c. They had good homes, were not allowed to drink alcohol, and lived in clean neighborhoods.
    d. They had the opportunity to attend Harvard University.

REFERENCES

Howe, J. W. (2015). *Memoir of Dr. Samuel Gridley Howe*. London, England: Forgotten Books.

Howe, S. G. (1846). *An essay on separate and congregate systems of prison discipline; being a report made to the Boston Prison Discipline Society*. Boston, MA: William D. Ticknor and Co.

Howe, S. G. (1993). The causes of idiocy. *History of Psychiatry, 4*(4), 590–603.

Klein, P. (1920). *Prison methods in New York State: A contribution to the study of theory and practice of correctional institutions in New York State*. New York, NY: Columbia University Press.

Meltzer, M. (1964). *A light in the dark: The life of Samuel Gridley Howe*. New York, NY: Thomas Y. Crowell Co.

Ruane, M. E. (2011). How Julia Ward Howe wrote "Battle Hymn of the Republic"—despite her husband. *Washington Post*. Retrieved from https://www. washingtonpost.com/local/how-julia-ward-howe-wrote-battle-hymn-of-the-republic-despite-her-husband/2011/11/15/gIQAnQRaYN_story.html?utm_term=.b349e770f53c

Schwartz, H. (1956). *Samuel Gridley Howe: Social reformer, 1801–1876*. Cambridge, MA: Harvard University Press.

13

ZEBULON BROCKWAY
The Father of Prison Reform

Prisons are not just for punishment. They should be for rehabilitation and reformation because the prison that emphasizes industry, productivity, and education will lead the way in preventing crime in our society.

Those words very aptly sum up the philosophy of Zebulon Brockway, a leading prison reformer and inspirational spirit of the nineteenth century. He's been called the Father of American Parole and a recognized leader in scientific prison reform. For forty years of his career, he was the highly influential superintendent of two model prisons—the Detroit House of Corrections and the Elmira Reformatory in Elmira, New York (Fuller, 2013).

Although very little is known about his personal life (because he chose to share almost no information about his family life or his personal struggles), still he left a significant number of details about his work in his autobiography *Fifty Years of Prison Service: An Autobiography* (published in 1912) and in his published articles and speeches. What is known about his work as a prison manager indicates that he had a facility for self-promotion and that there was a disparity between his theories of prison management and the reality of the operation of his prisons. The public perception was that his prisons were always innovatively run and the very model of benevolent, successful penal institutions. Historical records that have come to light long after Zebulon Brockway's death suggest that some of his pioneering reform efforts may not have been so successful after all.

One of seven children, Zebulon Reed Brockway was born on April 28, 1827, in Lyme, Connecticut. His father, also named Zebulon, was a wealthy businessman, politician, state prison commissioner, and philanthropist. In his autobiography, Zebulon Brockway refers to his father as a "man of importance in his time and place" (Brockway, 2012, p. 5). Among his father's specific accomplishments were his service for thirteen years as one of the directors of the state prison in Connecticut, and, in the 1850s, his elections to both the Connecticut House of Representatives and the Connecticut State Senate.

Although his father was not a religious person, Brockway's mother, Caroline, was. Her devotion was illustrated by her gift of a Bible to her son when he left home at age eighteen to pursue business (Brockway, 2012). Brockway writes that his father's rationalism served as a valuable counterweight to his mother's religious fanaticism. However, there was another incident in Brockway's life that left a profound impression on him. This happened in his early years in school. The young Brockway truanted from school, which resulted in his being punished. But his behavior did not improve, and he truanted again from school. His teacher, a Miss Nichols, made him stay after school and, instead of punishing him further, she simply talked to him. As he notes in his autobiography, she did not bring up his "bad behavior" and told him about her genuine affection for him. "This proved effective ... and left its abiding impression," Brockway remembers (Brockway, 2012, p. 13).

From the age of eighteen until he was twenty-one, he engaged in business, sometimes traveling as far away as Indiana, to carry on his business dealings. But at age twenty-one, he was hired to work at the state prison in Wethersfield, Connecticut, as a guard. Wethersfield is located four miles from the city of Hartford. And the state prison, which opened up to receive prisoners the year Brockway was born, was modeled on the Auburn Prison system, with four tiers of cells stacked on top of each other. When Brockway hired in, the warden of the prison was Leonard Wells. Wells had succeeded Amos Pilsbury. Amos Pilsbury had succeeded his father, Moses C. Pilsbury, who was the first warden of Wethersfield. It was Moses Pilsbury who was the first warden in America to require prisoners to earn their own support (Brockway, 2012).

Moses Pilsbury, the founder of a movement to improve prisons in the New England states, instituted the practice of daily Bible reading with inmates. Amos Pilsbury was just twenty-five years old when he became the warden at Wethersfield, where he continued to develop the practices his father had begun. The youthful Pilsbury demonstrated in his management of the prison that a penal institution could be sustained by prisoner labor (Brockway, 2012). In 1845, Amos Pilsbury would become the warden of the Albany County Penitentiary in Albany, New York, where he would remain for thirty years.

In his autobiography, Brockway wrote that the Pilsbury system of prison management, which not only included using prisoner labor to support a prison and turn a profit but also his form of discipline, was a sound basis for building what Brockway termed the ideal state prison system (Brockway, 2012). The discipline under the Pilsbury system was "stringent, but not severe" (Brockway, 2012, p. 35). Zebulon Brockway considered the discipline promulgated by Amos Pilsbury as humane, considerate, and conscientious (Brockway, 2012).

THE AMERICAN PRISON SYSTEM

At this point, it is instructive to look back at the history of punishment— and at American criminal justice. For hundreds, if not thousands, of years preceding the establishment of the colonies in what would become America, the primary punishments for violations of the social codes were basic and simple: death, slavery, maiming, or the payment of fines (Sullivan, 1990).

At the time of the establishment of the British colonies in America, there were hundreds of crimes that could be punished by the death penalty. Confinement at that point, in England and elsewhere, was just a way of detaining people before trial or before execution (Sullivan, 1990).

However, beginning in the eighteenth century, optimistic ideas of progress and the improvement of mankind influenced the "new science" of penology. This so-called science attempted to give a larger purpose to punishment. That grander purpose given to punishment was to eradicate evil behavior and purify the soul from sin (Sullivan, 1990). By the early years of the nineteenth century, incarceration became the central feature of American criminal justice (Rothman, 1995). The main idea that grew out of colonial America of locking up people was not to reform or rehabilitate prisoners; it was to frighten them into lawful behavior (Rothman, 1995). And prisons were, indeed, frightening places. They were dirty, drafty, and overcrowded. And they held a curious mixture of people, including debtors, the insane, and the truly dangerous (Oliver & Hilgenberg, 2006).

But reformers in the 1820s and 1830s discovered prisons, and they initiated attempts to make jails and prisons into institutions that would teach inmates the lessons of order and discipline. The prison should, the reformers insisted, transform the deviant into a law-abiding citizen (Rothman, 1995). That is, prisons shouldn't just exist to frighten people into good behavior; they should rehabilitate the offender. And that's where various reformers came into the picture. Some of the early reformers included Thomas Eddy, John Pintard, and Enoch C. Wines. In the post–Civil War period, though, one person dominated the movement to reform prisons—Zebulon Reed Brockway (Sullivan, 1990).

ZEBULON BROCKWAY THE MAN

We know that Zebulon Brockway was born in Lyme, Connecticut, and we know some things about his parents. But his autobiography includes remarkably scant information about his personal life, his family, and his children. Although he mentions that he married Jane Woodhouse, we don't know the year they married. He had two daughters, whom he refers to as Mrs. Caroline Butler and Mrs. Emma Blossoms. And he does reveal, literally at the end of his autobiography, that his wife Jane died on February 8, 1911. He writes that her death was "a calamity that must irrevocably overshadow the remainder of my existence" (Brockway, 2012, p. 386).

Otherwise, there are photos of Brockway that have survived that show him at different stages of adulthood and that reveal an imposing man, usually sporting a full beard. For the rest of what he believed and experienced, we are left to speculate. What he was remarkably clear about was his work and his philosophies of managing a successful prison. What emerges from his autobiography is a portrait of a man who had a sense of humor; espoused a steadfast belief in treating other people, especially prisoners, with dignity and respect; and boasted that he believed in—and practiced—an open-door policy in terms of communication with those who were imprisoned in his care. But, as will be clear in this biography of Brockway, he was a study in contradictions, and he would ultimately be exposed near the end of his career as a man who talked about treating inmates with dignity, but was, more often than not in private, brutal in his punishments of prisoners in his care.

HIS EXPERIENCES AT WETHERSFIELD, THE ALBANY ALMSHOUSE AND INFIRMARY, AND THE PRISON AT ROCHESTER, NEW YORK

Serving under Leonard Wells, Amos Pilsbury's successor and his brother-in-law, Brockway could observe firsthand the kind of prison the Pilsburys established at Wethersfield. From there he began gradually to form his own opinions about management of a prison and the handling of inmates.

He relates several instances in his book that many prisoners locked up at Wethersfield were dangerous, both to the guards and other inmates. In addition, as he reflected back a few decades to those years he worked at the state prison, Brockway said that "The prison population, viewed as a whole, subjected only to punishment and religious ministrations, constituted a forbidding and well nigh hopeless mass of full grown men. Enough of them were dangerous and manifestly incorrigible to check foolish sentimentalism and to impart to the whole matter of crime and criminals a grave significance" (Brockway, 2012, p. 40).

Starting as a guard at Wethersfield in 1848, he was promoted to a clerk position in which he was responsible for keeping accounts and records. He was also responsible for picking up prisoners from the county jail and transporting them to the prison. In 1851, he was hired as a deputy of the Albany County Penitentiary in Albany, New York. Since Amos Pilsbury was the warden at Albany County Penitentiary, it was apparent that Brockway had impressed Pilsbury, and he wanted the twenty-four-year-old Brockway on his staff. Albany was a larger prison than Wethersfield, and Brockway would work there for two years before moving to a new position. He regarded his stay at Albany as "severe but serviceable training" (Brockway, 2012, p. 50). It was Amos Pilsbury who recommended him for the position of warden at Rhode Island Prison (the job went to someone else) and then as superintendent for the Albany city and county almshouse and infirmary. He began his duties there in 1853.

The almshouse would be a unique experience for him, since the inmates there were an amalgam of women, men, and children who had been abandoned, left destitute, and living in extreme poverty. Others were insane, and some were sent there by immigration officials because they were trying to enter the country. Brockway spent a year at the almshouse before he was appointed superintendent of the new county penitentiary at Rochester, New York. During the next seven years, managing this prison, Brockway considered his time there as a period of "enlarged experience in management of contemplative penological inquiry, and of the emergence of deep religious feeling and the formation of a remarkable personal friendship" (Brockway, 2012, p. 58).

Although he doesn't reveal with whom he had this remarkable friendship, it is apparent that at this period in Brockway's life, based on his experience in several institutions, he was beginning to have a sense of what a prison should be. For instance, he went into this position with the notion that a prison should be self-supporting by virtue of the productive employment of inmates. He also experienced a new interest in religion and he began attending religious revivals; both he and his wife became Christians, joining the Plymouth Congregational Church. But after seven years of settling in as citizens in Rochester, he was notified of an opportunity in Detroit, Michigan. He was invited to become the superintendent of the new House of Corrections being built in there.

Brockway readily accepted and notes that he was ready to take on this responsibility because of his hope that he could bring about reformation of the prisoners in Detroit (Brockway, 2012). Helping to influence his decision to leave Rochester was a new state law passed in Michigan. This law, enacted in 1861, allowed for young felons to be housed at the Detroit House of Corrections (DOC) instead of being confined at the state prison at Jackson, Michigan. Brockway thought it was (and he may well have been right) the first law in any state that discriminated between younger people (ages sixteen to twenty-one) and older felons for the purpose of treatment in prisons (Brockway, 2012).

THE DETROIT HOUSE OF CORRECTIONS

The purpose of the Detroit House of Corrections was, as stated in a report to the Detroit Common Council in 1857, to "Occupy the position of a home to the friendless, rather than as a place of punishment. The city is to stand for the time being in the parental relation to those unfortunates who, deprived of their natural guardianship, are tempted on the threshold of crime … Its object is to reform and restore the young, who have been tempted, before it is too late" (Brockway, 2012, p. 71). In short, the Detroit House of Corrections was launched with the ideal that it would be a place for treating offenders for their "industrial, educational, and moral good" (Brockway, 2012, p. 72). And that coincided with what Zebulon Brockway desired to accomplish in running a prison.

The DHOC opened its doors to convicted felons in August 1861, and Brockway was there to begin welcoming residents. Both he and the Board of Inspectors of the DHOC fully intended for the facility to provide close supervision, strict discipline, and complete occupation for every inmate during their waking hours. They were not only to be kept busy, but they were to be engaged in work that was both instructive and profitable—for themselves and the DHOC. A further goal of Brockway's was to make sure that every inmate who was released would be supplied with employment and supervised for a period time when they were living on their own. But while they were living at the DHOC, there would be a plan for each inmate's education and for every resident's exposure to religious instruction (Brockway, 2012).

Did Zebulon Brockway succeed in reaching his and the Board of Inspectors' goals?

In his autobiography, he writes that the plan in both theory and practice was "remarkably fulfilled" almost completely during his years as superintendent (Brockway, 2012, p. 77). Brockway, as was his habit (perhaps established during his years as bookkeeper for the state prison at Wethersfield), maintained careful and meticulous records. He could, therefore, confidently assert that by the third year of operation, the DHOC was bringing in more money (basically though prisoner employment) than was expended in running the institution. And he could show that from that third year through at least the year 1900, the DHOC was still making a profit of anywhere between $25,000 and $36,000 annually (Brockway, 2012).

During his tenure at DHOC, his philosophy of running a prison was crystallizing. That philosophy revolved around the reformation of prisoners so that there was adequate protection of the public and that the inmate, once released, could find their way back into society as a productive citizen (Brockway, 2012). To bring this about, he believed in the practice of promoting inmates to semiofficial duties; this was different from the trustee system used in other prisons. Instead of designating them as trustees, Brockway found that by promoting them, their social status was improved and they felt better about themselves. In addition, he insisted that all inmates attend school two evenings a week with further opportunities for study and learning available to them on other evenings. This schedule only afforded them about 200 days of classes a year. Nonetheless, his prisoners were making twice as much progress as those students who attended Detroit public schools many more days a year (Brockway, 2012).

On the other nights of the week, when inmates were not attending classes, professors (from the University of Michigan, for instance) and other specialists came to the DHOC to give lectures. Brockway felt very strongly about inmates being exposed to these lectures because they "Quickened and ennobled the minds of prisoners and officers. It elevated and improved the general tone of the whole institution and greatly contributed to the reformatory efficiency" (Brockway, 2012, p. 105).

In 1868, Brockway obtained the approval of the Board of Inspectors and the city of Detroit to add a house of shelter to the DHOC. The purpose of this shelter was to provide a place of treatment for female prisoners, with the idea that women sent to the DHOC would be received into a family life where they could receive intellectual, moral, domestic, and industrial training under the influence and "sympathy of refined and virtuous women" (Brockway, 2012, p. 107). The house of shelter would be run by Emma Hall, who, Brockway describes as a pioneer of education in adult prisons in America (Brockway, 2012). Besides the house of shelter, Brockway established a mission Sunday school outside of the walls of the DHOC. This was a unique mission, one of the first in the United States. In time, this mission Sunday school became the Church of the Covenant in Detroit.

Brockway drafted a bill in 1869 which was first approved by the Board of Inspectors, and then submitted to—and approved by—the Michigan legislature. Among the several provisions of this bill was one that would commit young offenders, as well as women who were prostitutes, to the DHOC for a sentence of three years. Brockway's reasoning for the bill was that he needed three years to turn around the lives of young offenders and prostitutes. One of the results of the passage of this bill, according to Brockway, was a mass exodus of prostitutes from Detroit to other cities and states (Brockway, 2012).

Zebulon Brockway was one of three people appointed in 1875 to a commission to revise the criminal laws of the state of Michigan. One of the recommendations that came out of this commission was the adoption of indeterminate sentences in Michigan. However, five years before that, in 1870, in an address to the National Congress on Penitentiary and Reformatory Discipline in Cincinnati, Ohio, he strongly recommended indeterminate sentences.

NATIONAL CONGRESS ON PENITENTIARY AND REFORMATORY DISCIPLINE

One of the seminal events that led to the development of the Elmira Reformatory was the National Congress on Penitentiary and Reformatory Discipline in 1870, along with the new ideas on penal reform voiced at this conference (Pisciotta, 1983). Many of the nation's outstanding penologists convened to talk about reform at this congress, and before it was over, four people were selected to write a declaration of principles. Those four men were Ohio governor Rutherford B. Hayes, Franklin Sanborn, Enoch C. Wines, and Zebulon Brockway (Pisciotta, 1983).

The Declaration of Principles that came out of this collaboration between Brockway and the other three men proposed a new scientific approach to prison reform based on humanitarian and individualized treatment. The Declaration of Principles' thirty-seven paragraphs included recommendations for indeterminate sentences, a carefully planned mark system, progressive classification of inmates, meaningful academic education, industrial training, intense religious instruction, and positive reinforcement, along with mild disciplinary measures (Pisciotta, 1983).

In his address to the gathering, often referred to as the National Prison Congress, which he titled "The Ideal of a True Prison System for a State," Brockway said the following about indeterminate sentences:

> Another active cause of crime is the release annually of hundreds of prisoners in every state, who are unreformed by their imprisonment, which must always be the case under the present system of sentences. No man, be he judge, lawyer, or layman, can determine beforehand the date when imprisonment shall work reformation in any case, and it is an outrage upon society to return to the privileges of citizenship those who have proved themselves dangerous and bad by the commission of crime, until a cure is wrought and reformation reached.... Therefore, as for the other reasons suggested, sentences should not be determinate, but indeterminate. By this is meant (to state briefly) that all persons in a state who are convicted of crimes or offenses before a competent court shall be deemed wards of the state and shall be committed to the custody of the board of guardians, until, in

their judgment, they may be returned to society with
ordinary safety and in accord with their own highest
welfare. (Brockway, 1995, pp. 71–72)

In this address, Brockway went on to offer fifteen arguments in favor
of indeterminate sentences. Those fifteen points were that indeterminate
sentences:

1. Supplant the law of force with the law of love;
2. Secure the certainty of restraint and continued treatment, which operate to prevent crime, and which severity does not;
3. Make possible the arrest and "right training" of individuals early in
   their life before their character is fully set;
4. Employ the desire for liberty and to be released as motivation to reform;
5. Remove the feelings of animosity toward the law and its officers, thus
   making discipline of inmates easier;
6. Bring about personal contact with prison officials to help instill good
   character development;
7. Secure cooperation of the prisoner in order to achieve the mutually
   beneficial goals of reformation and release;
8. Leave the decisions as to when sentences end to prison officials, not
   to elected public officials who have neither the time nor opportunity
   to determine what is best in the case of each inmate;
9. Allow experts in prisons to determine the period of imprisonment;
10. Remove the determination of the date of release from the time of the trial
    and sentencing to a later time, when that decision is based, not on preju-
    dice and public furor, but on a longer view of the character of an inmate;
11. Render possible the corrections of errors and misjudgments often
    inflicted on first offenders;
12. Accomplish the return of reformed persons back into society at the
    right moment;
13. Retain for as long as necessary the guardianship of prisoners so that
    society is best protected;
14. Are constitutional and can be enacted by legislative bodies;

15. Are based on the writer's (Brockway's) experience that a reformatory system is not possible without indeterminate sentences, and they are indispensable to the ideal of a true prison system (Brockway, 1995, p. 72).

At the time that Zebulon Brockway gave this address in Cincinnati, he was credited with coming up with the concept of indeterminate sentences. In fact, as he states in his autobiography (Brockway, 2012), he, too, thought he had originated the idea. However, he would later learn that others had had the idea before him. For instance, in the 1840s, the Englishman Captain Alexander Maconochie had gone to Van Diemen's Land (which later was renamed Tasmania and became part of Australia) to report on prisoner transportation. In his report back to England, Maconochie proposed that convicts should be sentenced not to a specific period of time in the colonies, but to a certain amount of labor measured by a system of marks or points (Rothman, 1995).

LEAVING THE DETROIT HOUSE OF CORRECTIONS

By 1872, Brockway was discouraged by the narrow and extremely conservative views of the Detroit mayor, and he himself had a bout of rheumatism. Consequently, he resigned from the Detroit House of Corrections. However, two friends, James McMillan and John S. Newberry, owners of the Michigan Car Company, wanted him to stay in Detroit and offered him the vice presidency of their company at a very attractive salary. He accepted their offer, and for two years he was a vice president. His wife and two daughters and he moved from a house provided on the grounds of the DHOC to a home on Jefferson Avenue in Detroit (Brockway, 2012).

After two years with the Michigan Car Company, he resigned in August 1874, and at age fifty, he found himself unemployed—with no income to support his family. To help make ends meet, he took a job with a furniture company. However, in May 1876, he received a telegram offering him the superintendence of the new Elmira Reformatory in Elmira, New York. The offer came from Louis D. Pilsbury, son of Amos Pilsbury. Louis Pilsbury was newly appointed to the board of managers of the Elmira Reformatory. He was also superintendent of the state prisons of New York. Brockway accepted immediately. As of May 12, 1876, he was officially the warden of the New York State Reformatory at Elmira.

BROCKWAY AND THE ELMIRA REFORMATORY

The decision to build a new penal institution in New York was debated by New York State legislators for some time, but they were mostly in accord in terms of their fears that crime in New York, especially crime committed by males in their teens and early twenties, was rampant, and that present correctional institutions were not doing a competent job of dealing with criminals (Pisciotta, 1983). In particular, many citizens of New York were disillusioned over the effectiveness of penal institutions such as Auburn, Sing Sing, and Dannemora prisons. The plan on which those prisons were organized, referred to as the congregate plan (meaning that prisoners slept in solitary cells, but worked and ate together during the day), did not seem to result in rehabilitation and reformation (Pisciotta, 1983). In 1869, the New York legislature authorized the building of an "industrial reformatory" for males between the ages of sixteen and thirty (Pisciotta, 1983, p. 614). Although the legislature did not specify in their bill how the administration of this new reformatory would bring about rehabilitation of inmates, their hiring of Zebulon Brockway as the new institution's first superintendent was based on Brockway's prominence as one of the nation's outstanding penologists at that time and on his views that he expressed at the National Prison Congress (Pisciotta, 1983).

With his own views of the causes of crime and how inmates ought to be treated and rehabilitated, from May of 1876 until August of 1900, Zebulon Brockway's life would be intimately connected to the management of the Elmira Reformatory. The board of managers of the Elmira Reformatory delegated to Brockway the authority to develop the "Elmira system." This system would be related to Brockway's views, as expressed in the Twentieth Annual Report of the Elmira Reformatory published in 1896, that "all intelligent efforts to reform criminals must of necessity be based on some theory of the cause of criminal conduct" (Pisciotta, 1983, p. 615). Brockway came to reject the views of Cesare Beccaria regarding rational beings making choices based on free will. He adopted a more positivistic viewpoint that behavior was based on a complex interaction of biological, psychological, and sociological factors (Pisciotta, 1983).

As he had at the Detroit House of Corrections, Brockway began educational programs for the inmates at Elmira. It was his innovations in educational programming for inmates that reflected his forward think-ing and, as a result, he is directly responsible for much of the progress in nineteenth-century correctional education (Gehring, 1982). Gehring (1982) describes Brockway as a courageous correctional educational administrator and practitioner whose many instructional methods "would be considered progressive even today" (Gehring, 1982, p. 4).

In the beginning of his tenure at Elmira, Brockway hired Dr. D.R. Ford of the nearby Elmira Women's College to direct the educational program at the reformatory. The Reverend Thomas K. Beecher lived in Elmira and had created in the community a "large-minded liberalism and humanitar-ianism," which Brockway thought would help support "rational reforma-tory procedures" (Brockway, 2012, p. 161). Elmira had an academic school building that was three stories high and included twenty-eight classrooms and a library (Gehring, 1982). In addition, this building had a 600-seat lecture hall, a huge gymnasium, with rooms for hot and cold baths and massages, and a spacious military drill hall. Professor Ford taught phys-ical geography and natural science, while other teachers and professors taught such subjects as history, literature, geometry, physiology, political economy, and psychology. At one point, Brockway made the English literature class mandatory for parole (Gehring, 1982).

The vocational education department was initiated by Professor N.A. Wells of Syracuse University. The department had two divisions: the trade school, which focused on industrial education, and the manual training department, which emphasized vocational education for handicapped learners. Some thirty-six trades were taught in the vocational education department (Gehring, 1982). Brockway put the special education depart-ment at the center of the school program, and according to Thom Gehring (1982) this department was the real cutting edge of his pioneering efforts in correctional education. Special education programming at Elmira slowly evolved from 1883, when a program featuring terra-cotta modeling and special instruction in plumbing, tailoring, and printing was instituted, to 1889, when 150 students were in this program receiving basic instruction plus baths, massages, and prescribed exercises, to 1896, when manual training for "dullards" was provided along with special diets (Gehring, 1982).

The moral education department was started by Professor D.P. Mayhew, who had worked with Brockway at the DHOC. Various teachers and professors taught classes in ethics, health education, and the Bible, and many of the visiting lecturers came on Sundays to present their cultural programs. The moral education department also sponsored the inmate-produced newspaper, *The Summary*, which summarized news from outside periodicals (Gehring, 1982).

And, as expected, Brockway would employ his philosophy of indeterminate sentences at Elmira. He advocated for a state bill that would allow Elmira to use indeterminate sentences. He himself drafted such a bill in 1877, which the New York state legislature passed and which gave prison managers the ability to decide the duration of the term of imprisonment for inmates.

When the Elmira Reformatory opened, it immediately accepted the transfer of almost 200 prisoners from Auburn Prison and Sing Sing who had been given determinate sentences. Brockway was of the opinion that some of the worst prisoners were transferred to Elmira in order to cause disruption to the orderly working of the new reformatory (Brockway, 2012). Over time, though, these prisoners were released and new ones admitted who had indeterminate sentences. But as he observed the initial inmates given to him, Brockway was moved to write:

> Their physical degeneracy, intellectual weakness, moral insensateness, together with their industrial inadequacy, disclosed the complexity of and at the same time intensified the interest in the problem of the reformation of animals.... in order to arrest the customary harmful habits and to initiate salutary

corrective activities, a fine-meshed disciplinary regime
must be planned and exacted. (Brockway, 2012, p. 223)

By the second year of operations, a prison industry was established: brush making. Residents worked for 5 to 8 hours a day in prison shops making brushes, along with hollow glassware, brooms, and shoes (Pisciotta, 1983). And within 2 more years, several other industries were functioning. Yet, not everyone was happy about the productive jobs and training provided to inmates.

For instance, companies who made brushes found that the prisoners were interfering with their business, and the state legislature acted to bring about changes in the type of prison labor that was acceptable. That is, the legislature abolished the contract system. Then, in 1888, the legislature prohibited all productive labor in all of New York prisons, although soon after passing such a law it did allow a "state supply system" (Brockway, 2012, p. 268). This was a public-use or state-use provision that allowed inmates to manufacture goods for sale to state government agencies only—obviously a very limited market. This irritated Brockway and other wardens as well.

At the same time, the seeming success of the Elmira Reformatory led to recommendations that that success be more widely publicized. With greater publicity came thousands of visitors to Elmira, and other states began to call on their own prisons to be modeled after the Elmira Reformatory, where inmates were "wisely and humanely treated" (Brockway, 2012, p. 238). The Elmira Reformatory was widely recognized as a "new departure in the treatment of adult male felonious prisoners" (Brockway, 2012, p. 242).

While Elmira Reformatory was becoming better known, Brockway continued to enhance services to inmates. Not only was the weekly prisoner newspaper, *The Summary*, begun in 1884, but two years later, "scientific physical culture" was introduced to the inmates. This physical culture consisted of special diets, baths, massage, military drill, and calisthenics (Brockway, 2012). Brockway reports that after introducing a physical culture regimen, not only were those men who participated in the program healthier physically, but their school grades "doubled" (Brockway, 2012, p. 279). Pads of paper and pencils were supplied to each prisoner, and they were encouraged to make special requests or ask for an interview. Brockway states in his book that every written communication was answered promptly (Brockway, 2012). Over time, he further reports, the number of private interviews grew to at least 12,000 annually. Brockway noted in his book that throughout all of his years at the helm of Elmira Reformatory, prisoners always had free access to the superintendent, managers, and the Board of Managers (Brockway, 2012).

In his autobiography, he characterized his reformatory system as "Socialization of the anti-social by scientific training while under completest government control" (Brockway, 2012, p. 309). He writes that he did not believe in using intimidation to bring about appropriate behavior. Instead, he instituted a system of merits and demerits leading to better habits. If an inmate earned too many demerits, he could be retained longer in the reformatory. He also writes that if there was a motto for Elmira, it should have been: "Here ends your customary thoroughfare and to you opens the new and narrow way which leads on to happiness by way of welfare. The wise will choose the path and follow in it; the wayward remainder will be constrained" (Brockway, 2012, p. 315). The mark system was modeled after the programs developed by Maconochie at Norfolk Island and by Sir Walter Crofton, director of prisons in Ireland (Pisciotta, 1983).

In the mark system put into place by Brockway, inmates could earn a maximum of nine marks per month—three each for performance in school, labor, and general deportment (Pisciotta, 1983). By earning perfect marks, an inmate could advance, over several months, to the first honor division. Having attained the top division, if they earned three additional months of good conduct, they could be eligible for release on parole (Pisciotta, 1983).

Parole was important for Brockway's Elmira system. He believed that the optimal parole period was six months following release. But prisoners should be provided prearranged employment, which they could start immediately upon release, and it was, if possible, a type of employment for which the individual had been trained while incarcerated. By 1896, there were 36 different trades or branches of trades taught to inmates. Brockway cites his records showing that over a seventeen-year period, 81.9% of paroled inmates did not commit another crime (Brockway, 2012).

He states that corporal punishment was only used in the form of "paddling," and he was the only person authorized to use the paddle. Brockway also writes that such punishment was never to be "severe" (Brockway, 2012, p. 330).

The Elmira Reformatory School and educational program was recognized by the American Prison Association (which in 1954 would become the American Correctional Association) as the best in the country (Gehring, 1982). Because of the success of the programs he established, Brockway was elected president of the American Prison Association.

INVESTIGATION AND RESIGNATION FROM ELMIRA REFORMATORY

A rather thorough investigation of the Elmira Reformatory was conducted by the New York State Board of Charities in 1893 and 1894. Hundreds of people were interviewed, and hundreds of letters were reviewed. The results of this investigation called into question many of the proclamations made by Brockway in his writing, speeches, and in his book (Pisciotta, 1983). The final report of the Board of Charities was that "the charges and allegations against the General Superintendent Z. R. Brockway, of 'cruel, brutal, excessive and unusual punishment of inmates' are proven and most amply sustained by the evidence" (Pisciotta, 1983, p. 620).

What he was accused of and what was found to be the realities of his treatment of inmates was that Zebulon Brockway gave those people in his charge a choice: they could conform to his rules and dictates with unerring compliance, or they would meet swift and severe punishment (Pisciotta, 1983). Brockway contended that while he did administer paddlings or spankings when it was necessary to introduce a sort of shock therapy, he stated, however, that these spankings were always mild (Brockway, 2012). What the investigation found, though, was in stark contradiction. He frequently administered beatings with a heavy leather strap that was sometimes soaked in water ahead of time. What was corroborated by many inmates as well as employees of Elmira was that those beatings were often so severe that inmates were bloodied, scarred, and sometimes in need of medical care (Pisciotta, 1983). In addition to these "spankings," the Board of Charities also found that Brockway placed inmates in solitary confinement (for as long as 100 days), restricted diets to bread and water, punched inmates in the face, or whipped them with rubber hoses (Pisciotta, 1983).

Brockway denounced the findings of the Board of Charities as "persecution," but he never denied using the punishments detailed in the final report (Pisciotta, 1983). His defense was that there were no rules prohibiting such treatment of inmates. Furthermore, he did record the punishments he gave out in each inmate's "conduct Ledger" (although not in any detail) (Pisciotta, 1983, p. 624). When Roswell P. Flowers, New York's governor, read the report, he wanted his own investigation. When his investigators couldn't come to an agreement, Governor Flowers announced that Brockway had exercised "great moderation" in administering punishment, and all charges were dropped (Pisciotta, 1983, p. 626). Brockway continued to be superintendent, but in 1899, a new governor of New York, Theodore Roosevelt, appointed a new board of managers for Elmira Reformatory. The new board of managers severely criticized the operations of Elmira, uncovered a network of employees and inmates who were smuggling tobacco, opium, and other contraband into the institution, and they issued orders for Brockway to stop using corporal punishment, commenting that it "degraded and brutalized" the inmates (Pisciotta, 1983, p. 626).

Brockway's version of what happened is sketchy at best in his autobiography. He writes that the new board of managers wanted changes—changes that Brockway couldn't approve because he was of the belief that these changes would lower the standards. For one thing, he states that the board wanted to institute solitary confinement and Brockway was against such a practice. He failed to mention, though, the other changes the board ordered. But feeling he could no longer be associated with Elmira, he resigned in July 1900.

After leaving Elmira Reformatory, he and Jane moved to a house in the city of Elmira, where they lived with their widowed daughter, Mrs. Emma Blossoms, and her children. Instead of being idle with lots of time on his hands, he found that he was besieged with requests to speak and to work as a consultant. He lectured at various clubs, churches, and universities, including Brown University and Yale. In 1902 he became president of the board of managers of the Arnot Ogden Memorial Hospital in Elmira. Then in 1905, he was elected mayor of Elmira and served in that position for one two-year term.

His wife Jane died in 1911, and he may not have recovered from her death. He died in 1920 at the age of ninety-two.

HIS LEGACY

Zebulon Brockway was a leading prison reformer of his day. It seems appropriate to consider him the Father of Parole and also, as Thom Gehring (1982) argues, the Father of Correctional Education. Gehring contends that Brockway's innovations in prisoner education helped pave the way for future advances in the education of inmates. His vision and his widespread influence during the latter half of the nineteenth century was perhaps unparalleled by any other reformer at the time. And while he was a flawed individual, particularly when it came to the discipline of inmates, still, Elmira Reformatory changed the course of corrections and influenced many penal institutions well into the twentieth century.

QUESTIONS FOR DISCUSSION

1. In your opinion, what were Zebulon Brockway's most significant contributions to criminal justice? Give support for your answer.
2. As a superintendent or warden of penal institutions, what aspect of Brockway's programs may have been most helpful to inmates? Why?
3. What are your views of Brockway's educational efforts at Elmira Reformatory?
4. What was Brockway's theory of the causation of crime, and how did his theory influence his treatment of inmates?

IMPORTANT TERMS AND NAMES

Almshouse: Almshouses were houses that provided food and shelter to the poor, the aged, and the infirm, although sometimes they housed the mentally ill as well. They were begun in colonial America and were frequently referred to as poorhouses.

Auburn Prison System: The Auburn Prison System was put into place with the opening of Auburn Prison in Auburn, New York, in 1820. The system at this prison was known as the congregate system and featured inmates working and eating together, but sleeping in separate cells. This was in contrast to the Pennsylvania system, in which inmates were kept separately in solitary confinement.

Board of Managers: The Board of Managers, or Board of Inspectors, was a board given the task of overseeing the management and operations of prisons and reformatories.

Detroit House of Corrections: The Detroit House of Corrections was a facility built by the city of Detroit. It opened in 1861 with Zebulon Brockway as the first superintendent. It was designed to reform young men and women.

Elmira Reformatory: Elmira Reformatory was opened in 1876 as an industrial reformatory with the aim of rehabilitating young men. Brockway was the superintendent from its opening until his retirement in 1900.

Enoch C. Wines: Enoch Cobb Wines was a Congregational minister and a prison reformer. He attended the 1870 National Congress of Penitentiary and Reformatory Discipline and helped to write the Declaration of Principles. Following that, he was involved in the National Prison Association and helped to organize the First International Congress on Prison Discipline held in London, England.

Franklin Sanborn: Franklin Sanborn was a journalist, author, and reformer. He was one of the founders of the American Social Science Association and was involved with the National Prison Association. He attended the 1870 National Congress of Penitentiary and Reformatory Discipline and helped to write the Declaration of Principles.

Indeterminate sentences: Indeterminate sentences are prison sentences imposed without a definite end date. Determinate sentences, on the other hand, have a definite date for their end.

Moses Pilsbury and Amos Pilsbury: Moses Pilsbury and his son, Amos Pilsbury, made their mark in correctional history by being superintendents or wardens of prisons. Most notably, Moses Pilsbury was the superintendent of the Connecticut State Prison at Wethersfield for three years, after which he was succeeded by his son. Both father and son were noteworthy for their use of prison labor to bring in funds to finance the prison.

National Congress on Penitentiary and Reformatory Discipline: This congress was a convention of prison reformers held between October 12 and October 18, 1870, in Cincinnati, Ohio. Attended by many prison officials and prison reformers from across the country, it featured presentations by many people on a broad range of topics. It concluded with a Declaration of Principles, written by Zebulon Brockway, Rutherford B. Hayes, Franklin Sanborn, and Enoch C. Wines. The Declaration of Principles included a number of reforms which would later be adopted by prisons and reformatories nationwide. The National Prison Association grew out of this congress.

Rutherford B. Hayes: After serving in the U.S. House of Representatives, Hayes was elected governor of Ohio in 1867. He became active in prison reform, and he presided over the National Congress of Penitentiary and Reformatory Discipline, which was held in Ohio in 1870. He helped to write the thirty-seven principles in the Declaration of Principles that came out of the congress. He would become president of the United States in 1877.

Captain Alexander Maconochie: Captain Alexander Maconochie was a native of Scotland who volunteered to become superintendent of the English prison on Norfolk Island, 1,000 miles off the coast of Australia. He served in this capacity for almost five years, during which time he innovated such things as his marks system, which could result in reduced sentences for prisoners who demonstrated exemplary conduct.

Theodore Roosevelt: A Progressive politician and reformer, Theodore Roosevelt was elected governor of New York in 1899 and in this position appointed a new Board of Managers for Elmira Reformatory. That move ultimately led to Brockway's resignation from Elmira. Roosevelt would go on to be president of the United States from 1901 to 1909.

FOR FURTHER READING

Brockway, Z. R. (1995). The ideal of a true prison system for a state. *Journal of Correctional Education, 56*(2), 68–74.

Brockway, Z. R. (2012). *Fifty years of prison service: An autobiography.* London, England: Forgotten Books.

Gehring, T. (1982). Zebulon Brockway: 19th century CE hero. *Journal of Correctional Education, 33*(1), 4–7.

Pisciotta, A. W. (1983). Scientific reform: The "new penology" at Elmira, 1876–1900. *Crime and Delinquency, 29*(4), 613–630.

REVIEW QUESTIONS

True or False

1. Zebulon Brockway has been called the Father of American Parole.
2. In 1912, Brockway wrote an autobiography that detailed his personal and family life.
3. Brockway's first job in corrections was as a guard in the state prison in Wethersfield, Connecticut.
4. Brockway was investigated on at least two occasions for practices in his prisons that were questionable.

Multiple Choice

5. Brockway considered the following person to be a mentor in corrections
   a. Captain Alexander Maconochie.
   b. Thomas Eddy.
   c. Amos Pilsbury.
   d. Thomas Mott Osborne.

6. Starting with his tenure at the Detroit House of Corrections and continuing at Elmira Reformatory, Brockway's main goal as superintendent was to bring about
   a. Degradation of inmates.
   b. Reformation of inmates.
   c. College degrees for inmates.
   d. Treatment for psychological problems for inmates.

7. A hallmark of Brockway's philosophy of running a penal institution was
   a. Probation.
   b. Beatings of inmates.
   c. That inmates pay all of their own expenses.
   d. Indeterminate sentences.

8. Brockway rejected Cesare Beccaria's theory of crime causation and instead believed that
   a. All people, even criminals, are rational and make free-will choices.
   b. People commit crimes for a complex number of reasons.
   c. People commit crimes because they are immoral.
   d. People commit crimes because they live in disorganized neighborhoods.

9. In Zebulon Brockway's system of parole, all inmates could
   a. Be released after one year in prison.
   b. Be released if they agree to attend church regularly.
   c. Be released if they are supervised for one year or more after leaving prison or a reformatory.
   d. Be released if they have a job waiting for them when they get out.

10. Despite Brockway's reputation as one of the leading penologists in America, his treatment of prisoners was found to be
    a. Brutal.
    b. Fair and lenient.
    c. Therapeutic.
    d. Progressive.

REFERENCES

Brockway, Z. R. (1995). The ideal of a true prison system for a state. *Journal of Correctional Education, 56*(2), 68–74.

Brockway, Z. R. (2012). *Fifty years of prison service: An autobiography.* London, England: Forgotten Books.

Fuller, T. W. (2013). *Prison reform catalysts.* Lafayette, CA: Pleasant Hill Press.

Gehring, T. (1982). Zebulon Brockway: 19th century CE hero. *Journal of Correctional Education, 33*(1), 4–7.

Oliver, W. M., & Hilgenberg, J. R. (2006). *A history of crime and criminal justice in America.* Boston, MA: Pearson Education.

Pisciotta, A. W. (1983). Scientific reform: The "new penology" at Elmira, 1876–1900. *Crime and Delinquency, 29*(4), 613–630.

Rothman, D. J. (1995). Perfecting the prison in the United States: 1789–1865. In N. Morris & D. J. Rothman (Eds.), *The Oxford history of the prison* (pp. 111–129). New York, NY: Oxford University Press.

Sullivan, L. E. (1990). *The prison reform movement: Forlorn hope.* Boston, MA: Twayne Publishing.

14

THOMAS MOTT OSBORNE
A Prison Reformer With Vision

Thomas Mott Osborne is remembered today as a dynamic force in American prison reform (Fuller, 2013). However, his path to that destiny was out of the ordinary, maybe even a bit bizarre. He didn't work in a prison until he was fifty-five years of age, only after he had had a successful business career and following his becoming an influential force in both New York State and national politics. And if his path to becoming a prison reformer was odd, then his methods of learning about prison life were even stranger.

He was born on September 23, 1859, in Auburn, New York, the third of four children in the family of David M. Osborne and Eliza Wright Osborne. The city in which he was born and raised, Auburn, was a center of progressive political activity, particularly antislavery activism, both before and during the Civil War. His was a well-off family, due to the success of his father's farm machinery business, the D.M. Osborne Company.

On his mother's side of the family was a long line of Quakers, as well as a number of eminent reformers. In particular was his grandmother, Martha Coffin Wright, and her sister, Lucretia Coffin Mott, both of whom were organizers—along with Elizabeth Cady Stanton—of the 1848 Seneca Falls Convention on women's rights in Seneca Falls, New York (Chamberlain, 1935). His mother, Eliza, had such friends as Elizabeth Cady Stanton, Susan B. Anthony, and William Lloyd Garrison, who were frequent guests in their home at 99 South Street in Auburn. His grandmother, Martha Coffin Wright and other family members, including Eliza Osborne, oversaw the finances of Harriet Tubman, and Martha Coffin Wright's home in Auburn was part of the Underground Railroad where she harbored fugitive slaves (Chamberlain, 1935). If the city of Auburn was a center of progressive political activity, the Osborne family tradition was one of liberalism and militant revolt (Chamberlain, 1935).

THOMAS MOTT OSBORNE'S EARLY YEARS

At age 16, after attending public school, Thomas was sent to the prep school Adams Academy in Quincy, Massachusetts. A year later, though, his sister Florence died from an illness and Thomas became sick, too. To aid in his recovery, his parents sent him on a six-month world tour. During this tour, he wrote home frequently, and his mother had his voluminous and engaging letters bound in four volumes. He then returned to Adams Academy to finish out a four-year stint, during which time he became a proficient pianist, discovered the manly sport of football, and passed enough of his exams to get accepted at Harvard College in 1880.

As a college student, Thomas stood out because he was regarded as a good fellow, although something of a "prig" (Chamberlain, 1935, p. 61). That is, he didn't smoke, usually stopped drinking after the first one, and didn't like or appreciate course language or ribald stories. But he enjoyed the friendship of Samuel A. Eliot, son of the president of Harvard, Dr. Charles W. Eliot. And he played on the football team (which didn't please his mother), and he was a genius on the piano. He had the rare ability to look over the music of a song he had never seen before, and then, without referring to the score or sheet music, play it perfectly note for note. He could remember how to play hundreds of songs and, consequently, his room was a popular meeting place for students who enjoyed music. He also had a flair for theatrics and was said to be a moderately good actor (Chamberlain, 1935). He frequently went into Boston for theater performances, musicals, and the opera, but he was especially fond of Gilbert and Sullivan.

Among other students at Harvard during Thomas Mott Osborne's four years were William Randolph Hearst, John Jacob Astor, and Theodore

Roosevelt. While he was a sophomore, he and his roommate were taking the train back to Auburn for an Easter vacation when he met a red-haired sixteen-year-old girl by the name of Agnes Devens. Within two years, they were engaged, and two years after that they were married. Rudolph Chamberlain, one of Osborne's biographers, writing in *There Is No Truce* (1935), comments that Agnes Devens brought to the relationship things that Osborne lacked: poise, a sense of proportion, balance, and the ability to evaluate situations with calm judgment. His relationship with Agnes was his only love affair. Although she died in childbirth when Osborne was still a relatively young man, there would never be another woman in his life.

GRADUATING AND MAKING HIS WAY

Thomas Mott Osborne graduated from Harvard in 1884. He had a brilliant career at Harvard—in everything except his classes and studies. He made his mark in theatrics, music, and his social life. Fortunately, he was gifted with a superb memory, and that got him through his classes (Chamberlain, 1935).

Upon leaving Harvard, he returned to Auburn and took a position in his father's farm machinery business, the D.M. Osborne Company. Within two years, he had worked in a variety of jobs in the company, moving up the ladder of the company to a vice president position. Then, his father died unexpectedly and suddenly in 1886, and Thomas Osborne just as suddenly became president of a thriving company that within a few years grew to become North America's third-largest producer of agricultural implements, which employed nearly 3,000 people at one point. However, the new president had little interest in business; he preferred theater and the arts. To accommodate his real interests, he formed an amateur theater group. In 1903, the Osborne Company was sold to the International Harvester Trust. By 1905, International Harvester would take over management, but the sale and the money that came to Thomas Mott Osborne allowed him to indulge his ultimate pursuits—social reform and public service.

When he married Agnes Devens in 1886, her vivacity led the couple to join the social life of the community. But both Agnes and Thomas were friendly and hospitable, and their home was a place for many social gatherings. Osborne continued his musical interests, finding time every day to play the piano and to become a student of Richard Wagner's music. He soon was lecturing at Cornell University about Wagner. Around this time, also, he was elected to the Auburn Board of Education, and his interest in schools in Auburn was timely, since he and Agnes soon had a son. At one point, he became the commissioner of education, and his involvement in his community resulted in an appointment as a trustee of the Auburn Savings Bank.

He and Agnes would, over the next several years, have four sons, David, Charles, Lithgow, and Robert. But in giving birth to Robert, complications developed, and Agnes died within a month. With the death of the woman who had brought him such great joy, Thomas Mott Osborne was lonely and bereft. To deal with his grief, he threw himself into politics, social reform, and philanthropy (Chamberlain, 1935).

THE POLITICIAN

Thomas's father, David Munson Osborne, served a term as mayor of Auburn in the 1870s. The elder Osborne was a Republican, but during college, his son Thomas saw himself as a Democrat; in Auburn, he got involved in the Democratic Party. However, when it was suggested that he run for mayor, his response was that he would consider it if he could be nominated on a citizen's ticket, with no party affiliation. In 1896, he became a delegate from New York State to the Democratic National Convention in Chicago. That experience, serving as a state delegate, opened his eyes in many ways. He was not happy with the choice of William Jennings Bryan as the Democrats' selection for the presidential candidate. Nor was he pleased with the various planks in the Democrats' platform. Osborne returned home from Chicago with the idea of forming a third party movement (Tannenbaum, 1933).

Although he did not form a third party, he did establish the more traditional Democratic Club of Cayuga County. His venture into politics soon brought him recognition as a force in the liberal wing of New York's Democratic Party. This was helped along by speeches he began making about the country's currency and finances. Osborne soon saw that he enjoyed this, and that perhaps he was a potential candidate for political office. In fact, his name was mentioned as the possible lieutenant governor for New York on a ticket with Theodore Roosevelt. That didn't materialize, but in 1898, he decided to run on the Citizens' Independent ticket for lieutenant governor of New York. While he didn't win that election, he continued to make speeches, and he always drew crowds because people could always count on Osborne to deliver some sort of vicious—and sometimes even truthful—attack on his opponents. He finally did run for mayor of Auburn in 1902 and won. Then, he was reelected in 1904. But the third election was not a charm. Chamberlain suggests that his extreme statements and vitriolic attacks ruffled enough citizens that many switched their votes to someone else (Chamberlain, 1935).

While mayor, though, Osborne's penchant for theatrics and costumes found an outlet related to his job. Dressing as a bum, he set out to investigate the Auburn water department's pumping station. He found that not only did he enjoy going about incognito, but he learned much about what was going on in the water department's pumping station and also in other areas of his city by making forays into taverns and saloons late at night. At the time, no one knew how the mayor could have access to so much information.

In 1905, Osborne launched a daily newspaper, the *Auburn Daily Citizen*, as a progressive voice to counter the city's dominant daily, the *Auburn Daily Advertiser*.

SOCIAL REFORMER

In 1904, Charles Evans Hughes was elected governor of New York. He was well aware of Osborne's help in securing the election and soon selected Osborne to serve as a commissioner on the state's first New York Public Service Commission. Osborne turned down the job three times before Hughes came back with an offer to make him commissioner of the Public Service Commission. Since Osborne believed in the value of the Public Service Commission (PSC) in regulating public utilities, he accepted the appointment (Chamberlain, 1935). Through his speeches and articles about the work of the PSC, Osborne helped establish the general principles underlying the operation of the PSC. Those principles included service to the public as the primary consideration of all work of the PSC; the prevention of fraud and dishonesty; and the avoidance of overcapitalization.

Osborne quickly found that he enjoyed the duties that came with being the PSC commissioner. In fact, it can be said that he was eminently well suited for this role. He had had business training; he had a facility for honing in on the fundamentals of a problem; and he possessed a strong sense of justice (Chamberlain, 1935). Furthermore, he was especially intrigued by the idea of investigating problems. It was quite common when a complaint was lodged against a public utility for Osborne to dress up as a worker and go out and investigate.

He did exactly that when there was a complaint against the New York Central Railroad. He rode the freight cars, disguised as a worker, and his subsequent report was very specific about how some practices of the New York Central were "inadequate and unsafe" (Chamberlain, 1935, p. 154). But even when he wasn't conducting an undercover investigation, he would disguise himself as a hobo and go to the Bowery just to hang out with other hoboes.

Despite his enjoyment associated with being the commissioner, in 1910, Osborne resigned the lucrative position of PSC commissioner in order to take an unpaid post as chairman of the Democratic League. That same year, the newspaper the New York World suggested that Thomas Mott Osborne be nominated for governor. The World editorial staff wrote:

> Where will the Democrats of New York find a better candidate for governor than Thomas Mott Osborne

of Auburn? Where will they find a candidate who is a more faithful representative of independent Democratic thought and independent Democratic courage? Where will they find a candidate who would devote himself more completely to the work of giving New York a clean, vigorous, intelligent administration of public affairs.... What the voters of New York will be looking for next fall is a ... man who will bring to his task a trained mind like that of Charles E. Hughes and a rugged independence that is subservient to no boss, to no machine and to no corrupt corporation. That is the kind of candidate the Democrats must nominate, and that is the kind of man Mr. Osborne has proved himself to be.... (Chamberlain, 1935, p. 163)

Tammany Hall, a powerful political organization in New York that virtually controlled politics throughout the state from 1789 until the 1970s, had other ideas and asked Osborne if he would run for lieutenant governor, but he declined. Eventually, a compromise candidate, John A. Dix, got the nomination and was elected. Dix wanted Osborne to be part of his administration and offered him the position of Forest, Fish and Game commissioner. This was seemingly a ridiculous appointment, as Osborne knew nothing about fishing or hunting, nor did he particularly care to learn. But he took the appointment and stuck with it until a brief illness forced him to resign.

In 1912, Osborne attended both national and state Democratic conventions and played a role in whom the Democrats would nominate for governor and for president of the United States. Working with Franklin Delano Roosevelt, Osborne and Roosevelt actively lobbied the assembled delegates on behalf of Woodrow Wilson. After Wilson was nominated and then elected as president, Osborne was never shy about letting Wilson know what he thought about some of his appointments.

OSBORNE AS A FATHER

When his wife Agnes died soon after giving birth to their last child, Osborne was left with four young boys to raise. His goal, since he never considered remarrying, was to be both mother and father for his four sons.

As a father he encouraged the boys to be involved in sports. He especially supported their efforts to play baseball, and went so far as to start the Osborne Athletic Club. However, it was not just sports that he promoted for his boys. He would take them to every musical and dramatic event that was available in nearby Syracuse. When they were old enough, each, in turn, attended a preparatory school.

Sing Sing Prison With Warden T.M. Osborne and Two Other Men

Bain News Service, https://commons.wikimedia.org/wiki/File:Sing_Sing_(prison)_with_warden.jpg. Copyright in the Public Domain.

And all would go on to college. Although he himself had returned from college to be involved in the family business, he made it clear to his boys that they were free to choose their own careers. They each went in a slightly different direction. David ended up working in New York City; Charles took a position with a Boston firm; Lithgow entered the diplomatic service; and Robert became a businessman. Later, Charles would return to Auburn to take over as publisher of the family newspaper the *Citizen*. All of the boys saw military service during World War I. After the war, Lithgow came back to Auburn, too, and worked as a journalist at the *Citizen* before going into politics.

When the boys were growing up, Osborne had a library wing added to their South Street home. He had amassed a large library with books on almost any subject. He loved Victorian novels, but there were books on penology and other current topics that interested him. Among his books were the bound volumes of his own letters and articles, articles he wrote for magazines and newspapers. Whenever he traveled, he would write about his observations and experiences, and these got printed into bound volumes.

Besides raising his boys and being actively involved in their lives, reading, traveling, and writing volumes of letters, he also spent a considerable part of his fortune on charity and philanthropy. He often helped young people whom he judged had some kind of special talent that needed encouragement. Since he loved Auburn, he frequently invested in businesses that were failing. Thus, he acquired a bank, a hotel, and, of course, his newspaper. Some of the businesses succeeded; some went bankrupt, losing money for him. In general, Rudolph Chamberlain (1935) points out, Thomas Mott Osborne was a man who responded out of kindness to human need—wherever he found it. Which explains how he became involved with the George Junior Republic.

Asked to become a trustee on the board of the George Junior Republic, a self-governing youth colony, in 1896, within a year Osborne was elected president of the board, a position he held for almost fifteen years (Tannenbaum, 1933). The George Junior Republic was established by William R. George, who had developed an interest in social work among small boys in the slums of New York City. By the year 1890, George had begun taking young boys from New York City to the George Junior Republic, which was situated in Freeville, an area not far from Auburn (Osborne, 1916). The republic started out as a way for William George to provide slum children a fresh-air-type camp experience. However, the camp grew into a settlement offering a full-time living experience for many disadvantaged children, and gradually the George Junior Republic developed into an educational experience teaching disadvantaged youth how to accept and use responsibility, educational opportunities, and self-government (Osborne, 1916). When Thomas Mott Osborne arrived to take his place on the board, he had only read about the Republic, but he was intensely interested in how it operated. He found out that the Republic was not designed to accept violent or aggressive youth, but he insisted that they begin taking on more violent kids. He got his way by 1903—without any adverse effects on the program (Chamberlain, 1935).

FROM GEORGE JUNIOR REPUBLIC
TO PRISON REFORMER

Growing up in Auburn, Osborne, like every other resident of the town, was well aware of Auburn Prison, which opened in 1816. He even went on a tour of the prison when he was a schoolboy. As Osborne grew into adulthood, he knew there were problems in the Auburn Prison system—just as there were in every prison and every prison system. But he had no ready solutions. That is, he had no answers until he was fully indoctrinated into the world of the George Junior Republic.

In a 1905 speech in Syracuse, Osborne said that "prisoners are treated now like wild animals and are kept in cages ... The system brutalizes men and the keepers ... This is not reformatory. It does not create in the criminal a desire to work and respect the law ... I would propose a system like that of the George Junior Republic ... The prisoner's sentence would be indeterminate ... he would be self-governing and learn to respect law" (Chamberlain, 1935, p. 237).

A year later, he was asked to speak before the Congress of the National Prison Association in Albany, New York. In his address, Osborne offered three basic principles for rebuilding the prison system. Those principles were:

1. The law must decree, not punish;
2. Society must brand no man a criminal;
3. The prison must be an institution where every inmate has the largest practical amount of individual freedom. It is liberty alone that fits men for liberty (Chamberlain, 1936, p. 237).

These principles, formulated early in his life as a prison reformer (which was still almost ten years in the future), were themes that would be repeated often by Osborne and put to the test when he actually became a warden. When he wrote the preface to William R. George's book *The Junior Republic* in 1909, Osborne would indicate the genesis of these ideas for prison reform: "Mr. George opened my mind to the possibility of the same principles [self-government] being used as a basis for an intelligent and reforming Prison System—a system which would be a social sanitary drainage—not merely a moral cesspool. At first I laughed at the idea; then I saw the Truth" (Chamberlain, 1935, p. 238).

In 1912, sick in bed, Osborne was inspired to read *My Life in Prison* by Donald Lowrie, a former inmate of San Quentin Prison in California. The following year, Osborne advocated for the appointment of Charles F. Rattigan as warden of Auburn Prison. When Rattigan was given the wardenship, Osborne then was promoting the idea of a state commission on prison reform. When New York governor William Sulzer did institute such a commission, the governor made Osborne chairman of this commission. Given his background at George Junior Republic and his study of books on penology, Osborne threw himself into the chairmanship with a passion. But an opportunity came along for him to take on the chairmanship of the National Committee on Prison Labor, which he eagerly accepted (Osborne, 1916).

Spending most of his time investigating conditions in New York prisons by visiting prisons, he talked to many prison officials and to numerous inmates. However, he felt he needed to do something dramatic in order to make a difference as the chair of a commission on prison reform. Then, an idea hit him.

Pursuing his idea, on September 29, 1913, Thomas Mott Osborne entered the big gate at Auburn Prison and walked up the steps to the main building and entered the warden's office. There, he was booked as Thomas Brown, inmate No. 33,333X. Suddenly, he was one of the 1,400 inmates at Auburn Prison. And he would be just like every other inmate for the next week.

The day before he turned himself over to the warden, Osborne addressed the inmates of Auburn Prison, telling them he was coming there to learn what he could from them firsthand. "I have sentenced myself to a short term at hard labor," he told the inmates. Furthermore, he added:

"I am curious to find out, therefore, whether I am right; whether our Prison System is as unintelligent as I think it is; whether it flies in the face of all common sense and all human nature, as I think it does; whether, guided by sympathy and experience, we cannot find something far better to take its place, as I believe we can" (Osborne, 2013, pp. 14–15). Afterward, he would write a book about his life as Thomas Brown, inmate No. 33, 333X. Titled *Within Prison Walls*, it would be published in 1914.

He kept a diary while in Auburn Prison, writing in it as often as two or three times a day. He described his small cell (4 feet by 7-½ feet), his daily routines, the meals, the code of silence (except during his work in the basket-making shop), the medieval sewage system, the lack of exercise, the other inmates he met, the Principal Keeper, the guards, the warden, and his own thoughts and feelings. By the time he had spent just a couple of days as Tom Brown, Osborne was compelled to write in his diary that

> The way in which a man's family and friends are taken away seems superlatively cruel. A prisoner gets no wages for his work except his board, lodging, clothes, and the ridiculous cent and a half a day. In the meantime his wife and children may be starving on the streets outside; he is powerless to help them, and can write only one letter a month. In other words, as one prisoner once said to me bitterly, "At just the time we need our friends the most, they are taken away from us. We must write our one letter a month to a wife, a mother, or some member of the family having special claim. Our friends do not hear from us; they think we are hard and do not care—we are criminals; so they drop us and we are forgotten." (Osborne, 2013, p. 69)

Osborne would also write that prison was a brutal system in which the brutality of guards goes unpunished. In addition, he offered the opinion that inmates lost all respect for authority, writing that "it is a mistake to suppose that rigid discipline increases respect for authority; it usually does nothing of the sort" (Osborne, 2013, pp. 165–166). During the end of his week, he contrived to be sent to the "jail," which was the name of the solitary confinement cells. Spending just a few hours in solitary led him to observe that "The jail is admirably situated for the purpose of performing the operation of breaking a man's spirit" (Osborne, 2013, p. 181). He came to have special feelings of empathy for the other prisoners who were serving not just a few hours, but days, weeks, and months in dark, cold, vermin-ridden solitary confinement cells.

Finally, his week came to an end, and on his last day, a Sunday, of being Tom Brown, he again addressed the inmates at the Sunday service. He told them that his short week had altered the whole tenor of his life and that he had forged a bond between the men he had met and himself that would never be broken. Writing about his farewell speech afterward, he recalled what he said to the inmates:

> I said to these men last Sunday that I should try to "break down the barriers between my soul and the souls of my brothers." It was necessary so to endeavor in order to understand the conditions I came to study. But what has happened is that these men have broken down their own barriers; they have opened their hearts; they have dignified and ennobled my errand; they have transformed my personal quest for knowledge into a vital message from the great heart of humanity in the outside world—a heart that, in spite of all that is said and done to the contrary, beats in sympathy with all genuine sorrow, with all honest endeavor for righteousness. (Osborne, 2013, p. 232)

And although he didn't say this to the inmates and guards he had grown to like and respect, he concluded from his experience in Auburn

Prison that the system of prison discipline he encountered couldn't have been more misguided: "If a deliberate attempt were to be made to draft a code of punishment which should produce a minimum of efficacy and a maximum of failure and exasperation among prisoners, it could not be more skillfully planned" (Osborne, 2013, p. 240).

When his week in Auburn Prison was given publicity, he was criticized by some and praised by others. On the other hand, the publication of *Within Prison Walls* in 1914 made him the most prominent prison reform crusader of his day.

Thomas Mott Osborne With His Four Sons

https://www.loc.gov/item/89706563/, https://www.loc.gov/item/89706563/. Copyright in the Public Domain.

While he was Tom Brown, Osborne worked alongside Jack Murphy in the basket shop for his week inside the prison. He and Murphy would become good friends, and together they developed the idea of a Mutual Welfare League. With permission of Auburn's warden, Charles Rattigan, and the New York commissioner of prisons, John Riley, Osborne returned to Auburn Prison to initiate the Mutual Welfare League. This experiment in prisoner self-government was judged as a smashing success by both Jack Murphy and Osborne himself (Osborne, 1916).

WARDEN OF SING SING

After his book was published, Osborne was appointed Warden of Sing Sing Prison in Ossining, New York, on December 1, 1914, replacing Judge George S. Weed. Sing Sing was built on the east bank of the Hudson River, approximately 30 miles north of New York City. The original cell block was built by prisoners from Auburn Prison in 1825. Although Osborne had tried to change the worst conditions in New York state prisons while he was the chair of the governor's commission, still, when he arrived at Sing

Sing, it continued to be a very brutal place for the 1,500 inmates it held (Tannenbaum, 1933). It was a prison that took its toll on both prisoner and staff. Of the thirty-one previous wardens who ran Sing Sing before Osborne, the average term was a little over one year. Osborne recognized that one of the problems contributing to the frequent changes in administration was the fact that the position was a political appointment, and most of the former wardens were anything but qualified. Osborne learned that his predecessors included a steam fitter, a coal dealer, a drunkard, and a "flock of ward heelers" (Chamberlain, 1935, p. 290). Even on his first night in the warden's apartment, he became aware of a further problem—the warden's apartment overlooked the death house. That was a constant macabre reminder that wardens had to be responsible for executing death row inmates. However, while Osborne, who was strongly opposed to capital punishment, was warden at Sing Sing, he never attended an execution (Chamberlain, 1935).

On his first day as the new warden, Osborne did what every new warden of Sing Sing did; he stood in front of an assembly of all the prisoners in the chapel and made an introductory speech. But once that speech was concluded, he then did what no other warden had ever done: he locked himself up as a prisoner. His intention was to see Sing Sing from the inmates' point of view. After a week as a prisoner, he shocked the guards and the prisoners by frequently visiting the prison yard—unarmed and unescorted. He began talking to the inmates, listening to their problems, and paying attention to what they wanted to see changed. As a result, he was soon granting some of the reforms requested by prisoners.

By talking to the inmates, he discovered that there was a Golden Rule Brotherhood, which was an organization of inmates with a ready list of complaints and requests. He also quickly learned that the Golden Rule Brotherhood handled all discipline problems, not just the minor discipline violations (Tannenbaum, 1933).

One of Osborne's first major changes was to remove all but a few guards out of the various inmate shops. The few who remained were guards requested by the prisoners. Contrary to what the guards expected, after the armed guards were given new assignments in the prison, the shops still functioned successfully—and without any discipline problems. These kinds of reforms inside Sing Sing drew attention to what Osborne was doing, and he soon found out that there were people who were opposed to his reforms. Consequently, it was soon apparent that there were people who were out to get him. Despite becoming aware of a group opposed to his reforms, Osborne continued to make changes.

In one of his many changes, Osborne began working closely with the Golden Rule Brotherhood, transforming them into an organization responsible for internal self-rule. This wasn't the first time Thomas Mott Osborne developed a system of self-rule. He first did this at Auburn Prison with his Mutual Welfare League. The Mutual Welfare League at Auburn Prison brought inmates together in an organization given the task of making positive changes in prison life. In Sing Sing, the Mutual Welfare League grew out of the Golden Rule Brotherhood and became instrumental in abolishing the rule of silence, getting rid of the stool-pigeon system (which involved inmates snitching on each other in other to gain benefits, such as a reduced sentence), and eliminating Blue Sunday (the tradition that forbade most forms of activities for prisoners on Sundays). The Sing Sing Mutual Welfare League, in addition to getting rid of some hated practices, instituted outdoor sports and the formation of a grievance committee (Osborne, 1916).

If Osborne's Mutual Welfare League had many successes by instituting positive changes and allowing self-rule for prisoners, it helped galvanize criticism and opposition to Osborne's style of running a prison. In the eyes of some critics, including some influential newspapers, the Mutual Welfare League was synonymous with mollycoddling and the pampering of prisoners. But there was opposition to the changes even within Sing Sing, especially among a few prisoners who had used the old system to intimidate other inmates and used their financial resources to bribe guards for privileges. One of these prisoners who thrived in the old system was a former Manhattan banker who was imprisoned for larceny and used his financial and political connections to instigate a rigged "investigation" of Osborne's administration (Chamberlain, 1935). As a result of this one prisoner's dissatisfaction with the changes, Osborne was indicted for perjury, neglect of duty, and "unlawful [sexual] acts with inmates" on December 28, 1915, by the grand jury of Westchester County (Chamberlain, 1935).

After Osborne put up the $2,000 bail, he was pressured by the governor to take a leave of absence. Although he was reluctant to leave the job he loved, he finally agreed to take the leave of absence. However, Osborne would fight back by organizing a speaking tour of the state. He held two meetings at Carnegie Hall, with one of those meetings attended by the retired president of Harvard University, Charles William Eliot, who offered his name and resources in the cause of Osborne's defense. After the speaking tour and the support from people like Eliot, testimonials and endorsements of his prison reforms began to pour in. Many former inmates sent letters; the Grand Jury Association of New York passed a resolution supporting Osborne; one hundred leading citizens of Auburn signed a testimonial lauding him; and the prison guards wrote a letter in support of him as well. During the trial, witness after witness for the prosecution failed to deliver the kind of testimony the district attorney expected. The case for the prosecution slipped away, and finally the judge in the case directed a verdict of acquittal (Osborne, 1916). Osborne could return to Sing Sing in triumph.

Despite the criticism and the opposition to the Mutual Welfare League, the organization would survive for another fifteen years. Osborne could proudly point to the efficiency and effectiveness of the Mutual Welfare League. While the Mutual Welfare League was in existence and Osborne was warden, there were fewer attempts to escape from Sing Sing; there were fewer prison riots; the physical health of the inmates improved; and, perhaps mostly importantly of all from Osborne's vantage point, a large number of inmates went on to be released and became good, responsible citizens. These numbers justified his faith in "the enormous capacity of man to recover his moral balance after the commission of sin" (Chamberlain, 1935, p. 282).

While the Mutual Welfare League led to many positive changes for the inmates, Osborne had plenty of other ideas for prison reform. One of his ideas was to establish a convict honor camp for road construction.

Selecting twenty inmates in 1914, he started the first honor camp near the village of Meridian, about 16 miles north of Auburn (Osborne, 1916). After it got going, Tom Brown showed up to work on the road crew (Osborne, 1916).

After his acquittal in the trial and three months after returning to his position as Sing Sing's warden, Thomas Mott Osborne recognized that he was tired of battling his superiors and New York State governor Charles S. Whitman. So, in 1916, he resigned as warden. In his resignation letter, he blamed Governor Whitman, contending that Whitman had broken many of the promises he had made. Osborne also noted that he thought the opposition to his reforms were basically directed at himself rather than the programs; consequently, he thought that his usefulness was at an end.

COMMANDER AT PORTSMOUTH

Continuing to blame the governor, Osborne campaigned against him in the next election, doing what he said shouldn't be done: that is, inserting the operation of Sing Sing into politics. Besides that, Whitman won reelection as governor. Osborne was ready to retire to his Auburn home.

But in 1916, Josephus Daniels, the secretary of the Navy, at the likely suggestion of Assistant Secretary Franklin Delano Roosevelt, an ally of Osborne from his years in New York State reform politics, commissioned Osborne to do a study and submit a report on conditions at the Portsmouth Naval Prison in Kittery, Maine. That motivated Osborne to resurrect Tom Brown.

In January 1917, Tom Brown served a short term in the Portsmouth Naval Prison, where he could investigate conditions by living inside the prison like any other inmate. What Tom Brown, posing as a deserter, discovered was a facility desperately in need of his reforms. He soon realized that the government was making a bad investment. Although he observed that there was less brutality in the naval prison, it was also clear that the prison was plagued by "degrading" uniforms and "absurd" procedures (Chamberlain, 1935, p. 367). In particular, Osborne saw that the young men who were punished by imprisonment in the naval facility were not only locked up, but once their sentence was served, they were then dishonorably discharged. That made no sense to Osborne because America was in a war in which they needed the services of all healthy young men. Why not return them as able-bodied seamen to serve in the Navy?

After submitting his report to Secretary of the Navy Daniels, Daniels asked him to take charge of the Portsmouth Naval Prison. Osborne accepted, becoming immediately a lieutenant commander but also the first civilian to be in charge of a Navy prison (Chamberlain, 1935).

In August 1917, now a lieutenant commander in the U.S. Navy, Osborne took up the position of commander of the Portsmouth Naval Prison, a post he held for two and a half years. Immediately, he mapped out a common-sense program for the prison, but his main interest was saving manpower for the Navy, along with saving the "manhood" of each of the young men who were incarcerated in the naval prison (Tannenbaum, 1933). He certainly had a vested interest in the manhood of young men. Not only was the United States in a war, but his four sons were all involved in military service for America.

During his tenure as commander of Portsmouth, Osborne would institute many of the same programs he established at Auburn Prison and Sing Sing. One of the changes he brought about very quickly was the removal of Marines as guards for the prison. Then, he allowed the men to engage in outdoor sports, and, as usual in his prison reforms, he brought about self-government. When he resigned his command of Portsmouth, there was much he could point to as successful. In two and a half years, only eight men tried to escape, but, conversely, he returned more than 4,000 (of the 6,500 in the prison during his term) men back into the Navy. He established a dramatics club, even taking them on the road for performances. He listened sympathetically to men who voiced complaints and brought about a prisoners' court to hear grievances.

But Osborne often had to depend on his subordinates—all Navy officers—to keep him out of trouble. While he proudly wore his lieutenant commander's uniform, he generally had disdain for Navy traditions and Navy protocol. However, it was invaluable to have the staunch support of

Secretary of the Navy Daniels and Assistant Secretary of the Navy Franklin Delano Roosevelt (Chamberlain, 1935). In his biography of Osborne, Rudolph Chamberlain makes a point of noting that it was amazing that in two and a half years in this position, Osborne somehow avoided being court martialed.

Among his final suggestions to the Navy was that criminals and ex-convicts be recruited for the war effort. This idea was vetoed by the Navy, including by his son Charles, but that didn't stop Osborne from continuing to advocate for the idea.

When the war ended, Osborne felt it was time to leave the Navy and Portsmouth. Although his first resignation was turned down by Secretary Daniels (who persuaded him to remain on the job for six more months), his next resignation was accepted. Lieutenant Commander Osborne left the Navy in May 1920.

THE END OF HIS CAREER

With his Navy career finished, he returned home to 99 South Street in Auburn. There, he could enjoy his old interests—playing the piano and giving recitals, lecturing on music and the arts, and reviving his role as president of the Auburn Amateur Dramatics Club. But he took on some new activities as well. One of these was staging benefit shows for the local post of the American Legion.

He tried to get back into politics, but he soon would find out that the things he fought against—such as Tammany Hall—had, if anything, become stronger. Prohibition, too, had come along and, as he said, threatened to make drunks of everyone, because most people, himself included, still enjoyed a cocktail now and then.

And his prison reforms?

There were ongoing reactions against his prison reforms, and this left him feeling a sense of "impotence" (Chamberlain, 1935, p. 389). This was especially the feeling he was left with when the new warden at Sing Sing began rolling back the reforms Osborne had instituted there. A period of desolation set in, and he told a friend that he was "condemned to heart-breaking idleness; realizing what I can do to benefit mankind and not permitted to do it" (Tannenbaum, 1933, p. 287).

Nonetheless, from 1920 to 1924, he was in demand as a special investigator of prisons. There were some offers of wardenships at various prisons around the country, but none of these offers came to fruition. As a special investigator, though, he did complete reports about prisons in Maryland, Missouri, and Colorado, more often than not turning up instances of brutality against prisoners. And he could enjoy the international acclaim that came his way from countries such as England, Germany, and Greece.

His books, public speaking, and notoriety helped end the so-called "rule of silence," the floggings, and other kinds of prisoner abuses common in U.S. prisons at the time. But Osborne's cherished prisoner self-government plan, the Mutual Welfare League, vanished soon after his death. Although his initial experiments had been greeted by the press largely with derision, over the course of his life, he won grudging admiration from both the press and the public.

But he remained committed to the arts up until his final day. In fact, he planned to see one of his sons in a play, but he didn't want to just show up as the father of the actor. So, donning a disguise, Osborne headed for the theater. However, he didn't make it. He was found in his disguise dead in the streets of Auburn on October 20, 1926, at age sixty-seven.

A funeral service was held in the prison chapel at Auburn Prison. Osborne was buried in Fort Hill Cemetery in Auburn, dressed in a Portsmouth prison uniform.

THE LEGACY OF THOMAS MOTT OSBORNE

Thomas Mott Osborne was the foremost prison reformer of his time. Throughout his career as a prison reformer, he stood virtually alone as an advocate for democratic principles being applied to prison management. It can be reliably said that he alone, among all prison administrators, wardens, and reformers, was the only one who could say that they studied prison management from three different perspectives: that of the ordinary citizen; that of the prison official; and that of the prisoner (Osborne, 1918).

In 1933, the Welfare League Association and several other organizations Osborne had created were merged and reorganized as the Osborne Association. The Osborne Association, which still exists today, is devoted to helping released inmates adjust to their lives post-incarceration.

In his biography of Osborne, Frank Tannenbaum wrote that there was something of the saint about him—"Something about his love for his fellows that reminds one of Saint Francis of Assisi" (Tannenbaum, 1933, p. 291). Tannenbaum continued to say that his very presence made men better. "A word of his lifted spiritless men above themselves ... The most hardened of men mellowed under his touch and they loved him for the rare quality that made them stronger in his presence. Surely no man of our day and generation was so loved by the outcast and persecuted of the underworld" (Tannenbaum, 1933, p. 291).

In 1933, Franklin Delano Roosevelt wrote the introduction to Frank Tannenbaum's book *Osborne of Sing Sing*. In that introduction, Roosevelt said that Osborne had courage and he had vision. Roosevelt went on to write: "When Osborne first began his work in the State of New York, the cells, the food, the sanitation in our prisons had changed little from the status of 1850. Mr. Osborne was the great pioneer in calling our attention to these physical conditions" (Tannenbaum, 1933, p. ix).

Roosevelt also wrote in that introduction that he thought that Osborne's greatest contribution to modern civilization was his recognition that 90 percent of all inmates eventually come back into society. With that in mind, Roosevelt acknowledged Osborne's abiding faith in most men; that if treated with respect—and not with brutality—they could become law-abiding citizens. But the key to them coming back into society and becoming productive citizens rested on how they were treated in prison. If they were treated as men who could govern themselves and make their own decisions, they could reenter society as independent and democratic citizens (Tannenbaum, 1933).

Roosevelt closed his remarks with this: "Let us remember that penology as a social science is still in its infancy and that the greatest tribute which we can pay Mr. Osborne's memory will be to carry on the fight relentlessly, and with the high idealism which he so exemplified" (Tannenbaum, 1933, p. x).

And perhaps that is the most fitting tribute that can be paid to Thomas Mott Osborne: that he saw the capacity for change in some of the worst of men and he was never afraid to stand up and fight for the principles that he believed would transform criminals into decent citizens.

QUESTIONS FOR DISCUSSION

1. What were the most significant personal traits that Thomas Mott Osborne brought to his work as a prison reformer? Why?
2. How do you think Osborne's career as successful businessman and as an influential politician impacted his prison work?
3. In your opinion, did Osborne's flair for dramatics serve him well or not so well in his prison reform endeavors? Why or why not?
4. Could Osborne's views about democratic self-government for prisons have relevance today? Give reasons for your answer.

IMPORTANT TERMS AND NAMES

Auburn Prison: Built in 1816 in Auburn, New York, this prison established a model for prisons throughout the United States by using the Auburn system for discipline.

Auburn Prison System: The Auburn Prison System was put into place with the opening of Auburn Prison. The system was also known as the congregate system and employed corporal punishment, solitary confinement, and the practice of inmates working and eating together. This was in contrast to the Pennsylvania system, in which inmates were kept separate in solitary confinement and never allowed to meet together in groups.

Franklin Delano Roosevelt: Franklin Delano Roosevelt served as the thirty-second president of the United States from 1933 to 1945. However, prior to that, he and Thomas Mott Osborne worked together in New York State politics; when Osborne was the commander of the Portsmouth Naval Prison from 1917 to 1920, Roosevelt was the assistant secretary of the Navy.

George Junior Republic: Established by William R. George in the 1890s, it started as a camping experience for disadvantaged New York City kids but grew into a residential program that featured self-governing principles. Osborne served as a trustee and president of the board for fifteen years.

Josephus Daniels: Josephus Daniels was secretary of the Navy when he asked Osborne to conduct a study of the Portsmouth Naval Prison in 1917.

Mutual Welfare League: The Mutual Welfare League was an organization of inmates at both Auburn Prison and Sing Sing Prison that allowed prisoners to handle their own discipline problems and to take on a greater role in self-governing.

Osborne Association: The Osborne Association developed out of the merger in 1933 of two organizations started by Thomas Mott Osborne—the Mutual Welfare League and the National Society of Penal Information. The goal of the Osborne Association, since its founding, has been to help those people who have been incarcerated.

Sing Sing Prison: Opened in 1828 in Ossining, New York, this maximum-security prison adopted the Auburn system. Thomas Mott Osborne introduced some reforms when he was warden of Sing Sing from 1914 to 1916.

Portsmouth Naval Prison: A naval prison opened in 1908 in Kittery, Maine. Thomas Mott Osborne became the commander of this prison in 1917, bringing with him reforms to improve the operations of the prison.

Tammany Hall: A political organization in New York State from 1789 until the 1970s, Tammany Hall held considerable power in New York politics for almost a hundred years. It is remembered today as being associated with graft and corruption in politics.

Theodore Roosevelt: A Progressive politician and reformer, Theodore Roosevelt was elected governor of New York in 1899 and would go on to be president of the United States from 1901 to 1909. He and Thomas Mott Osborne attended Harvard at the same time. Later, they would be aligned in despising the corruption of Tammany Hall and promoting Woodrow Wilson for president.

FOR FURTHER READING

Chamberlain, R. W. (1935). *There is no truce: A life of Thomas Mott Osborne.* New York, NY: Macmillan.

Osborne, T. M. (1995). The true foundation of prison reform. *Journal of Correctional Education, 46*(2), 76–78.

Osborne, T. M. (2010). *Prisons and common sense.* Farmington Hills, MI: Gale.

Scharf, P., & Hickey, J. (1977). Thomas Mott Osborne and the limits of Democratic prison reform. *Prison Journal, 57*(2), 3–15.

Tannenbaum, F. (1933). *Osborne of Sing Sing*. Chapel Hill, NC: University of North Carolina Press.

REVIEW QUESTIONS

True or False

1. Thomas Mott Osborne actually came from a long line of reformers and activists on his mother's side.
2. As a politician, he was once the Democratic candidate for president of the United States.
3. In his political life, he had more than a passing acquaintanceship with Theodore Roosevelt and Franklin Delano Roosevelt.
4. In his position on the board of the George Junior Republic, Osborne came to develop his ideas about inmate self-government.

Multiple Choice

5. One of Thomas Mott Osborne's principles for reforming the prison system was

    a. That prisons must not pamper inmates.
    b. That society must not brand people as criminals.
    c. That the threat of the death penalty is essential.
    d. That the rule of silence must be maintained.

6. Tom Brown was

    a. The name of a schoolboy.
    b. The alias of a dangerous criminal whose real name was Jack Murphy.
    c. The alias Thomas Mott Osborne used when he went undercover.
    d. The name given to most new prison inmates.

7. A hallmark of Thomas Mott Osborne's views of the traditional prison system of his time was that prisons were

    a. A place that lacked common sense and defied human nature.
    b. A place where inmates were treated respectfully.
    c. A place where guards were too friendly with inmates.
    d. A place where punishment made real men of criminals.

8. Thomas Mott Osborne's Mutual Welfare League was
   a. An organization that mollycoddled inmates.
   b. An organization that sought to make prison life comfortable and pleasant.
   c. An organization whose aim was to bring together inmates so they could plan to escape.
   d. An organization of self-government that allowed inmates to be involved in bringing about positive changes in prison life.

9. Thomas Mott Osborne had a deep and abiding faith in the ability of prisoners
   a. To be recidivists.
   b. To escape from prison.
   c. To adjust to a routine of total silence.
   d. To change and become respectable citizens.

10. Along with instituting many of his typical prison reforms at the Portsmouth Naval Prison, one of the accomplishments that pleased Osborne when he was commander of the naval prison was
    a. Returning 4,000 men to active duty as sailors.
    b. Keeping Navy deserters in solitary confinement.
    c. Teaching Navy prisoners to swim.
    d. Hiring Marines to guard dangerous naval prisoners.

11. When he was president of the United States, Franklin Delano Roosevelt wrote that Thomas Mott Osborne was
    a. A man of courage and vision.
    b. A pioneer in calling attention to the poor conditions in prisons.
    c. A man with faith that prisoners could become law-abiding citizens.
    d. All of the above.

REFERENCES

Chamberlain, R. W. (1935). *There is no truce: A life of Thomas Mott Osborne*. New York, NY: Macmillan Company.

Fuller, T. W. (2013). *Prison reform catalysts*. Lafayette, CA: Pleasant Hill Press.

Osborne, T. M. (1916). *Society and prisons*. New Haven, CT: Yale University Press.

Osborne, T. M. (1918). Common sense in prison management. *Journal of the American Institute of Criminal Law and Criminology, 8,* 806–822.

Osborne, T. M. (2013). *Within prison walls: Being a narrative of personal experience during a week of voluntary confinement in the state prison at Auburn, New York*. DE: Create Space.

Tannenbaum, F. (1933). *Osborne of Sing Sing*. Chapel Hill, NC: University of North Carolina Press.

INDEX